Brian's Autobiography

Author Brian Willetts

My book also has answers to the way in which I have achieved so many successful results and how I have solved problems where others have failed.

It is important not to be afraid of making mistakes, because, often, these are the sources from which we learn.

Brian's Autobiography and Featuring Some of His Great Achievements

The Wonder of What One Can
Achieve When We Take the Time
to Build on What We Can Do

Brian Willetts

To order additional copies of this book, contact:
Xlibris
1-800-455-039
www.Xlibris.com.au
Orders@Xlibris.com.au
786087

The recommended retail price:

- eBook $11.99
- Soft Copy $29.99
- Hard Copy $49.99

You may order your book through online book sellers or the ordering desk at your local book store. There is also another way which is from the friendly Xlibris staff.

Talking to a living person on the phone; 1800 455 039

- Fax: (02) 8088 6078
- E-mail: InfoAU@authorsolutions.com
- Web: Xlibris Online Bookstore https://www.xlibris.com/Bookstore/BookHome.aspx
- By Mail, please send your order, along with a cheque or payment information to:

Attn: Book Orders
Xlibris LLC
Suite 1 A Level 2
802 Pacific Highway Gordon 2072

To order from online bookstores, visit the following web sites: www.amazon.co.uk, www.barnesandnoble.com, www.booksamillion.com.

To order at a traditional brick-and-mortar bookstore service desk. Our books are always available. (the signing off is not part of the suggested for advertising)

CONTENTS

PREFACE

My name is Brian Willetts, and I was born in New Zealand, where I spent the first 22 years of my life. I have resided in Australia for the bigger part of my life, and I have also spent 11 years travelling around the world twice, as well as spending quite a bit of time travelling back and forth between Australia and New Zealand while my parents were alive.

The majority of my book is about the experiences I have had in the journey of my life and the people who influenced the decisions that I made while taking that journey. The strongest influences that I had were my parents and schoolteachers. In this book, I have gone to a great deal of effort not to include people's names, except for my mother and father. (I have made an exception for the ranch in South Dakota because of the small likelihood of someone in South Dakota reading it.) The reason being that there is a possibility that some people may not be happy about the way I have represented them, or some other emotional problem may offend them. I have seen too many autobiographies which, after they have been written, and have ended up by having to deal with some heated debates that end up in the public arena and create a lot of misery. All that debating would not exist if they had used a pronoun or a substitute name instead of their real name. My aim in this book is to pass on valuable information to the next generation.

I talk about the great ethical value of results from the safety that my mother worked with, and I compared it with the way safety is dealt with in the modern generation. I also talk about the importance of learning from your Mum and Dad. However, while doing that, there are two facts that need to be taken into consideration. There is not a parent on the planet who is perfect, so do not waste your time looking for them. Siblings are the ones who determine what a perfect parent is, and each one has their own version of what they believe it should be. As the sibling gets closer to the age of 25, where their brain is now fully developed, which also becomes a good time for establishing what is good advice and sort out what is not worthy of repeating and what needs changing. Making a mistake is not necessarily a bad thing if it is used as a learning tool, although repeating the same mistake is.

I have dyslexia, and it is the major reason it has taken me over two decades to write this book. Even though it may be a bit hard to swallow, after taking so long to write this book and despite the contrary belief that a lot of people may have about dyslexia, I wanted to show that it does not only have a bad side to it; it also has some great advantages that go with it. In my book, I have written 36 pages about not knowing that I had dyslexia, and that also includes all the other people who were associated with my life. I did not know that I had dyslexia until the age of 60, and I gained all my knowledge of dyslexia when I was between the ages of 60-65. In this chapter, I wrote a lot about the difficult struggle I had with dyslexia when I was at school with the teachers, my parents, and all the adults of authority who were involved in my life, as well as myself. This lack of knowledge continued over a long period.

I have travelled around the world twice. The first job that I did when I started travelling involved working on a high-rise building; where I had a fear of heights, and I learnt to get past the fear. I worked in a 5-star hotel in London as a waiter and started off with no knowledge of being a waiter, and in three weeks, I became the highest-tipped waiter in the hotel. In America, I got a job as a cowboy; once again, I had no knowledge of the job and did not even know how to saddle a horse, yet I was able to come back to that same rancher, where I worked for six months at a time and the boss paid for one of my trips around the world.

In Australia, I worked in the outback as a cook in the biggest cattle station in the world at the time, and once again in the outback as a stockman on another cattle station, where I had to fight a large bush fire.

In regard to the medical field, I gained a lot of successful results. I am not a doctor; I am not a nurse. The only medical knowledge that I have comes from books, advice passed on to me by doctors, TV, and any other means that I can find. The greatest result that I got was when I had a stroke and lost half of my eyesight in both eyes; my doctor had given up on me, and I was able to restore all of my eyesight by working out a method of remapping the brain.

I have also had many other successful results. In the early years of my life, I had to go through three decades of having large amounts of uncontrollable sweat discharging from my feet and hands, and I have now stopped that problem from occurring. I have also had painful spurs in the base of my bone in both of my heels, and I have had gout. I have also greatly reduced the amount of plaque that forms on my teeth, and I have done a good job of maintaining good health after having a severe heart attack and after having to return 5 times to the hospital for having arrhythmia (atrial fibrillations). Most of those results come from what I can do, and I spend as little time as possible relying on what I can't do or what someone or something else can do for me. No man is an island unto himself, and there are times when we rely on what others can do.

There comes a time in our lives when we have a chance to review the difference that we make by being in this world, and very often with a quick revision, we would naturally start listing all the things that we have accumulated, such as money and other possessions. However, once we are dead, the only things we have to offer the world are the things we gave away. There are a lot of people who believe that, at the end of the day, money is the most important thing. I dispute that fact because I was once fortunate enough to hear the wisdom of a wise man, who said to me, "Pretend your mother is in hospital, and it is 100 per cent certain that she has only one hour to live. She has two choices left to her: she can have a big hug and a kiss from her son, or she can have two million dollars." (You can make your own mind up on that, should you need to make the same decision.) The two million dollars are rendered valueless to her once she is dead, and the time which she still has to live lacks the ability to do anything with it. But the hug and the kiss are something she can embrace and feel good about in the time that she has left. Who knows? It may even carry beyond that time. I am now 71 years of age, and I believe that I have just given a good reason for devoting my time to writing this book.

My book does not offer any miracles, although it does offer a better opportunity to get results for someone who is prepared to get out of the role of a victim and take a positive step into seeing what they can do for themselves.

CHAPTER 1

A Brief History of the Jobs
That I Have Done

My name is Brian Willetts. I am a New Zealander who was born in a small town called Ngaruawahia (Nga rua w hia), in the middle of the North Island, 12 miles or 20 kilometres north of Hamilton. I started my first job at the age of 16 as a *porter*, working for the *railways* in the city of *Hamilton*. After about a year or two, I got promoted to a *shunter* (a person who puts trains together so that the wagons can go to their respective destinations), and I worked in the railways for a total of 8 years.

The next thing that I did in regard to working for a living was to organise work for myself while I spent 11 years *travelling around the world twice*. This was not a complete journey that I had planned prior to starting it. This journey was more of a case of being something that developed as it went along. One of the reasons that strongly influenced me to take the journey was that when I was talking to my father at an earlier time in my life, he said to me, 'If you want to travel, do it when you are young and before you get married, because you have Buckley's chance of doing it after you get married.' A trip as long as the one that I was about to undertake requires a lot of financial planning, which means that a small part of the journey was set up for sightseeing while the rest was for doing work in order to finance the expenses.

The first place I went when I left New Zealand was *Australia*, where I lived with my oldest sister for a while and where I managed to get a job working on a construction site as a *builder's labourer*. After a few months, I left Australia to work in *London* as a *waiter* in a five-star hotel (the full story of my being a waiter is in the chapter of when I was in London. The First Step of My World Tour: Australia–London'). After spending about nine months as a waiter, I left and went to *Texas* in *America* to work as a *cowboy*. I was fortunate to get a good opportunity by having the boss that I was working for pay for one of my trips around the world. (This is explained in the article 'South Dakota and the Many Duties of a Cowboy'.) After about 6 weeks, I got transferred to *South Dakota* and continued doing my cowboy work. The rancher that I worked for had 5 ranches—2 in Mexico, 2 in Texas, and 1 in South Dakota—and he also owned a meat abattoir, in addition to 2 food lots for fatting up cattle.

After that, my visa ran out, then I headed back to *New Zealand*, where I worked as a *truckie*, driving a small four-ton delivery tipper truck for sand and road metal. I remember that I was a pretty good driver at the time, and one of the jobs that I needed to do involved backing down the steep hill of a driveway with a full load of sand in my truck. The driveway had a fence post on one side and a letter box on the other side, and it had no more than a 3-millimetre gap on either side of the truck, which I successfully negotiated. On the way back, I successfully drove forward, past the letter box, and then was left with two choices: to turn right or to turn left. I accidentally started turning to the left and, after a while, realised that I should have been turning right. So, thinking I had got past all the dangers, I carelessly did a three-point turn and ended up knocking over the letter box anyway. Boy, didn't that make me angry, and that's to say nothing of the trouble I got into when I saw the boss.

My next job had me back in *London*, where I worked as a *trades assistant* on the water mains, which were mainly situated deep below the ground. After that, I headed back to the ranch in *South Dakota* to work as a cowboy again on the same ranch that I was on before. There was one bloke who worked on the ranch and who spent a lot of time working as a part-time bulldozer operator. After a couple of months of me being there, he got sacked, and I was required to replace him. He got sacked from the ranch for two good reasons. He was a person who had a little bit of knowledge on many things and a master of none, and in his case, he created more problems than he could solve. He was a pretty good operator with the bulldozer and was having trouble with some hard ground that he was working on; he volunteered to give a solution to the problem, which cost the boss quite a bit of money and resulted in a lot of wasted time, as it went horribly wrong. He also got into a lot more trouble when he volunteered to fix the gearbox of a four-wheel drive for the boss which was on the ranch at South Dakota. When he failed to have enough knowledge to be able to complete the job that he said he would do, it got him dismissed from the ranch, with a firm message not to return.

I then headed back to New Zealand for a short period. Then I headed up to the *Gulf of Carpentaria in Queensland, Australia*, and got a job as a *cook* on the biggest privately-owned station in the world at that time. The station was called *Dunbar Cattle Station*. Dunbar is as much of the outback of Australia as one can get. This was a seasonal job which left me with some wild and exciting stories to tell. The next job that I got was in *Sydney*, and there I worked as a *brickies' labourer* for a company called *Austral Bricks*, which contracted us from another company that supplied a gang to repair the kilns used for making the bricks. That job expired after about 6 or 8 months. The next job I did was back north on a cattle station called *Miranda Downs*, where I worked as a *stockman* in *Queensland*, which is situated a couple of hundred kilometres south-west of Cairns. I was also part of a team that needed to extinguish a large bush fire which had developed at the station, in addition to going on other exciting adventures.

After working as a stockman, I went to *Mount Isa* and got a job with a company called Simon Carves, which contracted me to work for Mount Isa Mines as a *rigger, scaffolder*, and *dogman* (a dogman is a person who loads the crane up for when they lift the loads). Mount Isa Mines at Mount Isa was the place where I got my tickets as a rigger, scaffolder, and dogman. First I trained with others that had those tickets, and then I went to the technical college and passed the test for the three tickets. Mount Isa Mines was also a seasonal job which would last for about 4–6 months; this was a regular occurrence each year and was set up to take place just before the end of the financial year.

The next job I took on was that of a *rigger/TA* (trades assistant) in *ICI in Botany*, which was later bought out by a company called Orica a few years after I finished working there. ICI is a chemical factory where I worked on many interesting types of machinery, such as a chemical reactor where the heat was created by the mixing of different chemicals (if you mixed the right chemicals, you can create a very high temperature of heat), a gas furnace that melted sand and soda ash, and pumps with many different types of seals that needed to withstand the harsh treatments of the many different chemicals that the pumps had to work. There were also several different types of conveyors, such as belt and pan conveyors. I also worked on big compressors that worked in three stages in order to reach a working load at 200,000 PSI (pounds per square inch). I spent 8 years in ICI, where I bought my first piece of real estate—a one-bedroom flat in Hillsdale, very close to the ICI factory—for $34,000. Within 2–3 years' time, the price for my flat had skyrocketed in the housing boom up to $90,000, so I left the job and went to Perth, where I could purchase cheap housing ranging from $70,000-$80,000 for a three-bedroom brick house.

Perth turned out to be a bad time for me in the journey of my life thus far, it was the first time that I was unable to gain employment as soon as I wanted it. There were several reasons that I thought I could get a job as soon as I wanted one. The main reason being that, in my past, I had often gone to places that I had never been to before and to jobs which I had never done, and I still managed to successfully get the job. Perth did not turn out to be as successful as I had planned. For the first time in my life, I had trouble getting a decent-paying job because *Perth* is pretty much like a giant retirement village and does not have much industrial or building activity. The availability for getting manual work in Perth is extremely difficult when you're over 40, and it is most likely to be lining up with the fact that nobody wants to even know your name, because the younger generation has a longer span of working time that they can contribute to the job and often has more energy. The employer is also able to pay them less for doing the same job. The story continues to deteriorate (to get worse) there was also a surplus of young people looking for work, which put the older people who were looking for manual work in the scrapheap. This shattered the goal I had and also cost me many thousands of dollars while I was trying to survive. I was now forced to go back to *Sydney*, where I would be able to gain some sort of employment.

Back in Sydney, I managed to get a job working for a company called *Skilled Engineering*. Skilled Engineering does not own any company or manufacture anything; they just supply people who are hired out to temporarily cover the workload in different companies when required. While working for Skilled Engineering in Sydney, I found some of the most interesting machinery that I have ever worked on, which was the machinery at Kellogg's, where I was employed as a *rigger/TA* for the maintenance of the machinery. *Kellogg's* had three interesting machines that I sometimes had to work on. This was where they made *Special K breakfast*, *Shredded Wheat*, and *small cartons of breakfast cereal*.

After a while, I found that I was not getting enough hours per week while working with Skilled Engineering, so I also started up with another company that did a similar type of work, called *Drake*. Where one of the jobs that they gave me was as a *packer*, which involved packing chemicals, in a company called *Ajax Chemicals* in *Auburn*. Eventually, I ended up becoming a permit worker with them. This job lasted six years, until a company called *APS* bought Ajax and all their equipment, along with the men working there. Men and materials were transferred to *Seven Hills*, and this included all the workers' entitlements. When I got to Seven Hills, my job was changed to that of an *acid plant operator*. This paid me bigger money and was also a more interesting job to have. This job lasted for another seven years. The factory which I was working in at Seven Hills had a staff of about 130 people. Even though they had 6 different branches—2 in Sydney, 1 in Queensland, 1 in Victoria, 1 in Papua New Guinea, and 1 in New Zealand—the branch they decided to close down was at Seven Hills. Then we were all made redundant. After we all left the site, it was subdivided; I believe that they made a lot of money through it. I did all-right financially but would have much preferred to have stayed on for at least seven more years until I retired, or even longer. I got 64 weeks for my redundancy pay, in addition to sick leave and holidays. But unfortunately, because of my age, I was not able to get back into the workforce and had to go on social security for the first time in my life. This was also at the time of the financial crisis—a chapter of my life that I would much prefer to have missed out on. After a couple of years of being out of work, I worked out a way to do work that I really enjoyed doing, which is *handyman's* work. Handyman's work is something I have done a lot of during the course of my lifetime and is something I have a lot of experience in. Since being made redundant from the chemical factory, I have spent a lot of time working hard at being an author. I also study chess, a game that keeps the brain very active.

In regard to taking my father's advice about travelling before you get married, well, I am now 70 years old, and I didn't get married until I was 49 years old. I have lived happily ever after since then and have not gone around wishing that I did not take the opportunity to travel when I had it.

CHAPTER 2

My Parents' History and the Influence That It Had on Me

Writing this story about my Mum and Dad meant that I needed to obtain most of the information from my mother, along with other records that I was able to find. The reason I was not able to take advantage of the history of my father was that he died in **1970**, before I started gathering some of the history that I needed to know; I had to rely a lot on what my mother passed on to me.

It was many years later, after I had my heart attack in **1996** when I started writing my autobiography. Another thing that adds to the difficulty of writing this book, is that everyone in the family has also made the same mistake as me, by never keeping a journal, which makes it harder to line up the dates of the different events that occurred in my life, although I am fortunate to have good long-term memory.

My father's name was Alfred Laurence Willetts, and he was always referred to as Don, not by his two Christian names. My Dad was born on **14/04/1916** in Thames, New Zealand, and on **23** November **1970**, he died of bronchial asthma at the age of **54**, when I was **23**.

My mother's maiden name was Joyce Eileen Walker, and she was born in Gisborne, New Zealand, on **28/1/1919**. My Mum died of heart failure on **10/11/2014** at the age of **95**, when I was **67**.

Our family was part of the first white settlers to arrive in New Zealand. I was born in a small town called Ngaruawahia, which is in the middle of the North Island of New Zealand. It was also the place where I spent the first 16 years of my life, living with my Mum and Dad, my two elder sisters, and my younger brother. *Ngaruawahia* is the name of the town and is the Maori name meaning 'the meeting of the two rivers', it is also where the Waiapu River flows into the Waikato River.

New Zealand is made up of two main islands, the North Island and the South Island. Even though the land mass for the two islands are roughly the same, the North Island makes up approximately three quarters of the population, and the South Island makes up the remaining quarter. The next biggest island is Stewart Island, which is situated south of the South Island and is very small compared to the other two islands. It only has a population of about 381. The total population of New Zealand is 4.4 million. The strait that separates the North Island from the South Island is Cook Strait, and the body of water that separates the South Island from Stewart Island is called Foveaux Strait.

My mother was born in New Zealand, in a place called Gisborne, during the war years, and Gisborne was also where she started her schooling. The only way for her to get to school was by walking 1½ miles. When she reached the age of 13, the family moved to a dairy farm in a place called Hauturu. Her nearest school was 6 miles (9.6 kilometres) away, too far for her to be walking to the school, and she was left with no other means of transport for getting to school. The only option left for doing her education was through correspondence. The correspondence came from Wellington, which was more than a hundred miles from where they lived, and it was passed back and forth once every fortnight through the post. Mum said that she found the teacher's remarks on her assignments to be very encouraging, which inspired her to work harder.

The place where she lived was very isolated; the nearest neighbour was 1 mile (1.6 kilometres) away. The reason it was so very isolated was because she did not have a car and was without any means of fast transportation, and their only alternative was to walk. They did not have access to modern technology such as computers and TV, and in the earlier part of her life, they had no telephone of any sort, which made life a lot more difficult to get through. However, the toughest problem of all was not having access to modern transport, which changed the whole way that one thought about getting through life. Given the era, I suppose that it is reasonable to think that the family may already have had a horse. In fact, the family did have a horse, although it is important to point out the lack of instant accessibility to transport when you view it through the eyes of the era of Mum's childhood, as compared to the modern transport and the way that we understand transport today. To the readers who are not conversant with only having horses as your sole means of transport (apart from walking), it creates a host of problems that you do not have with a motor vehicle. The total time it takes to get to your destination when travelling by horse may vary, from being slower than it would take to walk there to being two or three times faster. This depends on several factors: A longer distance usually means you have a better chance of doing it quicker than walking. It also depends on how hard the horse has been worked and how hard you are prepared to work the horse. The things you need to watch out for are saddle-sores and foot injuries that can escalate should the horse not have time to recuperate when the injury or injuries first occur.

The first problem that needs to be addressed when using a horse for transport to and from school is that the first thing you need to do is catch it. Even if you have a barn, you can't leave it in the barn all the time, because it needs freedom to move around so it can get its natural exercise as well as having something to eat. Also, there is the fact that the family was most definitely, not able to afford the special food that would be required for keeping it in the barn for any lengthy period. After you have caught the horse and saddled it up, you come to what most people consider to be the fun part, which is riding the horse to school. Well, the thing that can take the fun out of riding a horse is that it can sometimes start bucking, especially when it is cold, and can end up causing you to fall heavily on the ground. However, as a rule, that does not usually happen; it mainly depends on how passive your horse is. Unlike a car, when a horse stays in one place for a long time, it is going to spend a lot of time eating and will need to have a constant supply of drinking water. Another problem that can arise while it is waiting for you to return home from school is that it can be spooked (suddenly frightened). Even something as insignificant as a piece of paper being blown around can cause it to run away in a frightened state (bolt), and in the process, it can end up hurting itself by running into a fence or some other solid object that will result in the horse being injured. When the rider has saddled up and is returning home, then they are still at a low risk while travelling along their journey of being easily knocked off the horse; even when it is slowly walking along, it can be spooked by a sudden movement or when something unexpectedly appears (spooked). Spooked—this is when a horse moves suddenly to one side without warning. Sometimes, when it is frightened, it will bolt, which means that it will take off running very fast and jump over any given obstacle or sometimes suddenly sidestep an obstacle that comes in its path before you have a chance to get it under control. This may result in the rider falling off and getting some sort of injury. Also, there is a host of other problems that need to be taken care of.

Don't get me wrong, riding a horse does have some enjoyable moments when all is going well, which is more often than not. However, to understand the era Mum was living in also means understanding the unknown baggage that comes with it. So, the people who are not used to riding horses as a means of transport are more than likely to be missing out on understanding the difference between the comforts of having a motor vehicle as opposed to having a horse for transport. Most of the time, when experienced riders ride a horse, they complete their journey without falling off. People who ride horses daily for long periods at a time rotate the horses that they ride.

Mum's entertainment was a lot different from our entertainment today. Hers was done by doing things such as household chores and schoolwork and, on the lighter side, by swimming in the creek and being able to have as much fruit as she wanted, by eating from the fruit trees when they were in season, which was a very enjoyable place to be during the fruit season. In those days, they didn't have any fences around the creeks or any supervision while they played around the creeks.

It was considered smarter and less expensive to teach the kids the dangers of the creek and to make sure that they *fully understood and knew that they could get hurt.* As a matter of fact, not only were they told that they could not get hurt, but also their rules were purposely established so that they knew that they would definitely get hurt if they did not adhere to certain rules, and fully understood that their safety depended on it. The things which were important to know where the basic facts of the dangers of drowning in the creek (the key to preventing yourself from drowning is knowing how to swim, and knowing the different ways that you can drown). So, it was very clearly understood what the consequences would be of any wrong actions that they may have thought of or what would happen if they didn't think about what they needed to do in order to stay safe. I think this is a far better method than the method that we use today, wrapping children in cotton wool (overprotecting them) and letting the children believe that there will always be someone who will protect them and that they will never be harmed in any way. This reverts to promising the future, and the future which is not ours to give. Besides, regardless of how well-intended someone's intentions are, they are impossible to keep. Furthermore, who is going to fulfil the task of protecting them when you are in the toilet or when you are sleeping or, more importantly, when you die? In short, one would have to accept that you have given the children a bad start to life by allowing them to have a lack of understanding of the various dangers that confront them in life and by letting them believe that someone will always be there to protect them. My belief is, when it comes down to the protection of the children, it is going to come back to how well they deal with their *attitude* in understanding the dangers, the *balance* of how much attention they do or do not pay to the dangers, and the *choices* they end up making.

I have worked my way around the world twice and have encountered many dangers, such as working on high-rise buildings, working with wild animals, and working with dangerous chemicals. The only thing that protected me from those dangers was the methodology that I had and fully understanding the dangers about safety, so I don't become a victim to it and by knowing what I need to do in order to protect myself.

When I was a child, I had no idea of the dangers I was going to be exposed to, and as a matter of fact, nobody knows because we are dealing with the future. This story is not only about my mother but is also about the concept to the values of what we need to know about safety and by the way that she taught me to fully understand the dangers that are presented throughout my life. It has been my best tool in life for staying safe. Since I wish to convey good thoughts, it also includes anyone else who wishes to understand this proven method of safety in life. Having the knowledge about the dangers to the safety in our lives saves lives and is the best protection we can have and it is not cotton wool.

Water is a very big part of our life. Without it, we cannot survive, and if we have too much, especially in the wrong places, then it can end up killing us. I have a brother and two sisters, and throughout our lives as children, up to when I was 16, we always had the Waikato River at the back of our place. We did not have any physical objects to keep us away from that wide fast-flowing river. There were gates and fences which were built to contain cattle but which were something that any child could easily climb through. Instead, we were taught of a far greater gate and a far greater fence. The one I am referring to is understanding and respecting the fact that even though this water is wonderful, it can also very easily kill you by drowning you. We were clearly informed about how that could take place. There was also a weed in certain parts of the river, called river weed, which added to the dangers of drowning. Should you happen to be caught in the river weed while you are swimming in the river, it requires using slow movements with your hands and feet. The faster you move, the tighter your limbs will get entangled in the river weed. If you panic and start moving quickly, it will entangle your limbs and prevent you from being able to move; unless someone is around who is capable of pulling you out of the weed, then you would also be standing a good chance to sealing your fate for drowning. This is a scary situation when you do not understand the basic rules of how you can drown. However, when you do understand the basic rules, it is going to be the very thing that is going to keep you safe and alive when you are separated from your carers.

When it came to my learning how to swim, one day Mum took me to a place in the river where there was no river weed. She took me out a short distance into the river so I could learn to swim and then told me that I needed to move my arms and legs. After that, she got me to lay face down, and as I did, then she put her hand underneath me so that I could keep my head above the water. Then she slowly moved me through the water and told me to start moving my hands and kicking my feet. Being a typical child of about 5 years old, I didn't put as much enthusiasm into doing what I was told, and as usual, I relied on her to make this swimming successful. However, as she started to lower her hand away from my belly, I quickly got the message and learnt the requirements of swimming. I learnt to move my hands and feet a lot more quickly, because there was no question what I needed to do, and I got a taste of what it is like to drown really fast. This also gave me a good lesson on how easily one's life can be taken away, and it left me with a good understanding of the dangers of water. I was also taught about other dangers, such as electricity, what happens when you touch something that is hot, and the danger of cars, how they can be your friend, and the different ways that they can injure and kill you. There are many other dangers that we were taught to face in life. The lessons Mum taught me left me with a clear knowledge about the many dangers in life and were the best tools that I was given for maintaining safety in my life. It was also a good platform to work from when it came to confronting new dangers that I had to deal with, along my journey in life.

Another thing I learnt as a child is that your Mum and Dad are always right unless proven wrong. A good example of what I was taught regarding illegal drugs. All my father said to me when I was about 8 years old was to "not touch them, because you don't need them to live on and they will *wreck your brain*". Dad also had a good sense of humour which intensified the strength of his message as he added that I only have one brain and that even that one is in doubt. After hearing the warning he gave me about not taking drugs—coupled with a lot of things I was struggling to understand and wishing that I had better brainpower to sort out the problems that I already had—it became very clear to me that I was never going take a some silly drug that can wreck my brain which I neither needed or was it required for me to live on. After reviewing his witty comment many years later and seeing the dangers of illegal drugs, the damage that it does to the people taking them, and the destruction that it causes the loved ones around them. This proved to be the most powerful way that he could have helped me fully understand that important message, especially since I struggled badly with my grammar, which constantly had a tendency to point my intelligence level in a strong downward direction. When Dad would ask me to do something, I would do it first and ask questions later. He could have very simply said 'Don't touch them son, because they are no good for you, and I forbid you from taking them'. Fortunately for me, he was very wise when it came to getting someone to fully understand the message he was passing on, and he knew that the way he presented it was the most effective way for me to understand the dangers of drugs.

There was one other important message, my father passed on to me, and this time it was a more difficult one to be passing on. The reason was because though out my life time I have always seen my father as a smoker, and it is not easy for him to tell his children to not be like him and smoke. As usual my Dad worked out a great way to stop me from taking on that bad habit of smoking. He said, as you know I smoke, and if you ask my advice about it, I would advise you not to smoke, but I do not expect you to take my advice about it. This comment came as a surprise, because when Dad told me to do something then I would do it first, and if I was brave enough later, then I would think about asking questions. He then went on to say, "before you do start up smoking", ask three of your friends who are of the same age as yourself, who have been smoking for at least a year, if they had their chance over again, would they start up smoking again. I ask two of my friends who have been smoking and they said that they were trying to give it up but they couldn't. This left me with no uncertainty that there was nothing cool about smoking and that there was no way that I was going to take on that bad habit.

Let's get back to the topic of being on the farm. Mum was constantly kept occupied with such things as collecting wood and fuelling the wood-burning stove, doing her school assignments, milking the cows, and operating the separator, which was to be operated twice a day, every day of the week. The separator would separate the cream from the milk; the remainder of the milk, after the cream is extracted from the milk, is called skim milk. This operation, which was done by hand, required turning the handle of the separator at least a hundred times—or even more likely, a lot more-which depends on the quantity of milk being separated. Approximately ¼ of the milk would be turned into cream, and the rest of the milk was turned into skim milk. The skim milk was largely wasted because we were unaware of its true value, and no one else in our circle of friends had knowledge of its value either. When skim milk matures, it turns into cottage cheese, something that we missed out on at the time. However, it did not turn out to be a total waste, because the skim milk was stored in a 200-litre drum (44 gallons), and when it was filled, it would be poured on the ground and left for the domestic birds to eat; the birds ended up being fed some very expensive bird food. I guess the reason that they did not develop a better understanding of the value of the cottage cheese was that they had no other information available to them at the time, and since they were already using it to feed the domestic birds, they more than likely thought that was as good a value as it got.

In regard to me using the term *domestic bird* instead of *chicken*, I was brought up on a poultry farm and know for certain that what is often referred to as a chicken which is actually a domestic bird or a fowl. A domestic bird can also mean a duck or a turkey. The authentic definition of a chicken is this: When a chicken is first born, it is coated with soft, fluffy yellow fur; it has no feathers on it whatsoever for a few short weeks. The next stage it goes into is a pullet, where the fluffy yellow fur is replaced with feathers and remains as a pullet up to its first year. Then it becomes a domestic bird or a fowl, and the colloquial name for it is a chook. My best understanding of why they call it a *chicken* instead of a domestic fowl is the marketing problem that the word *fowl* can create.

Fowl is a homophone of *foul*. (A homophone is a word that has the same sound, but is spelt differently from another word, and each word has a different meaning to it.) *Foul* means 'very bad' or 'a nasty smell'. When a chicken is called by its proper name, fowl, it leaves a major problem to the promoters who are trying to market the fowl by trying to get the potential customers to want to buy them. The homophone *foul*, which is going to turn their nice presentation into a nasty thing that nobody would want to buy due to the bad perception while trying to promote the selling of the fowl—which also extends to the presentation of a fowl ready to cook or one that has been cooked, as well as the selling of their eggs—which is going to constantly lead them back to the homophone's stigma of a foul, something which is nasty and smells.

Not all of the cream from the farm was sent to the butter factory; Mum used some of the cream for making butter. This was done by hand, which is very time-consuming, and it required a lot of hard work. The electricity which was used for domestic use in that era was mainly used for lighting, and it later progressed to being used for other appliances as life progresses into a later date in time. Another thing that needs to be taken into consideration is that not everybody was rich enough to have had it connected to their house. This also required being able to afford the cost of paying for power that one is consuming. Mum's stove was powered by burning wood, and unlike electricity, which you just turn on when you need it, the wood stove is very labour-intensive and requires collecting a lot of wood, as well as having to regularly top it up with the fuel of wood. Although the stove had the advantage of keeping the room warm in the winter, unfortunately it did not provide the same luxuries in the hot summer days.

Mum had 3 sisters and 3 brothers, and the workload on the farm was something the whole family had to share; there was always something for them to do at any given time. Her eldest brother was killed in the Second World War and died at the age of 22, and her youngest brother was wounded in the war and was able to gain a good outcome to his life because he fully recovered from his injury.

He worked as a carpenter. Although the war was not able to kill him, some sixty years later the asbestos that he had to work with, while being a carpenter, did what the war was not able to do. It became very obvious in the last few years of his life that his lungs had slowly stopped working, and he ended up dying in hospital.

Due to a lack of family finances at the time, Mum went out to work at the age of 16 as a live-in nanny. A part of her wage included free accommodation, and her job required doing the housekeeping and looking after the young children. The wage she received was low for two reasons. The first one was that her food and accommodation were included. The other reason was that the people she was working for were very often, not much better off than she was financially. Most of the jobs that she did were before she got married and was as a live-in nanny on different farms and her first job lasted for one year. The next job Mum got as a live-in nanny which had a better pay; she was working for a barrister and his wife, who had a new baby boy. Mum held this job for two years and considered it her best job before she got married. She also took a lot of pride in knowing that, many years later, that baby she took care of became a top coroner in the courts. I believe that this higher-paying job made her enough money to buy a pushbike, which kept her fit and was also her main means of transport. This also meant having to clock up a lot of miles; it required a lot of hard work to reach the end of each journey. Mum got two more jobs as a farmhand, and at the age of 19, she started dancing regularly at the Frankton town hall in Hamilton, where she met her husband. Then 3 years later, they got married.

After they got married, Mum and Dad went to work on several different farms and started having children of their own, which eventually led to them having their own farm. Despite spending several years working on a dairy farm, they both lacked the knowledge to make cottage cheese. The irony of it all is that some 30 years later, when Mum left the farm and went to live in the city—well, let's put it this way, she now enjoys eating cottage cheese most days of the week.

In regard to my father, there was a strange bit of history concerning his name. Even though his Christian names were Alfred Lawrence, it was never used. Everybody called him *Don*. This name came upon him before he got married and was after he won a prize from the sport of wrestling. The prize was a pink ornamental duck with a top hat on it, and after winning that, he was teased and called Donald Duck. The name was later shortened to Don and ended up being the name he was always addressed by.

Dad had 2 brothers; the elder was Jack, and his younger brother was Arthur. At the age of three, he lost his mother, and at the age of eight, he lost his father. However, the three boys always managed to stay together and were passed around various foster homes. As children, they were brought up on dairy farms; typical of those times, the farm work was always put as top priority, because the way they saw it was that the work on the farm brought in the money that they needed for their livelihood. Their education was always put in the category of 'It will be dealt with if and when it can be done', and their school homework was left out a lot more than it was included. As ugly as that may seem in today's standards, with the children's education having such low importance, I feel that if you are going to judge them, you need to understand the mood of that era and the options that were available to them for them to be able to supply the needs for the household to survive.

The unemployment payment didn't start until **1938**, which meant that when it first started up, there was very little financial backup given—or very often, no financial backup at all—when things went wrong. Even the people who did qualify for benefits, found them to be very small benefits that did little to bridge the gap of their financial needs. Having to work with a mentality different from the one we have today was required in order to survive that era.

Dad's mother died when he was **3** years old while she was trying to give birth to a baby girl. The story continues to deteriorate after his mother's death, and **5** years later, his father died, when he had an appendix operation and fell out of bed. Well, as my Mum explained to me, it was the complications from the operation that actually killed him (more than likely the infection that developed). It was also sometime around this period that my Dad nearly died from pneumonia.

After that, he lived at his grandma and grandad's place, and in my way of assessing the given knowledge that I had at hand, I did not see him getting too much loving in his childhood. His grandfather used to have a whip on the kitchen table at mealtime, and should it be *considered* "*in their opinion*" that he was misbehaving, he would get a flick from the whip. When one looks at those last two paragraphs, then you would have to concede, that My Dad had an extremely bad life to live through as a child.

The principal rule at the time was to get as much work out of the children as quickly and as soon as possible; I need to point out that at that period of time it was mainly considered a way of surviving, and there were not a lot of options available to the parents, as compared to what we have today. After surveying the facts of Dad's history, I strongly believe that they were severely deprived of loving and affection. It is very hard to give affection when you have never received it, although given his upbringing, I believe that he did an excellent job when it came to sharing his emotions.

The grandparents looked after the three boys during this five-year period after their mother and father died and what I believe was lacking their moral code in life was that they were mainly deprived of their childhood and was left to creative the things which they knew how to do, and that was to constantly get into mischief. Bad times continued in a downward spiral; their grandparents ended up finding them too difficult to handle. Their grandparents gave up on Dad and his 2 brothers, who were then placed to be wards of the State. From there, they were sent to numerous foster homes on various farms, and as usual, their carers first priority was to see how much work they could get out of them; this would be put ahead of loving and education. It's not that a lot of the foster carers could have done a lot more, due to the conditions that they were required to live in, but in hindsight, one can see some fine-tuning that could have made a big improvement in his life, such as giving them a hug and kiss every once in a while, and getting rid of that whip on the table. There are a lot of better options available and different skills that could have been used to control them. Who knows, my Dad and his brothers may have been conditioned to such a degree that they were no longer able to accept the love of hugs and kisses at that point in time. There is a good chance that he may have ended up seeing the hugs and kisses in the world they lived in as being some mean trick that someone was trying to play on them. I am not saying that was what happened, just that it is a probability that, in the early part of his life, something along those patterns of thought may have been something that happened to him.

I guess it is easy for me to sit back and throw around this good advice since I have the luxury of already knowing better ways to control the same situation; it is not so hard when you have had several decades of hindsight to come up with answers that they did not understand or possibly may not have had available to them at the time. Despite the tough times, Dad still had very good knowledge of the things we need to know in life and also managed to do wrestling and played football. When he got married, he continued both sports with a slight difference: with wrestling, he became an instructor, and with football, he became a referee and later a first-aid officer for the footballers. In the later stages of their lives, they got back into dancing.

When I summarise the events of my parents' lives, I believe that they did a good job when it came to rearing their family. Sure, there were things they could have done better, and when I think about it, one could just as easily look back at *my* life and say there were also things that I could have done better. I feel that it is important to understand that there were a lot of valuable things I have learnt from my parents that gave me a good start in life. We always need to bear in mind that there is not a parent on the planet who is perfect, so there is no point in looking for them. The siblings of the parents make up the rules, and each sibling is more than likely to have a different expectation as to whether they are considered to be the perfect parent, or to being monsters or somewhere in between. I believe the trick here is to work out what they have done right and then work out a way to make that right decision a part of your life. The things you consider to have been done wrong, try and correct them. In addition, there are some things you just go along with. However, you need to bear in mind that these decisions are largely stamped on the slate of who you are.

In the case of my Dad, he taught me many great lessons that proved to be valuable throughout my journey in life. Knowing about the stupidity of taking illegal drugs was important. Another valuable lesson he gave me—and it is astounding how many people who should know better still get caught in this trap—is the one of being conned. My father told me that there is nothing in this world that is free. When he told me that, I laughed and said, 'What about the free cup of tea that I had at Mrs Russo's place?' I was surprised at his answer.

He said to me, 'No son, that cup of tea was not free. Because if you have any decency in you—and I believe you have—then not only will you pay that cup of tea back again, but you will give her another one as well when you can.' So, in continuing what my father was saying to me, once you wake up to the fact that nothing is free in this world, you can no longer be conned. The thing you always need to do is to look back down the trail to where this free thing is coming from and then ask yourself the moral questions: Are you still happy receiving it when you know where it is coming from, and do you still want to be receiving that so-called free money or free gift? Because someone had to pay for it somewhere down the track, is it fair for you to be receiving it?

My Dad was a very big part to the things I learnt in life, and unfortunately, in the early part of my life I had no thoughts at all of becoming a writer or doing any sort of writing. Writing a book was not even on the consideration list. This leads me to the sad fact that there was valuable information I should have asked him while he was alive, such as the knowledge of the history that he knew of. I also now believe that if I would had asked those unasked questions, I would have been able to put more valuable information in this book, and by failing to do so, means that I have also missed out on allowing him to feel even more valued as a father, which has turned out to be a sad opportunity missed.

Mum also taught me many things, like how to wash clothes, wash dishes, iron my clothes, and sew by hand. I know how to do **4** different stitches in sewing, and now that I am working as a professional handyman, I find the experience of gardening that I got from my mother very useful. I remember one day, when I was feeling bored, I made the terrible mistake of nagging and repeatedly telling my Mum that I was bored. She informed me that it was not her job to constantly entertain me and that it was my job to entertain myself. She then went about giving me a lot of meaningless jobs that lasted all day, and then she informed me that maybe next time I would be able to make a better choice for the jobs that need to be done. I took her up on that advice, and over the next sixty years and beyond, I have avoided mentioning the word *bored* again. As a matter of fact, I steer clear of the word *bored* altogether, and should I hear anyone using that word, I say to them that it is their job to entertain themselves.

The extra time I was able to spend with Mum has enriched my life in many ways. In this case, I was able to gain a considerable amount of information of our family's history; some of it was about certain events that I was not aware of at the time, and sometimes she was able to fill in some of the gaps for events that I was not sure of. Something that made this story even harder to compile was the fact that Mum was living in New Zealand and I was living in Australia, and our communication was done either when I went home to visit Mum, by correspondence, or by telephone. Even though she has departed the world we know, I would still like to express my gratitude to Mum for the help she gave me in filling in a lot of the details of our family history and, while looking through that history, looking for the things that added value to my life or the things that went wrong that needed to be modified. Or maybe they need to be completely disregarded, because there is no use holding on to a legacy when you already know that it is wrong and is only continuing to make misery, should that be the case.

CHAPTER 3

The Age of Three and
Our First Two Farms

When I was 3 years old, our family took on a very challenging task, well that part of the statement is not really true. It was our parents who took on the very challenging task, and the children were just a part of a very difficult situation which they were placed into, which lacked the answers to a lot of real possibilities to several dangerous problems, that should have been addressed before my parents took on the challenge of the farm. The dangers I am referring to is when my parents, who had four children and bought their first dairy farm, which had 10 cows and was situated on the side of a very steep hill. While we were living there, there were only two flat places on the property: one was the small area around the milking shed, and the other one was the small area around the house. The farm was roughly 20 acres (2.471 acres = 1 hectare, and 1 hectare = 10,000 square metres) in size. At the base of that hill was the road, and once you got across the road, which was a few yards further on, there was a river. The river was wide and fast-flowing, and it was called the Waikato River.

In regard to working the farm, Dad needed to go to work in order for the family to survive financially, which left Mum with a mammoth job on her hands. As they were living on a hillside, she had to look after her four young children while she milked 10 cows twice a day during the week, as well as having to separate the cream from the milk, each time she milked the cows. Her duties also had to take care of the family chores in the home. Her first concern was an extremely difficult one that required being able to somehow take care of her two daughters, aged 10 and 4, and two sons, aged 1 and 3 (I was the one who was 3 years old). While Mum was doing the job of milking the cows, which required her full attention for at least an hour or more likely a lot longer, this also required the time-consuming job of separating the milk that she got from the cows which were milked by hand, so that she can make and sell the cream. Since my Dad was working five days a week, then I don't believe that he would have had much of a chance to be able to do a lot of the jobs during the weekdays, especially when it came to milking the cows. There are also a lot of other chores that need to be done on a dairy farm besides milking the cows, such as maintaining fences and improving the working conditions on the farm, although the one dominating thing which always hovered over their heads was the financial expenses that needed to be met, like paying off the mortgage on the farm, along with the daily living expenses.

This was a tough time in my parents' life and is something that Mum did not like to spend a lot of time talking about. The dangers that she had to deal with while milking the cows and looking after her children at the same time. She also had to make sure that the children didn't get out of control by falling down the steep hill and hurting themselves. The natural place anybody goes is usually down a hill because it is the easiest way to travel, and the fence at the bottom of the hill was for the cows and offered no protection in regard to stopping the children from passing through it—well, the best it could do was slow them down a little bit. At the foot of the hill was a road that cars travelled along, and a short distance across the road was the fast-flowing Waikato River. Any one of those three obstacles could have badly injured or killed any of her children had circumstances got out of hand. However, she was able to get a considerable amount of help from her oldest daughter, who was very useful in assisting in the managing of the other three siblings. I personally do not have any memory of living on that farm and have had to rely on information handed down to me. My mother informed me that our stay there was no longer than a year. From there, we moved on to a farm that only consisted of 4 acres, which was flat, apart from three short and gentle slopes; we were now living on the other side of the Waikato River.

The new farm was totally different from the first one we were on, and even though I don't believe that it had started out this way, the only way I remember the farm while I lived on it was that it had 3 milking cows, 500 domestic birds, 1 pig, and up to 7 sheep at a given time, which were used for the supply of meat for our dinner table. One of the realities we had to deal with as farmers was in how we were able to eat the meat which we had on the farm, and we were somewhat under no illusion that the lamb roast did not come from a tree or from some other mysterious way.

My first memories always involved participating in some of the chores that needed to be done around the farm, and as I got older, the pace of the workload kept on increasing. I don't know for sure to all the times that I started each job, but I do remember it better from when I was 5 years old. At the age of five, I was taught how to ride a small pushbike; it required riding 2 miles (3.2 kilometres) each way to and from school, mostly over rough gravel road, which was, more often than not, laced with potholes. However, every so often, a road grader, which is used for smoothing out the potholes in the road, would come along.

I remember that the pushbike had a unique ability to make the journey rough and uncomfortable, especially because of the seat, which caused my butt to be sore from time to time, this was due to the roughness of the road, and which also took its toll on the bike, causing it to require a bit of maintenance. Somehow this got to be turned around to mean that were not looking after our bikes properly, and the reason I say 'our bikes' is that my brother and my two sisters, as well as my Mum, had the very same problem, although my Mum did not use the bike nearly as often as her four children. I guess if the truth is really known, I would have to say it was the lack of finances that created the comment that we did not take proper care when it came to looking after our bikes; it had very little to do with the way we did or did not treat our bikes, and if we looked at the bright side of the journey, there was some bitumen on the road which was in the immediate vicinity of the town, in the shopping area.

As with all dairy cows, our cows were required to be milked twice a day, 7 days a week. In the winter, there would be a period of about 4 to 5 weeks when the cows would have no milk, while waiting for them to get pregnant again. In order for a cow to produce milk throughout the year, the cow first needs to become pregnant and have a calf.

In the morning, I would get up at about 5 a.m., and I would go with my father and milk one cow while he milked two. I also had to separate the milk, which would be converted from milk to cream, 1 quarter of the milk was turned into cream and the other 3 quarters of the milk was turned into skim milk. The skim milk was poured into a large 44-gallon drum (200 litres), where it would form curds (a crust) on the top of the whey (the liquid which is left under the crust). We did not know at the time that the curds had matured into cottage cheese and had no idea of its value, and at that time, nor did we know anybody who had even heard of cottage cheese. This turned out to be the chooks' good fortune, because they were the ones that got to eat it, and the cream was sent to the butter factory. After breakfast, I would wash the separator before going to school. I am not sure of the timing to when I started working on the other chores, but it would have been in a shorter period of time, rather than the longer period, to when my Dad would have thought that I would be old enough to be increasing my work load.

On my way home from school, I had to pick up the mail from the post office, as well as half a loaf of brown bread, plus two full loaves of white bread from the bread shop. When I got home, I still had many chores to do, such as chopping the kindling wood, as well as the big wood, which needed to be chopped for the fire that kept us warm at night. We had 500 chooks, or you could say fowls or chickens. We used to call them *chooks*, which is the colloquial term for a domestic bird or a fowl. Most of us now refer to a domestic bird as a chicken. The substitute name of *chicken* is derived from a marketing plan that is designed to make them appear very fresh and pleasurable. A real chicken's life starts when it is first born by breaking out of an egg, and it starts off having a soft, furry yellow covering, without any feathers. It is small enough to easily fit inside the palm of one's hand. After about 6 weeks, the yellow fur is replaced with feathers. When they have all their feathers and have not yet fully grown, they are called pullets. When they are fully grown a year later, they become a fowl, a chook, or a chicken. I guess it is clear to see why the people marketing the fowl (a domestic bird) are reluctant to use the generic name, because something foul is offensive by having a bad odour or taste. In regard to marketing, it is a bad homophone (homophone; is a word which sounds the same, but the two words are spelt differently, and have two different meanings) although from a marketing point of view, it is clearly not the way to entice a potential customer to want to eat a lot of their product.

We also had up to 7 sheep from time to time for the purpose of supplying a lot of the meat that we ate. The sheep also had to be taken care of; one of the things that we did for them was push them through a special trench full of liquid chemicals that got rid of blowflies, ticks, and many other things that were harmful to the sheep. We also had a small young pig; it would take several months of feeding before it was sent to the abattoirs and returned for our future meals.

Getting back to the daily chores that I needed to do when I came back home from school, I had to feed the chooks and collect the eggs. We also had three cows; in the afternoon, my brother milked two of them, and I milked one. Each time we would milk a cow, it would produce about 10 litres of milk, and I still had to separate the milk for a second time (once in the morning and once in the afternoon). The separator was operated by hand, which meant turning a handle around for about 20 minutes; it also required being turned constantly at a certain pace. I also had many other chores that I had to do on the weekend, and some of them were digging the gardens, weeding the gardens, cleaning the fowl sheds, having to pluck the feathers, and gutting the chooks so that when we sold these chooks, they were ready for the customers to eat at their dinner table. There were also other chores that needed to be done, although I did get some time on some of the weekends to do other things.

I remember one time when I had managed to get ahead of my workload; feeling lost for something to do, I made the mistake of saying to my mother that I was bored and had nothing to do. The result of that turned out to be one hell of a mistake. She gave me so many meaningless jobs that firmly left me with the message that it is smarter for me to take care of my own schedule of work and find a way of entertaining myself because I have a far better chance of making it a lot more pleasurable. Many years later, I am still picking up on that valuable exercise, which Mum taught me about being bored, and that is: It is not for someone else to make the job interesting for me. Instead it is for me to work out a way to make each and every job I do an interesting one, because taking the initiative leads to me gaining self-satisfaction from the job; from my perspective, it is a far better option than being given an order to do the same job (one is a chore, and the other is a gratitude of self-satisfaction).

Another great thing Mum did for me was that she taught me that it was important to learn the ladies' jobs as well as it was to learn the men's jobs, because you never know the knowledge that one may need to have as you progress through life. She taught me 4 different stitches with the needle and cotton; she taught me how to cook, wash and iron my clothes, clean the dishes, and keep a good standard with house cleaning.

I remember when I was about ten years old and living in the farm in Ngaruawahia, where there was a job that was not often done which required Mum and her four children to get on their bikes. Each one would grab a 9-litre plastic bucket so that they could go blackberry picking. This required doing about an eight-kilometre journey with our pushbikes over a gravel road. Blackberries are not the friendliest things to be working with. The blackberry is a long, thin vine that usually entangles with other vines to form a long dense bush that has a lot of prickles which are similar to the prickles on roses. The dimensions of the bushes could be up to 2 metres high, 2–3 metres wide, and sometimes several kilometres long. I guess if someone were to view the scene of us riding our bikes, a good analogy would be from *The Sound of Music*, when Julie Andrews took the 7 children of the Von Trapp family on a joyride with their pushbikes. The big difference was that we were not doing it for a joyride; instead we endured many a prick from the blackberries and also many delicious meals from the blackberries that made all the pricking we received worthwhile.

CHAPTER 4

My First Job and My First Time Being Away from Family

This story starts when I was **16** years of age, and it is about the history of where I lived, as well as a brief history of my first job at the railways where I worked. New Zealand has a small town called Ngaruawahia (Nga rua wa hia), which is situated in the middle of the North Island, **12** miles north of Hamilton. I know that for anyone who is not a New Zealander, they are going to find *Ngaruawahia* hard to pronounce; it is not important to be able to pronounce it, only to know that it is where I lived for **16** years prior to starting my job, and it connects the history to my first job, where I worked for **8** years.

I was about to leave the home of my mother, father, two sisters, and brother. Which is a big step when you first leave the protection and safety of your home that you have taken for granted for so long and to be making all those decisions that someone else would have made for you.

The railways in the North Island have two main roots. The first one is from Auckland to Wellington, which opened in **1908**, and then in **1925**, the line was extended further north from Auckland to Otiria. The second main line is the East Coast line, which goes from Hamilton to Kawerau, and it was opened in **1928**.

In **1963**, I started my first job at the age of **16**, working on the New Zealand railways as a porter in the city of Hamilton, in the suburb of Frankton. The Frankton railway station was a big and important railroad station because of its location and was the junction that connected the Auckland–Wellington line to the East Coast line.

The only job that I was able to find at the time was working as a porter in Frankton. The distance between Ngaruawahia and Frankton is 20 kilometres. As nice as it was to be able to gain a job so quickly, I was still left with the problem of travelling back and forth to work. The options I had available to me were these: Catching one of the government buses which would use up two hours of travelling time, as well as having to pay a moderate fee. Walking was out of the question, and so was riding a pushbike. The only other option was to move into the railway hostel in Frankton, which was affordable and very close to my working facilities. The cost included getting a bed and three meals a day that would be automatically deducted from my wages. This appeared to be the best option by far and was the option that I took.

The railway hostel was only a 2-minute walk from the job. I was also able to avoid the worry of managing the financing of my accommodation, because the railway took it directly out of my pay before I got it. In some ways, it was good because they took into account how much you could afford to pay, although they were far from generous with their assessment of how much I needed to live on. The railways deducted the payment from my wages each fortnight, leaving me with £2 a fortnight to live on. Even in 1963, £2 ($4) a fortnight was still considered a very small amount of money to be living on. Fortunately for me, that was as bad as it got. Having such a small amount of money taught me to be thrifty, and it kept me out of trouble because I wasn't able to go out and buy things such as alcohol and other things that I did not need. Even buying a new item of clothing would have been in excess of my fortnightly allowance and would have required the need to save up for it. Wasting money was not an option. But in all fairness, the hostel did come with a good package deal. The only thing that was not fair was the low starting wage I was given. The package deal I was given by the railway hostel included a single bedroom with my own key to lock the bedroom door and three hot cooked meals—breakfast, lunch, and tea—which were provided at the back of the hostel. Since most of us were shift workers, we were entitled to have a late meal, which would be left in a warming oven with a top plate covering that prevented the food from drying out, or in lieu of the hot meal, a cut lunch of sandwiches when required. The hostel also provided a large room so you could watch TV or play table tennis. I did not fully realise at the time that the free entertainment room they were supplying us with which allowed us to save money and set us up to have better ability to manage our finances. The railway hostel was a fairly big place which consisted of 44 rooms, 40 single rooms and 4 double rooms. One thing that they were really strict about was having no girls in the bedrooms. It would only take one time of being caught with a girl in your room, and you would be evicted. However, you were allowed to have them in the entertainment room when you got permission to do so, and the ones that would be given permission would more than likely be some sort of relative.

Another great thing that happened, was the person that managed the hostel, Jack Davies, who had a generous heart and treated myself and most of the boys like he was a second father to us. I was most grateful that he treated me that way, and I certainly appreciated all the extra help that he gave me. He also had a second job as a train driver and lived in a house next to the hostel with his wife. His son and two daughters lived in a separate flat at the back of the hostel. I was fortunate because he was always ready to help with any problem that came our way. I was typical of most teenagers who started out in life by seeing every problem like it was a major problem. Jack was very good at melting the problems back to where they really belonged when it was often required to be put in its right perspective. If it was important, he would help you through it, and on the odd occasion that he didn't know the answer, he was more than likely to find out from someone who did know.

When I started out on the railways, it was as a porter. Unfortunately for me, after a week or two of working in Frankton, I was transferred to Hamilton station, and if you liked the idea of still working on the railways, it would be a good idea to take the transfer. This most certainly did not work in my favour because it required walking about 3 miles each way every day, although after a few months I was able to save up enough money for a second-hand pushbike for going to work. Another thing that did not go down well with me was that I had to start at 6 a.m., and that meant that I had to get up at 5 a.m. and get a cut lunch instead of the standard cooked breakfast. The upside to it was that I finished at 2.30 p.m., which gave me some free time to do other things in the afternoon. At this point, I feel that it is important mention that the mealtimes for the benefit of understanding the rest of the story. Breakfast was 6 a.m.–7 a.m., lunch was 12 p.m.–1 p.m., and (evening meal) tea was 5 p.m.–6 p.m. Now let's get back to that tricky bit of getting up at 5 a.m. each day. This continued for quite a few months, and being a typical teenager, I wasn't too wise when it came to the sleeping arrangements; I used to go to bed between 11 p.m. and midnight on a regular basis. I guess it was one of those dumb choices that we teenagers make when, for the first time, we have our own choice of when to go to bed, not realising that our parents were right all along when they insisted that we go to bed at an earlier hour. This became more obvious when I started realising, after a few months of starting at 5 a.m., which meant only getting 5–6 hours' sleep each night, which was creating the problem of me getting overtired. At the same time, a 5 a.m. starting time did come with one upside to it, which was the free time I was able to have by getting to the hostel by 3 p.m. Well, this lack of sleep ended up leaving me with the thought that it would be a good idea to sneak in a couple of hours of sleep before mealtime so that I would not feel so washed out. So far, so good, but here's the thing: After having that sleep and when I woke up, I found that it was 6 o'clock. Now I know this sounds really crazy, but I couldn't work out whether it was night or morning. I was thinking that I had slept too long for it to still be night but not long enough for it to be morning, and to go and ask someone whether it was night or morning was too absurd for it to be put up for consideration. So, I needed to find another way to work it out. I thought that I had come up with a good idea, so I looked outside and even then, I still could not work out whether it was the dew from the morning or the dew from the night. Not being one to give in real easily in my quest to find out whether it was night or morning, I thought of another way to work it out. So, I went to the canteen and thought, *here's a place that I should be able to work it out*, but when I went down there, I still was reluctant to ask whether it was night or morning, because I could not work out whether they were getting ready for breakfast or cleaning up after tea. But when I saw the porridge pot, all the doubt was taken out in one big jerk. *It was definitely morning, and I was running late for work.* I had slept for 15 hours straight, and the one thing that I learnt from that long sleep is that when you sleep for such a long period, you end up in a deeply disoriented state. It is one of those things that you need to experience in order to fully understand it. I guess that I spent about a year in the Hamilton station before I got my transfer back to Frankton station, this also meant getting pay increases. The first job when I got back to Frankton was to work three rotating shifts: day shift, 8 a.m.–4 p.m.; afternoon shift, 4 p.m.–12 a.m.; and morning shift, 12 a.m.–8 a.m. After a few months, I was promoted to railway shunter, which required working even more different staggered hours of shift work. My time on the railways was split up between spending 2 or 3 years working as a porter and the rest of the time working as a shunter.

A railway shunter is a person who puts the railway wagons in the right order to assemble them into the different destinations for the duration of the train's journey and very often, when a train comes into a major station, it may need to be pulled apart, so that it can be sorted into the different destinations that each wagon needs to go to.

The amount of money I was earning kept on increasing as I got promoted through the ranks of porter and up the different promotional positions that a shunter can achieve. The overtime that I got before getting the transfer to Frankton was zero, but after the transfer, I would be given overtime in groups of four hours or no overtime at all; the reason for that was that the overtime was to cover a shift, which was when someone would be absent, by not working that rostered shift. Having two people working four hours overtime was the way the shift was covered. Having a lot more money in my pocket didn't turn out to be all glory, because it raised the problem of rostered hours becoming more staggered, with less palatable starting times, such as 2 a.m. You can name almost any hour of the night or day, and it could have well been the time that I started work. The starting time that I found the worst to work was 2 a.m., for many reasons. First of all, when you are working an 8-hour shift then end up finishing at 10 a.m., this presents a bad time for getting 8 hours of sleep. The things you have going against you are that there is daylight when you finish your shift and the sun in the summer has already heated the room you sleep in, which makes the room too hot for sleeping. The meal breaks that I had to adhere to broke up the mealtime schedule, and also, when the boys returned home from the hostel to have their mid-day meal, they had a tendency to make enough noise that would result in me waking up. Personally, there was not one advantage that I could see that the 2 a.m. starting time had for me, although the bosses had a legitimate reason for a different point of view.

After about 4 or 5 years, and now that I was collecting the wage of a shunter, which supplied a much higher financial level to work from, I found that it had opened the door to new opportunities of what I could be doing with my life. Most of the people living in the hostel were Mario's, (Mario: a native of New Zealand) who I had a good friendship with, and they often invited me to parties. A lot of my Mario friends left the hostel and rented a house. About 4 of them pooled together and shared the expenses for the food, rent, electricity, etc. The advantages of sharing a house with your mates are that you can have a girl stay any time you want, cook your own food, and have whatever food you want to eat. You can also save money if it is managed correctly, and besides, it was a big step forward for me to be managing my own life. I teamed up with three of my Mario railway mates and rented a house which was about 4 houses down a side street away from the railway hostel. This turned out to be a good experience, and one of the first things I learnt was that we all have a different way of living. For instance, I was used to storing the bottle opener (which did two jobs: open bottles and open cans), and when I was at home, I would put it in the knife drawer; I thought that it was where everybody would have put it. But as I later learnt, it is not everybody's choice of storage. It was my turn to do the cooking, and when I could not find the can opener, I went and asked the last person who had it. When I asked him where it was, he simply told me, 'It is where it is supposed to be.' So, I asked where that would be. He said, 'In the fridge.' I said, 'How did you work that out?' He said, 'When you open a bottle of drink, it is in the fridge, isn't it?' I had to agree, although that is only if you are putting no importance on the fact that it opens tin cans as well. He ended up winning that battle with the can opener because I did not care where it was put, only that I could find it when I wanted to use it.

There was one very unusual incident that happened while I was working in the railways in Frankton, which was when I experienced an earthquake that occurred in the marshalling yards while I was working. It is rather funny when you think about it, because neither the bloke I was with, nor myself had ever experienced an earthquake. When we walked out of the lunchroom and into the marshalling yard, we both looked at each other, with neither one of us prepared to say what we were seeing. The bloke I was with asked, 'Can you see what I am seeing?' as he waved his arm towards the direction of the railway wagons in the marshalling yard. Then I said, 'Do you mean . . . ?' and I repeated the same arm-waving motion as him. Then I nodded in agreement. We got a lot braver since we were a lot more confident in confirming in our minds that we were not going mad, and for the first time he verbally said, 'Do you mean the railway track waving up and down in a sequence of waves?' Obviously, we were both willing to say yes by now. The reason the railway wagons showed signs of waving was that the ground supporting the wagons was literally waving, which was caused by the earthquake. The first time you see an earthquake and see the earth waving, it is hard to comprehend that what you can see is really happening, and that is because it has never been programmed into your brain, that it is feasible to take place, since you have never seen it happen before.

I continued working on the railways for 8 years and would have most probably stayed a lot longer, had it not been for two factors. The first one was that the railways was a government job, and most of the people who had not worked by doing one of the many government jobs that generally ran with the perception that people who worked for the government were inefficient, lazy, and lacked interest in what they did. That point of view is a long way from being entirely true and is a stigma that government employees have to wear. This also led to another problem that I needed to handle, which was when the foreman kept telling me and anyone else, when he got in a bad mood with them, that we wouldn't last 5 minutes in a job outside the railways. I found his speech to be very irritating and degrading, and I did not consider the comment correct.

The second reason that got me into the travelling mood was one of the wise things my father told me before I left home: 'If you want to travel, then you better do it before you get married, because you've got Buckley's chance after you get married!' So, I took up the challenge of being not good enough for anything but a job working for the government. I had enough of the foreman's degrading comments, so not only did I decide to change jobs, but I took it a stage further and decided to travel around the world. Fortunately for me, at that time one didn't need as many visas as you do today while working in other countries, and the conditions set out for working were a lot more flexible, which made it easier to tour the world.

In Memory of Jack Davies

Jack Davies spent many years of doing a magnificent job of managing the railway hostel. In my case and along with many of the other young people who stayed in the railway hostel, where he would take them in like being a second father to them, while they were away from the family and loved ones. When someone first leaves home and when you are young, then everything seems to be a major problem, although Jack had a unique ability to be able to turn what we may have considered to be a major problem and turn it around to pointing of what it really was, which was usually one of a minor problem. Regardless of whether it was major or minor he would find some way of solving it.

Jack gave not only me, but many people who stayed in the hostel a safe place to fall when they got into trouble and set them up for having a good start in life. Even though Jack has passed away I would still like to thank him for all the helpful things he did for me when I most needed the help.

Brian Willetts

CHAPTER 5

My Motorbike Accident and the Interesting Story That Followed

This story starts when I was **18** years of age, when I had an accident while riding my sister's Vespa motor scooter. If I remember correctly, it had a **125**cc engine. I was coming down a hill, doing about **60** kilometres, and while I was proceeding down the hill, I noticed a car coming out of a side street on my left-hand side. When I first saw the car, I thought it was going to stop. Instead it just kept coming, so I swerved to the right in order to avoid a collision. But the more I swerved to the right, the more he kept coming, until he hit my scooter with his car. Both the motorbike and I lay damaged on the road. I thought that I was all right because I did not have any pain. I decided that I wanted to get up. Both my legs were facing down to the bottom of the hill, so it should have been easy to stand up. Ah, but there was a problem! I wasn't able to stand up, despite the fact that it should have been an easy thing to do. Since I was unable to feel any pain for a short period of time (unbeknown to me, I was suffering from shock), and not being able to get up led me to believe that I was paralysed from the waist down.

At that point, a lady came over and asked me if I was all right. I said, 'No, I am paralysed!' She said, 'Don't go anywhere, I am getting an ambulance for you!' I was grateful that she rang for an ambulance for me, but I was completely confused as to how she thought I was going to go anywhere. I guess that the ambulance took about ¾ of an hour or maybe even 1 hour before it arrived. The pain kicked in after about a ½ hour and it kept intensifying as time progressed. After an hour, it became severe, and after the second hour, it had reached the peak of its severity, which was extreme. They were no longer able to give me anything for the pain because it would interfere with finding out the extent of the damage done by the car accident.

After doing several tests on me and just before sending me to be X-rayed, they gave me morphine to relieve the pain. The X-rays confirmed that I had two broken legs. On the left leg, I had broken off a small piece of bone from the fibula, which goes down the side of the ankle. The small piece of bone was screwed back to where it came from, and this was the correct treatment for when this happens. On the right leg, I broke the main shin bone (the tibia), and the normal procedure is to put the leg in traction to keep the bone growing straight. Failing to do so will cause the muscles to pull together too tightly, and the bone will end up knit in a crooked position.

Unfortunately for me, the orthopaedic surgeon treating me was a lot dumber than he gave himself credit for, and we need to bear in mind, the time that I am referring to is the mid-60s, when the mentality was set up a lot differently than what it is today. Here is where things started going wrong. First of all, when I asked the surgeon 'What is going on?' he replied, 'The less you know, the better off you are son.' How very convenient that answer was for him when I was the guinea pig for his bad experiment. What he did, in my opinion, lacked logical thinking in the equation. The experiment was this: He put me to sleep with an anaesthetic and then put a pin through the heel of my bone. Then he stretched the leg and wrapped the leg in cotton wool. He then finished it off by wrapping plaster around the leg and letting it set. His intention was that the plaster being set with the pin in it would hold it in position and substitute for the traction. To this very day, I cannot understand how he was not capable of understanding that cotton wool is very soft and has lots of give in it and will never be suitable for holding the tension. Because of his bad decision, my right leg is an inch or 25 millimetres shorter than my left leg, which has caused me many problems throughout my journey in life. Even if he had stuck to the normal treatment, there still could have been some shortening of the leg, but nowhere near as much as his blunder. I also got a lot of extra pain, which I could have done without.

I spend six weeks in hospital and about six months before everything settled back to normal. As you can see from the rest of my book that I have been able to continue with a successful life, and that the broken legs work out to be a distraction that I would much preferred to have not been a chapter in my life.

CHAPTER 6

The Bay of Islands and My Gift to Mum before Going on My Two World Tours

This holiday started in 1971, when I left the railways in Hamilton, and it was just before I went to travel around the world twice (although to be quite honest about it, at that point my belief was that I was going for one trip around the world). It was the first time that I left New Zealand, and it was not all that long since my father had passed away in November 1970. I thought that since I had gone through a bad period of sadness with my father passing away and since I was going to be gone for a few months for a tour around the world on a working holiday, then it was an important time to think of all the wonderful things that my Dad and Mum had done for me throughout my life. Even though it was too late to do anything for Dad, it was certainly not too late to do something for my Mum before I went on my world tour.

After I went to work for the railways, my mother changed her place of dwelling from the country town of Ngaruawahia and moved to the city, in the suburb of Melville, which is in Hamilton. Hamilton is 20 kilometres further south of Ngaruawahia. Ngaruawahia is also the place where I spent most of my childhood, and I have a lot of fond memories of it. Even though the two places are only 20 kilometres apart, there is a big difference between the country atmosphere and the city atmosphere. Yet the city still had an upside to it, and it was that Mum was only about 3 kilometres away from where I was living, which made it easier to communicate with each other. I realise that I have deviated a bit from the original story, but I feel that it is important for me to express the emotions of my character.

The next thing I did after leaving the railways was to go around to Mum's place and ask her if she wanted to go on a trip before, I left to go overseas. Mum was excited about the idea and suggested that we go to a place that she had always wanted to visit, which was the Bay of Islands, up the top of the North Island in New Zealand. This was a trip that would take a few days and was somewhere that I had never been to before. So, I said, 'OK, let's do it!' We both sat down and worked out a plan on how we were going to do it. Since I was going overseas, I had to be careful with the amount of finances I was about to use up, which led to Mum offering to pay for the accommodation and the petrol. Mum also got some good advice from some of her friends, who informed her that it was better to use the bus tours once we got to Kaikohe. The trip from Hamilton to Kaikohe is 356 kilometres, and there is a significant amount of money you can save when you drive your own car for that long segment of the journey.

I supplied the car and did all the driving to and from Kaikohe. I felt sure Mum would enjoy the trip, because it was a place that she had always wanted to go to. I did not think that I was in for the same luxury and said to myself, *At least I am doing the right thing for Mum.* Well, in hindsight, I found that I couldn't have been any more wrong, because it is one of the best trips that I have ever done.

It is important to take the bus tour at Kaikohe for three reasons: When one takes the advantage of using the tourist bus, then you also gain extra information. The guide on the bus announces the different scenes one sees which have historical value. If you were driving in your car, you would more than likely miss out on the historical knowledge you are driving past. An example of what I am referring to is that I noticed some very old small buildings which were not much bigger than a giant doghouse; these turned out to be the huts where the gum-diggers used to live. I didn't even know that there were gum-diggers, so having the tour guide on the bus explain the history, which put a whole new spin on the way I understood what I was seeing. The guide on our bus tour became even more important, when you take in the times when there is nothing of interest to watch for maybe half an hour or maybe more; so, one can rest up a bit, and the guide will announce when the next interesting event is about to happen.

The guides also supply a lot of humour that makes the trip so much more interesting. One of the more memorable jokes was when we were travelling along this high and winding narrow ridge which had a drop on either side of about 200 feet (70 metres). Mum and I were sitting in the first row of seats, just behind the driver, and we could hear the other passengers expressing how nervous they were about travelling on that winding and very narrow ridge. The bus driver got on the loudspeaker and said, 'For those of you who are nervous, do like I do. *Close your eyes.*' The whole bus burst into laughter, which obviously changed the mood of the passengers.

There is another story for people who used their own car and who may have missed out by not knowing about the quicksand, which lacks distinguishable identification for letting someone to be aware of the fact that it is even there; that part of the beach looks like any other part of the beach unless one knows better. The portion of quicksand on the beach that I am now referring to is between Ninety Mile Beach and Cape Reinga. The history of why the quicksand is there was explained to me by the tour guide from the bus.

The story goes that a long time ago, there was no quicksand, and instead there was a waterfall of about 125 feet. Gradually after that period, the sand and the wind continued to build up until it was level to the rest of the ground, and in effect, the water was trapped in sand and formed quicksand. Quicksand is firm enough to withstand the weight of a vehicle, providing one keeps moving over it. If someone leaves their vehicle in one spot for long enough, especially if they leave the motor running, then it will slowly sink, and I was informed of a car that stood still on the quicksand and disappeared below the surface of the sand in just two months.

Many years later, I did research on the Internet to test the accuracy of the history of what we were told by the tour guide. The Historian had one hell of a job for being able to be accurate with their history. The biggest problem that confronts them is that when you go back through New Zealand history, they have a very poor way of recording the documentation of their history. Most of it—or all of it, to a certain point—was handed down by word of mouth. When it comes to the story about Ninety Mile Beach and how it got its name, the answer is not as simple as you might think. It is because, in fact, Ninety Mile Beach is only 55 miles long, and there are two stories as to how that came about, although neither one of those stories is officially correct. Both stories come up on the Internet. The first one is that the missionaries used the beach as a way of travel by riding their horses down it for three days. They thought that they were travelling 30 miles a day, but in reality, they were only travelling 18.4 miles a day. The second story is that farmers used it as a road to drive their cattle to the market, and it also has the same story of how long it took them to do the journey. There is also a third version that I was told by the bus driver while touring Ninety Mile Beach, and that was that the gum-diggers used to ride their horses down the beach and came up with the same theory as the other two stories. I prefer the story of the gum-diggers, although all three stories are plausible. There is still another odd story to tell about Ninety Mile Beach, and that is that it is an official highway in New Zealand, with a speed limit of 100 kilometres an hour. By the way, the story gets a lot more bizarre than that. When the tide is out, it becomes the widest highway in the world. It is also only considered usable by four-wheel drive vehicles, and if you rent a car that is not a 4-wheel drive, then you are not allowed to use it on Ninety Mile Beach.

CHAPTER 7

The First Step of My World Tour

Australia–London

While writing this article about my adventures of travelling around the world, I have given my memory a good workout. This is due to the fact that I did not have a journal to work with over that period, and I have gone several decades before I started to write my story. In addition, I inadvertently lost my first passport, which would have been useful for references to dates of travel. These are a few of the stumbling blocks that I expect to encounter while venturing through my journey of writing and contributing to what will eventually be a part of my book.

When I first left New Zealand, I got an international driver's licence, and that was on **17/12/1971**. The date I left for Australia would have been only a few days after the **17**[th], because I remember having my first Christmas away from home with my sister Betty and her husband, Michael, who were living in Sydney, in a semi-detached house in the suburb of Vaucluse. Vaucluse is a posh part of Sydney which is elevated fairly high up and provides a very good view of Sydney Harbour. At night, you can see the harbour bridge and all the bright lights surrounding that part of the harbour.

Betty is my oldest sister, her husband is Michael, and they also have a daughter called Mary, who was about **4** or **5** years of age at the time. Betty and Michael made a big effort in order to support me with accommodation in their semi-detached house. The reason I say that they went to a lot of effort—and this is also something that I did not clearly understand or fully appreciate at the time—is that the house was small and had a lot of people living in it. It consisted of a small garage, a sunroom, a dining room, 2 bedrooms, a bathroom, and a small laundry area. To compound the matter further, they also had another family staying with them. The Caballero family was composed of a mother and father who had two daughters and a son. The eldest was a girl of about 12 years old, and the second eldest was a boy of about 7 years old, with the youngest being another girl of about 3 months old.

I arrived late at night, and after my arrival, Michael continued to show me the sights around Sydney. The next day, Mr Caballero and Michael were working on Michael's car (it was a Sport Volkswagen). The two of them were repairing the floor by taking all the rust out of it. While working on the floor, they spoke in Portuguese (because Michael's friend didn't know very much English) while they were both sitting in the car, repairing the floor, and they only had one putty knife, which they shared. Well, this led to a confusing problem. After about an hour or two, I got tired of what I thought was swearing. I said to Michael that he did a lot of swearing. He said, 'I haven't been swearing.' My reply was 'That's not true.' Then he quickly worked out the reason for the misunderstanding on what I was talking about. He said, 'You mean the word *knife*.' I said, 'No, the word I am referring to does not sound like *knife*.' Then he enlightened me about the way you say *knife* in Portuguese, which is *faca*, although when you hear it in English, the word sounds more like *fucka*. They did pass that putty knife back and forth to each other a lot. Quite often, when you listen to a foreign language and you think you recognise an English word, it can sometimes get you into a lot of trouble when you get it wrong.

My wife writes in 5 different languages and speaks 6 different languages, one of them being English; when it comes to spelling, I go to her for advice, not the other way around. She speaks Italian, French, and Arabic fluently, and she speaks good German and Greek, although she is not fully fluent in German and Greek. While we are on the subject of languages, there is an interesting story about the German language that I feel needs to be told. This story happened a long time after I finished touring the world. I had a German friend that I was working with who happened to end up being the butt of me playing with the German language. In the German language, the word for poison is *gift*, and it is even spelt the same way. So, one day I went up to my German friend and said that I would never accept a gift from him. He quickly replied and asked me why not. I said, 'Because everyone knows that a German gift is poison.' There is a lot of fun you can have when you mix up languages. I suppose I best get back to the story of my journey.

The first thing that I needed to do before continuing my journey; meant that I needed to get a job in Australia, in order to have enough finance to continuing with when I got to London. In that time (1971), the newspaper was by far the best way to get a job, via the 'job vacancy listed' columns. Most of the different types of jobs had a list of a column or two and sometimes had up to half a page listed. The one that had the longest list of jobs were for labour's, and it usually had 4 or 5 pages. In order to get the job, you were not required to write out a résumé or a covering letter to apply. It just required being ready to start work as soon as you were told that you had the job and turning up to the place where the job was advertised for. There was something else which was important to adhere to, and that is that you did not just stand anywhere while waiting to get the job. If you just stood anywhere you wanted and ignored the queueing system or if you breached the queue (broke the line) in any way, you would automatically be disqualified from getting the job. It did not matter if you did not understand that you needed to queue, because their understanding was that if you were not smart enough to work that out, then you were not smart enough to do the job.

The jobs would usually start at 7 o'clock in the morning, so getting there at 6 a.m. was usually a good way to start. Around 6.45 a.m., the foreman you would be working for was the one who would be standing at the front of the line, and there were two ways that he would go about hiring you. He would walk down the queue and say 'I will take you, you, and you', or he would sometimes ask you a couple of quick questions—or both. How long you had the job was determined by how much he decided that he needed you. He did not need to have a reason to sack you (dismiss you). You could have the job for a day or several months, and your survival relied on his version to how much he still needed your skills. In regard to how much you were paid, well, there was a going rate that would slightly vary from site to site. To even bring the subject up of how much you were going to get for doing the job could have meant that you were too much trouble, and someone else was more than likely to get the job. The verbal résumé I had to offer was that I was young, fit, healthy, used to doing hard work, and very dedicated to doing good work.

The first job I got was as a builder's labourer on a five-storey building. Since I was employed under harsh rules, I thought it was fitting that I was able to throw in a harsh rule of my own. The thing that I neglected to tell him was that I had a fear of heights and that the fear would usually kick in after the second floor. To make matters worse, as I progressed past the second floor, so did my fear of anxiety increase, and the further up I went, the greater the intensity of fear became. My thought at the time was that the top priority for me was to hold on to a job for a few months and to get rid of this fear of heights that had a good grip on me. At that point, I had no idea how I was going to achieve that goal, and I firmly believed in the theory that if someone else could get past that fear barrier, then so could I. After all, I am a part of the human race. The one thing I did know for sure is that I needed to start from somewhere, and since jobs came and went so easily, that led me to think that this was a good place to start. The one thing that stayed constant was that the fear factor was only improving at a very slow pace when it came to my ability to control my fear of heights. One thing I urgently needed to do was find a way to overcome this fear of heights; giving in to the fear was never going to be an option.

One of the jobs that I was required to do was to take turns with four other labourers to receive the load from the winch, which would take the load up to the top of the roof of that five-storey building. The load was material that was required for the job that we were working on. This job required standing on the edge of the roof of the five-storey building with nothing to hold on to and to lean ford in order to land the load on the roof. I managed to do all right for myself for a few weeks by avoiding the job. Well, so I thought at the time. This was until I was unable to avoid taking my turn to pull the load in from the wench, which was on top of the roof. When it came to the fear factor, it couldn't have been any worse, because it was equivalent to being on the sixth floor, as high as you could possibly get on that site, which was very daunting (scary) for me, to say the least. I had managed to dodge that job until now, but the boys were no longer going to let me off the hook; I had to face the task of leaning over the outside of the building in order to pull the load in. Since they all knew that I was scared of heights and that I had dodged the job that I was supposed to be doing for so long, this ended up creating an audience that had gathered; quite a few of my fellow workers wanted to watch me perform that task. Up till now, the boys had found my avoidance of the job to be good entertainment value, and now they had decided to take it to the next level by forcing me to do the job I was employed to do. I have to admit that I wasn't too sure how I was going to get out of this problem, taking into consideration that I was scared out of my wits standing on top of that roof even before getting to the edge of it. I managed not to panic and just stood still there for a short while, trying to work out what I was going to do. Eventually, I saw a long piece of reinforcing rod. I grabbed one end of it, bent it over and made it into a hook, and then used it to pull in the load while staying in the middle of the concrete roof. The boys were very disappointed for two reasons: First of all, the way I did it was safer. The second reason was that I avoided having to go to that fearful place (the edge of the roof, where I would have nothing to hold on to) and still managed to get the job done.

After finishing that job on the five-storey building, I went to a new site. I made up my mind while starting this new job that it was time for me to deal with this fear of heights; it was imperative for me to find a way to overcome that fear and at least make the effort to climb out of the state of being a burden to my fellow workers. I guess the reason I managed to figure it out for myself and how I got past this fear was that I listened to other people who were not afraid of heights and who would tell me "What is there to be scared of?" When I got rid of the "inflated version of fear" that I had in my head, I worked out a way to get rid of the fear. I was also aware that if I was going to get over this fear, I needed to ask some questions about my attitude towards high places, and if I was ever going to succeed in conquering my fear of heights, then I also needed to require myself to change my attitude; otherwise, I would end up back where I first started—as someone who was not skilled enough to be doing the job.

The new site was equivalent to being 10 storeys high, with eight levels to it. Nobody asked me to do what I did next. Well, that's not entirely true, because the person I asked to step up to the plate and resolve the problem of my fear of heights was myself. I came to the conclusion that the answer to this problem was a lot easier to find than I gave it credit for, because it came down to analysing myself and being very logical by remembering a very easy phrase: 'What is there to be scared of?' To this very day, I am still amazed at how powerful those 7 words turned out to be for me. This gave me an idea to work on. After repeating the phrase 'What is there to be scared of?' many times in my head, I put the theory to the test. The only way it could work was by me climbing to the point where I felt scared and asking myself the questions which needed to be genuine, and above all, it required having very logical answers to them. So, I climbed to a height where I felt nervous, and then I got very logical and honest about why I was feeling nervous. So, the first question I asked myself was 'Why am I nervous?' Answer: I can fall. There were Handrails all around the platform which meant that I had to rule that out; when I am on the ground, I don't fall, even without handrails, and there was no reason for me to fall up there either. The next excuse was 'Maybe the platform I am standing on could fall'. I had a good look around the structure of the building; it became very obvious that the answer was that the building was many times stronger than it needed to be, so that was also ruled out. Then I spent a considerable amount of time walking around on that level and continued calming my fear by embracing the logical answers that I had supplied myself with, and each time I would say one of those phrases, I would always finish it off with '**There is nothing to be scared about**'. This was by far the most dominant phrase I would use. As I continued to gain confidence, with the phrase 'There is nothing to be scared about' which was turned into a way of mocking myself, and the more I mocked myself about it, the more confident I became. After I became confident with the level that I was on and felt good about losing the fear, with the new feeling of confidence that I had gained, I proceeded up to the next level and kept repeating the process until I had reached the eighth floor. The time factor was governed by my ability to proceed with the successful journey of feeling comfortable at the top of the building without most of the fear. The thing I had to conquer was the balance between fear and confidence. It is important not to waste any time on being overly worried about being overconfident in these early stages of conquering your fear of heights. At the same time—and now I am referring to being much further down the track—as your confidence continues to build, remember that it is healthy to have a small reserve for the respect of fear to the high places and not to let the fear dominate you like it did before.

I am not sure, but I think it was Michael that told me about a job advertised for the Portman Hotel in London, the very place I was going to. The place he referred me too was a five-star hotel—not that I had any clue as to what five-stars even meant at that time, apart from knowing that it was one of the classier hotels. Sure, I clearly do now! After topping up my money supply for travelling, I got on a plane and headed for London.

After arriving in London, I found that it did not take long before I was able to find accommodation in a rented one-bedroom flat. The flat was 6 kilometres from the Portman Hotel and is the place where I was seeking a job as a waiter. The Portman Hotel is situated across from Hyde Park, in the centre of London. If you go to the street-block of land across from Hyde Park and at the left-hand corner of the block is the Church Hill Hotel and when one walks around that block and goes to the diagonally opposite of that block is the Portman Hotel. The nearest big land mark is Buckingham Palace which is 4 kilometres from, Hyde Park. When it comes to transport, by far the fastest way to get around London is the tube (the metro), and it was the method I used for travelling to work.

The next thing I needed to do was get that job as a waiter in the Portman Hotel from the advert in the paper. Here is how the interview went: The manager, Sue asked, 'Have you ever worked in a hotel before?' My reply was yes! Then she asked me for the name of the company that I had worked for as a waiter. I said that it was only a small company in New Zealand and that she wouldn't know it. The finer details of that answer are that I had only waited for my mother in bed. I figured that too many details to that question wouldn't make for a very good résumé, so I left quite a few of the details out. After taking such a liberty with embellishing my verbal résumé so heavily, I worked very hard at watching the other waiters in order to work out the proper procedure of what I needed to be doing. Somewhere down the track, I needed to do what I said I could do, and this part I took very seriously; after all, that was my excuse for all the embellishment. It took me 3 weeks to become the highest-tipped waiter, and I learnt the essential things that I needed to learn. I also paid attention to the fact that a lot of the people that came to that five-star hotel were people who were lonely and missing the company of their loved ones at home. So, I would talk to them a lot, which was obviously appreciated, judging by the tips. One person I talked to was an American, a professor of English, and I remember him asking me if I swore. I told him I did, although I failed to state that I thought it was a cool thing to do because I thought that I was able to control the times I used it, as well as the level at which I was using it at any given time. He said to me, 'Do you know why people swear?' I remember what my Dad had told me from earlier days in my life. If you want to know the answer to a question that someone is asking you, don't be a know-all and say yes; otherwise, they are more than likely are, no longer going to tell you the answer. So, since I wanted to know the answer to that question, I told him no. (The truth of the matter is that I did have many dumb answers ready for that question.) He replied by saying that it is because *"people who swear are out of control and lack the ability to put in the appropriate word needed for their sentence."*

After receiving that great bit of wisdom, I went home and gave what he had said a lot of thought. After spending a lot of time analysing what he had said, and by gaining a great deal of clarity from my previous belief, well, let's put it this way: I was advertising myself as someone who was conducting himself like a complete fool. This also meant that I was out of control and lacked the ability to use the only language I know, the English language, and was unable to use it well enough in order to say what I needed to say. From that day on, I stopped swearing, and I work hard to make sure that I have the appropriate words that I need for expressing what I want to say. That doesn't mean that I am always going to get it right by putting in what I think is the correct wording, but it does mean that I endeavour to get it right and that swearing is definitely not the place that I intend to go any more. It only represents a fool who is out of control.

Another thing that happened at the Portman was that the boss asked me to work on Christmas Day. I said to her that this was the one day of the year that I always had off and that I did not wish to work on that day. She said, 'If you don't work, then you will be sacked.' I said, 'What do I get paid if I work?' She said, 'The same as usual except you will get one paid day that you have off.' I said that I still didn't want to work, but I would work that day so that I would not lose my job.

The landlord of the place that I was renting and her husband had invited me around to their place on Christmas Day for the evening meal, and she agreed to come and pick me up after I had finished my shift. Part of the wage at the Portman was that we were supplied with a free hot meal each day. I worked that Christmas Day, and the only extra thing that they gave us for it was 1 glass of wine. Not much of a bonus, given the circumstance! So, after lunch, I spent a considerable amount of time making up 2 large piles of folded serviettes, which I placed on the bottom of the trolley. Then I got a carafe from the bar, which I filled with a nice white wine, and placed it between the 2 piles of serviettes that I had on the bottom shelf of the trolley, and I topped it up as required. I also informed the other girls who worked with me about the wine and who also drank the wine, nearly each time that they walked past the trolley. At the end of the day, the boss said, 'I know you have been drinking, but I don't know where in the hell you got it from.' We all got good tips that day, so it couldn't have done the Portman any harm. The landlord was an Irish woman, and she and her husband picked me up at work after the end of my shift. I had a nice time at their place, and I also had a good time despite the boss trying to give me a hard time.

There is one strange thing left to say that happened in the Portman Hotel, and still to this very day, I have not been able to explain it. Before starting this story, I would like to explain the belief that I had about ESP (extrasensory perception). I remember talking to my Dad about people who claimed to have ESP, and his response was to mock the claims, due to the naive misunderstanding that he had of it. While I would naturally believe him to be correct and disbelieve that it is even possible to do, I have since changed my opinion on that theory and have a good reason for doing so.

My first experience of ESP started long before I had any idea that it had started its course. I am referring to when I had a dream, and this was when I was about 8 years old. It was one of those dreams that I remember very clearly in detail. In the dream, I was walking through two double swinging doors, then I turned right as soon as I got through them. I walked along this corridor. Then I came to another set of double swinging doors on my left, which I walked through. Then I walked a little way and slipped, and as I landed on the floor, I very distinctly remember that I heard a female voice laughing at me. I couldn't see her face, and all I could hear was her laughter.

Now an important thing that needs to be taken into consideration at this point is that the event of the ESP taking place 16 years after I had that dream, along with the fact that this event had shifted from New Zealand to London, at the Portman Hotel, in a country that I had never been to in my life. Here is what happened in the restaurant of the Portman Hotel: I had travelled through all those doors and corridors like I did in the dream, and at the end of that journey was the coffee machine, where I picked up a freshly percolated pot of boiling coffee. It was still boiling as I took the coffee off the percolator and as I walked along to take the percolated pot of coffee to the customer. I slipped and spilt the coffee all over my chest (the attire I was wearing was a thin cotton shirt, a black pair of trousers, and black shoes). The boss was sitting in a cubicle bay with very high-sided seats that were higher than her head, so I couldn't see her. She was laughing at me, and when I heard that laughter, I knew instantly that it sounded exactly like it did in the dream that I had when I was 8 years old. Even the layout of the place, with double swinging doors and the corridors, was identical to what I saw in my dream. I didn't move at all, and I just stayed, lying there, for about 2 or 3 minutes or maybe more. All I could think about was how explicitly the details of that earlier dream matched up (the accuracy of the laughter, the double doors, and the corridor). That was not the only incredible thing which had just happened. The other part of my story, which I am still unable to explain, is that when I eventually got up later, I didn't have a blister or a burn on me, only a slight sign of a red mark. How does someone explain such an event? I don't know, but one thing I do know is that I have never laughed at anyone claiming to have ESP. As a matter of fact, I have a lot of respect for what they have to say.

There is one more experience that I have had with ESP and I do not have any answers to this one either. I know how to divine water by using two metal rods bent at 180°. I hold the rods pointing forward and as I walk over the place where there is water both rods turn without me doing a thing, and where the rods without any assistance from me move across the path of my body. I have got other people to try the same thing and found that some can do it and that some cannot to it. I have also found that no matter how hard some wants it to work. If they do not have the power to do it, then it does not work for them.

CHAPTER 8

Touring America and Becoming a Cowboy in Texas

So now I had left London, and I was on my way to Los Angeles, America, with a bit of money in my pocket, which meant it was time to relax a bit and take in some of the sights.

As a child, I was occasionally allowed to go to the movies, as well as some of the comedy movies that Walt Disney did not make, by far the best movies I saw were Walt Disney's. Not once did I ever see a bad movie of Walt Disney; they always had very good morals in them, and the presentation of them was always held to a very high standard. Walt Disney always held unique way of putting in something special and adding a much higher value to his ideas, such as not falling for the trap of trying to be, "the biggest, the brightest, and the best". He also went with the assumption that unique will always triumph over biggest brighter and best. Both my parents saw them in the same way as I did, as a matter of fact. That is the same standard that I hold my movies up to today, although I do not see many movies reaching that benchmark. That is why it was so important for me to go and see Disneyland. I spent eight days there, and the sights and all the action were every bit as good as I thought it would be and more. Disneyland is situated in Anaheim, roughly 50 kilometres south of Los Angeles. The next place I went to visit was Knott's Berry Farm, which is roughly 35 kilometres south of Los Angeles, in Buena Park. It's an amusement park with the theme of the West in the 1940s (a bit like being in a Western movie); this I also found very interesting and very well presented, and the next place that I visited was at one of the film studios I toured, they showed how they did the parting of the Red Sea, from the movie *The Ten Commandments*. We were taken around on a mobile train that had pneumatic tyres, and seeing that great event happen in reality was still incredible to grasp.

I am not sure, but I think the next place I went to was the wax museum of Madame Tussauds. She made wax figures of great movie stars such as John Wayne, Humphrey Bogart, Jane Fonda, and Marilyn Monroe, to name a few, and they were so lifelike that I kept looking at them with the anticipation that they would start moving at any moment. I know that all this sightseeing may have seemed very good and wonderful, and it was. But it did have a catch to it, and that was that the money was running out at a fast pace. I suppose by seeing Knott's Berry Farm, and the infatuation I used to have in watching cowboy movies, and the fact that I had always thought it would be a great thing to do was what motivated me to get a job as a cowboy.

I caught a plane to Laredo, Texas, because I figured that would be my best chance of getting a job as a cowboy. Now my money was in a very poor situation, and I really needed to get a job fast. I took a taxi into town with the intention of checking newspapers, and on the way, I asked the taxi driver if he knew anyone who was trying to hire a cowboy. As luck would have it, he said yes and that he had a friend that was looking for a cowboy. So, I said to him that if he put in a good word for me, I would give him $10. After paying the fare, that was all I had left. I know that was really dumb by letting myself get that low in finances, but I got away with it. I suppose if I had, had a more mature and responsible attitude then, I would have handled it differently.

Here is how the interview went. Q: 'Have you ever done this job before?' A: 'Yes, I was brought up on a farm in New Zealand.' Q: 'Do you know how to ride?' A: 'Yes.' Q: 'How well can you ride?' A: 'Well, that is not for the individual to say, but what I can tell you is that I have never fallen off.' I suppose he must have got tired of the evasive answers I was giving him, so he asked, 'How soon before you can start?' I gave him the answer he wanted to hear: 'Right away.' I don't think he had anyone else lined up; otherwise, he wouldn't have told me that he wanted me to start right away. The detailed version of the verbal résumé (the one that he never got to hear) was that I was a young child at the time I was working on our dairy farm at home and that I only had 2 hours' experience of riding at a riding school, on really quiet horses that were already saddled up and ready to go when I hopped on them. Then the boss took me to a restaurant, and we had a Mexican lunch. When you are a cowboy, meals and the accommodation are part of the wages. I knew that, so that was why I wasn't concerned about giving my last few dollars away. Then the boss (a big, tall solid-looking guy) got me to pick up my gear so that we could load up the car and get started on our journey. He also had his wife with him in the car. She was a very attractive lady with blonde hair and a slim body. When she spoke, she had a very heavy Texan accent, which I thought was tough to listen to, but she was a nice person. After we had spent a few hours driving, we arrived at the ranch in a place called Brackettville in Texas. The next day we picked up some supplies. The first job was to build a fence for the cattle and it was also where I got my first taste of bull -ants. I saw them there but paid no attention to them until they started stinging me by crawling up my trousers and injecting formic acid into me. I know it may look very funny to onlookers when someone is having trouble with ants in their pants, but the victim sure does receive a different point of view (it is a bit like getting bee stings).

The next day, we needed to do some mustering, so I went with the boss to get a horse to ride. He had two horses in the barn. One was quiet, and the other was a bit wild. He told me that I could have my pick, but he was having the quiet one (a bit of Texas humour). With horses, you must always climb on from the left side of the horse because that is the way they are trained, and they have a strong tendency to get very shy and spooked when you mount them on the wrong side and which can also leave you feeling sad and sore. I talked to the horse a lot, trying to calm it so that it wouldn't throw me off, and had no idea which side I needed to mount on. Guess which side I mounted on? That's right, you got it—the wrong side. But the horse didn't do anything. It just let me hop on. The boss said to me, 'Either you are one hell of a horse rider or you are dead stupid for hopping on the horse from the wrong side.' Obviously, the latter was true but I guess that the way I kindly talked to the horse got me out of trouble.

Another thing that did not work out too well for me was that when cowboys are moving around a ranch on horseback, they normally do it trotting, because horses use less energy trotting than galloping, even if it is a slow gallop. The boss said to me, 'Red (he used to call me Red), if you don't stop bouncing all over that saddle, I will get to thinking that you can't ride.' (He got that part right, but that didn't mean that I stopped trying to get it right.) By the way, if that wasn't bad enough, I got bushed and ended up pushing the cattle the wrong way for a small part of the journey, and if I missed something that I should have seen, he would say, 'Red, you've got your head up your ass again!' That night, we left the cattle in the holding paddock, and the next morning, we had three other helpers from another one of his ranches who were Mexicans and could only speak Spanish. One of them was the foreman. The boss, (the owner of the ranch), also spoke Spanish, and he brought the other men because of a lot of work that needed to be done.

The cattle were loaded into a holding chute and at the end of the holding chute was a squeeze chute, where we hold the cattle one at a time. This enabled us to do all the things we needed to with the cattle as well as making it easier and quicker. The first thing we needed to do was to put a spray in the cattle's mouth to treat worms, and other pest. Cutting off a small piece of the ear is a requirement for part of the registration, along with branding them with a hot iron for when you sell them and for proof of identification. Another job is cutting off the horns if they are considered to be too long, so they do not injure the other cattle and the men working with them. When you brand any letter or number that is not placed in a 90° angle, then it is called lazy. One of the distant neighbouring ranches had a weird brand name which had a 2 at a 90° angle, then another 2 laying on its side and a P, and if you read it as a brand, it reads *two lazy two pee*. Branding was far from being one of the jobs that I liked doing, but it is what came with the territory. After we had done all the cattle, there were about a dozen calves that only needed to be branded. The boss decided that he was not going to put them through the squeeze chute like we did with the rest of the cattle, because it would take too long to herd them up again. We had to do it by hand, which meant throwing them on their side and holding them down while someone else branded them. He left me on my own for a while to see how well I did it. Well, after a lot of hard work in getting the first one down, I was left close to being all but worn out. So, he said to me, 'Do you want to see the easy way to do it?' (No prizes for that answer.) He showed me how to get the calf around the neck. Then standing next to its front shoulder, you grab it from the far front leg, then pull it and bump it with your shoulder at the same time. This method worked, and without a shadow of a doubt it was a much easier way to do the job. You've just got to love the Texans' humorous methods, another thing that it created was by eliminating all the ifs and buts and all other presentable arguments for doing it differently. The next day, the Mexicans went home; they were working on another ranch not far away. I was left to stay in a caravan and repair all the fences, with only horses for transportation. (This proved to be quite a task, each time I came to a gate, which meant having unloading and loading of the equipment every time I went through a gate.) Every so often, the Mexican foreman would drop by and bring the supplies and also give me instruction of what he wanted done *in Spanish*, which gave me a hell of a job working out what he wanted done. He refused to learn English, and I had to pick up some Spanish really fast; however, the communication did work most of the time. One experience I got while I was over there was the flash flood. The place would be bone dry one minute, and the next, there would be rivers and creeks everywhere. It is quite a scary feeling when it first happens. It is pretty much the same as you would see in Western movies, when they would have a heavy downpour.

After three months, my boss wanted me to go to Fort Pierre in South Dakota, to work with another team of cowboys. This meant travelling from the most southern part of America to almost the most northern part on a Greyhound bus. I am not sure, but I think that it took either two or three days to get there. The one part I am sure of is arriving in Dallas at 4 a.m. and having to wait until 8 a.m. for my next bus, which meant having a lot of time to kill. It was a big town with lots of shops to look at, so I decided to walk the quiet streets where there were hardly any cars and even fewer people. While walking along the street, I noticed a small car with four big blokes inside who pulled up and parked about 20 car lengths in front of me. All four of them got out of the car and started to walk towards me. Fortunately for me, I had done some training in karate, and one of the most important things I learnt was that regardless of the situation, you need to stay calm and relaxed. So that was what I did. I didn't speak; I just kept the same pace and walked straight towards them. They kept coming for a while, and then they turned and quickly went back into their car and left. I guess having my cowboy outfit on was a help, and by me staying so calm and walking towards them must have made them think that I had a gun that I was willing to use. One thing I know for sure is that I was really glad that I didn't have to take that bluff to the end of its track, because I didn't have a gun. It would have been touch-and-go whether I would have fared so well should I have needed to enter a full battle with them. I believe that I might have been able to bring down three of them, but I was not so certain about getting all four of them. So, then I went back to the bus depot without delay and stayed there till the bus arrived. Who knows, they may have gone back to get guns of their own, and I was not about to put round two to the test. The rest of the journey was filled with wanting the kilometres to pass and trying to sleep on a moving bus. I arrived in Fort Pierre, South Dakota, safe and sound.

CHAPTER 9

South Dakota and the Many Duties of a Cowboy

I completed my trip on the Greyhound bus from Texas, which my boss paid for, and arrived in a town called Fort Pierre in South Dakota. The foreman of the ranch, Bill, came to pick me up from the bus depot in a four-wheel drive pickup truck, and to take me to the ranch, which was about 15 kilometres out of town. We ventured off the public road and into a private one that led to the ranch, still having about another two or three kilometres to go, along a fairly rough dirt road that led to the log cabin. When I arrived at the log cabin, I met the other three cowboys—Joe, Rosado, and Robert. The first three were Mexicans, and Bill and Robert were white Americans. There were also two more: Tom, an old white American man who just did odd chores and looked after the ranch when it was shut down for the winter, and a Mexican cook named Manuel, who put chilli in almost everything he cooked. Rosado and Manuel could hardly speak any English at all. Joe could speak just a little bit of English. Spanish was the majority of the language spoken in the log cabin, and unfortunately for me, I was the only one that did not speak Spanish. But things picked up when we were working outside the log cabin, because the majority of the spoken language then turned to English.

The ranch owner owned two pickup trucks. One was about two years old, and the other was a lot older, maybe about ten to fifteen years old. This was our main form of transportation around the ranch; it is a lot easier and quicker than a horse, although there are some things you cannot do in a pickup that you can do on a horse, such as working cattle. The size of the ranch, going on memory, was about 6 × 8 kilometres.

The majority of the work was fixing fences, and the hardest part of that job was digging five-foot (1.5-metre) post holes in the ground for the fence; some were even deeper (six feet for the main post), and all were dug by hand. Another big job was fixing the water line from the second artesian well that the boss had done by a drilling company. The water from both wells was drinkable but had a horrible, oily taste to it that we still had to drink. I noticed that the boss brought his own fresh water whenever he came to the ranch. An artesian well is water coming up from the ground from its own natural pressure, and getting it to come up through the surface required drilling through the ground until you reached the water. The next trick would be to remove the drill bit and cap the water so that you had control of turning the water off and on. The water would be sent to the highest point of the ranch, where a large tank was set up to store the water. Then they used the two-inch lines and later on were reduced to one-inch lines of PVC piping which would be placed 4 feet (1.3 metres) in the ground. The digging for all these pipelines was done with a machine called a Ditch Witch Digger, which would dig the trench and travelled at about a quarter of a kilometre in about 4 hours. All the lines needed to be glued together and then, after being tested, put in the ditch.

One of the biggest problems was stopping the cattle from walking on the pipeline around the storage tank and, in the process, the cattle would end up by breaking the pipeline (they could smell the water, and that was their fastest way they knew of getting it.) We put a fence around the storage tank, only to find the next day that they had smashed the pipes. So, we repaired the fence and the pipework and made it even, better and stronger. The following day, when we came back, we found that they had broken it again. Bill was hopping mad with the steers' success of getting through the fence and smashing the pipeline again. With great anger in his voice, he said, 'Those *steers* can smash a goddam *steel ball* with a *rubber hammer.*' However, this time we fixed it well enough that the steers did not break it again. Another activity that was happening at the time was that Robert spent most of his time working on making a dam with a D2 Caterpillar bulldozer. There were three dams that needed to be built.

Another job that we were required to do was use a lasso to rope the steers. Before I get too deep into the topic of that activity, I feel it is important to give you a clear picture of the terrain that we were working in. In the summer, it could get as hot as 50°C, and in the winter, it could get as cold as −40°C. As a result of that very cold weather, there would be a lot of snow that would form; when it warmed up, the snow would melt, and the run-off water would cut big gorges in the land, some as deep as 60 feet (20 metres), leaving very steep banks. Fortunately, they all existed in just a few places on the ranch. Most of the ranch had fairly moderate slopes. OK, let's get back to the great work of the lasso. I had never done the job of roping a steer with a lasso before, and in my spare time, I would spend it with the boys, by practicing the art of using a lasso by catching a peg in the ground. It is a lot easier to be roping a peg in the ground than it is to be sitting on the back of a horse and trying to throw the lasso over a steer's head. The other thing that needs to be taken into account is that no one needs to be wearing the horses out for nothing. We roped the cattle for one of two reasons: One was that if they didn't have any brand on them, we would cut a small piece off the ear for identification purposes. The other reason was that if they had an infected eye, we would give them an injection which would heal it. The breed of horses that they had on the ranch where Quarter Horses, which were highly trained. They knew that when you were chasing a steer, they would have to keep going at a full gallop until you threw the rope, and then they would stop very fast for the purpose of keeping the rope held firmly. Now came the day for putting the rope-throwing skills to the test. The boys roped a few steers, just to let me see how it was done. So then came my turn. I found a steer that needed to be roped, and I set off after it. Unfortunately for me, that was as good as it got, because while I was chasing the steer, it headed to one of those steep gorges in the land that I was talking about before, which was at least a 60-foot drop. The steer kept on heading right towards it. One thing is for sure: I had no intention of galloping down that deep gully. I tried desperately hard to stop the horse, but no matter how hard I pulled on the reins, it just kept going. The steer jumped down that big drop, with the horse following it, and that was when I started sucking air really hard (and by now I am sure you can gather where that air was being sucked from—not the nose or the mouth). The inevitable happened: we hit the bottom of the gorge. The horse still kept galloping, and like me, it was sweating profusely. I didn't know what else to do, so I threw the lasso on the ground, with the hope that it would stop the horse. Boy, did it stop; I went very close to flying over the top of it. If it hadn't been for the fact that I had grabbed hold of its mane and held on to it, well, let's put it this way: the next port of call would have been me hitting the ground. I reckoned that it sure would have been nice if I had known *how* the horse was trained before I commenced the chase, instead of having to find out later. The horse sure knew what it was doing, and sad to say, it was much better trained than me. The other boys roped between 6 to 10 steers each that day. My count was zero. I guess that was why I got to do more of the fencing and less of the riding, except when it came to mustering.

Another thing that the Americans liked was their guns. The old pickup had a rack at the back of the cabin with two rifles in it. One was a .22 Western with a lever action to it. On our days off, which was sometimes one day a week, we would go out and put up some tins for target practices. I would sit there and watch them. Then one of them asked me to have a go at shooting the rifle. Well, the only experience I had with a gun was once in New Zealand, with a shotgun. I was about 12 years old at the time and was told to hold it tight. When I fired it, well, it almost landed me on my butt and gave me a sore shoulder and left me wondering how anyone could find enjoyment in shooting it. The boys told me that this one had no kick to it at all. Reluctantly, I gave it a go, and they were right—it didn't have any kick to it. But that didn't change the fact that I was still hopeless at hitting the cans. I guess that I lacked the enthusiasm to be shooting something that was causing me no harm. I still don't like guns, regardless of which end of the barrel I am standing at, but at least I now know a little bit more about them. For example, where the safety catch is! How many rounds are kept in the magazines is useful information that one day may save my life, or at least, it lets me know when I'm watching a movie if they are firing more rounds than the magazine is capable of holding. Let's face it: if a gun is only capable of firing six rounds, then after they have fired the sixth shot, the gun is then empty and needs to be reloaded before it can fire again.

At the end of the season, all the cattle needed to be herded up into holding pens so that they could be loaded into large trucks that would transport them to feeding lots so that they can be fattened up by being fed with lots of alfalfa before being taken to the abattoirs. When the cattle are being loaded into the trucks, all hands are on deck; it is a very big job and needs to be done as quickly as possible in order to minimise the stress for the cattle and to keep the cost of transport down to a minimum. The job of loading them is very dusty and requires staying very vigilant because the cattle are frightened and do not like being pushed around and will do you harm if you don't pay attention.

I returned a second time to work as a cowboy in South Dakota. However, that only lasted for a couple of months before a bloke who worked on the ranch and operated the bulldozer got sacked as a bulldozer operator. He later got totally dismissed from the ranch for two good reasons.

He was the type of person who had a little bit of knowledge about many things, but his lack of wanting to complete what he was learning ended up leaving him in a bad place. He had been working on the bulldozer, trying to make a dam, and he ran into a very hard layer of clay. It was so hard that the bulldozer blade was only skidding over the top of the surface. The bulldozer operator's name was Robert. The boss was looking for ways to fix this problem, so Robert took it into his heart to tell the boss that he was good with explosives and that he had an explosive licence and that he would blow the hard surface off with dynamite. The boss agreed that it was a good idea. So, Robert brought the explosives and spaced several sticks of dynamite in separate holes in the hard ground and blew the dynamite up. This did not go too well for him, because it only ended up leaving a lot of useless holes around the place that were about 6 inches (150 millimetres) in diameter. The boss was far from impressed with the results. Robert told the boss that he knew what he had done wrong and that he could fix the problem, and he said that instead of putting one stick of dynamite in each hole, he would put ten sticks and also pack the holes with fertiliser. The boss agreed, hoping to make good of the money he had just wasted. So, Robert got the fertiliser and dynamite and blew up the hole again, only to find that all he had done was make a much deeper hole; it didn't serve much use for clearing that hard surface. Since Robert was the only one who could operate the bulldozer, the boss gave him an ultimatum: get the dam finished with the mess that he had made or pack his bags. Robert managed to finish building the dam. A few weeks later, the boss had trouble with one of the four-wheel drives; it needed a new gearbox.

Once again, Robert put up his hand and said that he could save the boss a lot of money by putting in the new gearbox. Once again, Robert was in over his head. Several weeks passed by, and he was still not able to put the gearbox back together again. This time, the boss had had enough of him and told him that he would keep him on another month if he taught someone how to operate the bulldozer. The boss was aware that I had never operated a bulldozer before, although he must have still had it fresh in his mind when he remembered how I had pulled the wool over his eyes in order to get the job in the first place. I was now assigned to learning how to operate the bulldozer. I didn't let him down, and I learnt how to operate the bulldozer in a little over two weeks. The bulldozer was a Caterpillar D2, which had a lot of play on the blade (a lot of free movement between the response of the control and when the blade moved), and I was required to turn a gully into a dam. I had to make two dams, and with both of them, I had trouble with the ground. It would be soft for a short section, and as I would proceed, it would all of a sudden become very hard. It was a bit difficult, but still I managed to do a good job on both of them. Then I headed back to New Zealand, because the work in South Dakota was seasonal, which was due to the very cold winters; the snow made it too hard to work.

It was early December, and it had come time for the ranch to close down and for me to head back to New Zealand, with a promise to come back the following year. Part of the wage for being a cowboy is that the boss pays for your transport to the ranch but you pay for your own way back. Fortunately for me, it was cheaper to get a ticket from New Zealand to London than it was from New Zealand to America. So, the boss had lived up to his end of the bargain and paid for me to traveling halfway around the world twice. It was something I hadn't counted on, but since I was not the one who enforced the conditions, I figured that I would take the good with the bad. And let's face it: that was good. More importantly he had no regrets for hiring me as a cowboy.

CHAPTER 10

Australia: Dunbar Cattle Station and the Adventures of a Cook in the Outback

Dunbar Cattle Station is a large station which is 3,700 square miles (9,583 square kilometres) and is situated in Queensland, which is a part of the Gulf Country (Gulf Savannah Region), and the nearest big town is Normanton, which is 141 miles (227 kilometres) south-east of Dunbar. The cattle stations sometimes change in size over the course of years due to the fact that when the stations are sold, they are sometimes broken up into several stations, or sometimes they are sold by being joined together with a neighbouring station. I was told that at one time, Dunbar was the largest privately-owned cattle station in the world. It also has an airport, which in reality is just a runway that has a cleared strip of land so that it can land small aircraft.

My experience of working on Dunbar Cattle Station as a cook, started around 1976. I remember that I was looking for some sort of work on farm or cattle station. My journey for this quest started with my Ford station wagon in Sydney, where I drove my way up through Queensland while trying to find some permanent work. So far, all I had managed to achieve were a couple of jobs where I did a few months of work along the way. When I reached Cairns, I found a job which was both very interesting and challenging. By now, I had learnt through experience that the pub is a good place to look for this type of work, because when stockmen take a break from their normal work, it is where they quite often head to. So, I went into the pub, where I happened to come across the head stockman. When I asked him about getting a job as a stockman, he then informed me that he had already hired plenty of stockmen but was short of a cook. This was not the job I had in mind to be doing, but I was low on cash and decided that this was not a good time to start being fussy. He asked if I knew how to cook. I told him that I have been cooking since the age of about 10 for the family, and the reason I cooked at that early age was because both of my parents were working. Then he asked me if I would be happy to work as a cook at Dunbar Station, to which I answered yes. The next question he asked was 'Do you know how to make bread?' I had to sadly answer no. This led me to believe that I had now lost my chance of getting that job, because this was one of those questions you could not bluff your way through; the reason for that, is that yeast changes the rules of how most cooking is done. Fortunately for me, he must have been struggling to get a cook, because he said that it was OK and that he would teach me, and he gave me the job.

Dunbar Cattle Station: In Australia, there are several large isolated areas which are referred to as the outback. The outback is a very large and isolated place, where the nearest shop is quite often more than a hundred kilometres away and where your nearest neighbour is also a great many kilometres away from you. For most people who have only experienced living in the city, well, the way they are more than likely to view the outback is by seeing it as just a lot of wild bush with some cleared areas. Water is very important for survival in the outback. When you read it on paper, you will see that Dunbar has a lot of water; however, as the hot dry season continues, so do all the water sources continue to diminish in size. Should you happen to get lost while you are out there in the hot dry weather, the water may end up being hard to find, due to the vast amount of land, along with the land mass gaining in size as the different sources of water continue to dry up.

Water on Dunbar Station: There are two Mitchell Rivers in Australia, one is in the state of Victoria, and the other is in Queensland. Dunbar Station has 2 rivers flowing through its property, the Nassau River and the Mitchell River in Queensland;'

13 creeks; and 8 lagoons, or as the stockman prefers to call them, large waterholes. It also has more than its share of insects, and by far, the

majority of the insects are flies, mosquitoes, and termites. It also has some animals, such as kangaroos and wild pigs, and unfortunately, the wild pigs dig a lot of unwanted holes that lead to a chain of other problems. It is not wise to eat the wild pigs, because a lot of them are contaminated with TB (tuberculosis) and end up becoming carriers of TB, which is a bad disease that can be very deadly to human beings. One of the better animals on Dunbar are the wild Brahman cattle, which is the wildest of all the cattle breeds that you can be working with, along with being the breed that is most suited to the outback's harsh conditions. This is just a brief description of what the outback is like, and I will add some more details via the experiences which I have had at Dunbar. As much as I enjoyed the outback, I think it is fair to warn people who may be thinking of visiting it and who have only lived in the busy cities that they are more than likely to find the isolation overwhelming and not liking it at all.

To venture into the outback is a unique experience that very few people in Australia have had the luxury of sharing. Unfortunately, it is hard to explain and is something that one needs to experience first-hand in order to truly understand the life and gain a mental picture, to what I have seen of those very exciting events that took place. Most of the campsites that we worked on had no buildings, and the stars were very often the roofs that we lay under while we were sleeping at night. I remember one campsite had a building that was built with a corrugated tin gabled roof, which was mounted about 18 inches (.5 of a metre) off the ground, and the hot sun made it a very hot place to live in, especially when it came to being 50% c in the middle of the day. Everybody had a swag, which is made of canvas and which substitutes for your bed and also for a suitcase that carries your personal belongings. It would be rolled up with leather straps that made it easy to carry, and if it rained, you would need it to wrap yourself with the canvas in order to stay dry. So, when we went from one campsite to another, we would load up the truck with the swags and food supplies. This was one of the reasons the cook was taken special care of.

Explaining the duties of what a cook does in the station leads me to believe that it will give you a better feel for the environment I was living in while I was in the outback. A very important feature for living in the outback is being able to have someone provide us with a regular supply of essential things for living. Some of the supplies we were able to provide for ourselves, such as having to kill our own meat for our meals, and making our own bread. We got our supplies from a 12-ton mail truck that would bring in the mail and food, and it also supplied us with anything else that we needed. I think it may be wise if we first define what the people in the outback consider regular. Due to the isolation, one would consider that they are getting a good deal if they got supplies once about every two weeks, when the truck would more than likely arrive. One of the biggest obstacles the truck had to face while travelling to Dunbar were the dirt roads, which were very rough and required driving over a few hundred kilometres each day. An obstacle that one might consider as only a little annoying is the dust which is created as you are driving, and especially the dust which is referred to as bulldust. Bulldust is an extremely fine red powder (as fine as talcum powder) and is derived from the clay on the road that was very finely ground by natural resources, such as the wind that travels across the road and motor vehicles. The biggest contribution to that problem came from the wild pigs.

Due to the bulldust being so very fine, it gets in everything that is in and around the vehicle. It also presents a danger should you run into a dense patch of it; if you happen to hit that dense patch at too fast a speed, it can end up throwing your vehicle out of control. The bulldust still hasn't finished with the damage it can cause you. It still has a good chance of blocking the air filter to the point where the motor becomes very sluggish, and if you do not do anything about the dust problem, it'll keep blocking the filter, to the point where it stops the motor from working. There are also other obstacles the mail truck needed to be concerned about, such as the road being riddled with large potholes that one cannot avoid hitting from time to time. To make matters worse, the pothole may have a hard rock at the base of it. Another thing that could be very damaging is rocks protruding from the surface of the road. Cars are more likely to be prone to serious damages due to the fact that they travel lower on the road, and it is on the underpart of the vehicle is where the damage is going to occur. Another thing that the truck driver always needed to be wary of was that there is always a chance that it could rain, which has the potential of stopping the truck for days at a time. Even though the men working the cattle stations in Queensland work between the monsoon seasons, where it usually hardly ever rains, along with the fact that you can go years with it not raining between the monsoon seasons, it can also be the case that you get a couple of years, where it might rain heavily for many hours or sometimes for days, which causes everything to become very wet and slippery. If you happen to get caught at the bottom of a once dried-up riverbed, you would have a lot of reasons to be very concerned. The thing the driver of the mail truck driver had to be concerned about, was that when it does rain between the monsoon seasons, it usually comes with very little warning, and that rain normally comes in the form of a heavy downpour. There is also the fact that when it does rain, very often you do not have enough time to reach a safe place, and you can be left stranded for a time with the inability to go anywhere. The monsoon season usually starts in November and lasts until about sometime in April.

In regard to the base camp cook on Dunbar Station: It has a large building that has a diesel generator and gas for cooking. Away from the base camp, the camp cook who is constantly moving from one camp site to another and the stockman who travel with him. Their camp sites have no buildings, no electricity and no gas. The need to move frequently and are left with only one option—making a campfire. This requires digging a large shallow hole everywhere we go and gathering lots of firewood, because the fire needed to be kept burning 24 hours a day while we were at that site. Another important requirement, especially in the bush, was to make sure that I extinguished the existing fire before moving on to the next campsite. The kerosene fridge was very weak when it came to keeping the food cool, and I could only add small amounts of food at any one time; otherwise, the whole fridge would lose its coolness. There was also the fact, that the flue would clog up with soot every so often, and when it got clogged with soot, then it would also start losing its ability to stay cool or when it got bad it would completely close down. However, the upside is, when you move from one site to another, the vibration from the truck will end up automatically cleaning the flue for you.

When it came to the food which I had available for cooking with, the only fruits and vegetables I had come from cans; the number of how many of these I was allowed to use was heavily restricted. Meat was the one thing that we had in abundance, and the way our meat was supplied was like this: The stockmen would take the herd of cattle under a tree, and one of them would sit up in the tree. As the right steer that he wanted went by, he would shoot it with one clean shot to the head so that it would cause the least stress as possible to the animal. Another important fact is, if the animal did get stressed, the meat would become tough and stringy. After the animal was slaughtered, one of the stockmen would butcher it for me. Most of the meat was salted because it was the best way of preserving it, and it is what we know as silverside, which also largely helped to ensure that none of the meat was wasted. The one thing that did surprise me was that when the meat was so extremely fresh, it tasted different and had a much stronger taste compared with the meat from the city that I was used to eating. The best cut of this very fresh meat is, surprisingly, the chuck steak, or as most people know it, the neck. Anyone in the city would consider this to be one of the cheapest cuts of meat that you can buy; that is due to the fact that in the city, that cut of meat is tough, but that is not the case when it is very fresh. The other thing that I found strange was that the top cuts of meat, such as the rib-eye, tenderloin, and scotch fillet steaks, are very often thrown away because they are situated behind the ribs and because it requires a saw, along with a lot of extra work, to get to that cut of meat. Since it is such a small cut of meat, along with the fact that the meat is so fresh, it no longer has the advantage of being of a high quality when compared to the other cuts of meat.

The majority of the food eaten in the meals was meat (meat for breakfast, lunch, and tea). I had to have their breakfast ready for the stockman at the first light of day, which was 6 o'clock in the morning, as well as having a cut lunch ready for them when they went to work. I would boil the billy for a cup of tea, which was something that we had with every meal. The method used for making the tea involved boiling the billy on the fire and then putting the tea in the water as soon as it started to boil after giving the billy a few taps with a wire to make sure that none of the leaves floated and was also the time for taking the water off the fire. When it came to lunchtime, the stockmen would make their own cups of tea. They also needed a lot of bread, the making of which was quite a time-consuming chore that required a lot of preparation and required cooking in a camp oven. The camp oven was a large cast-iron pot with a lid on it, and when you baked the bread, you needed to put red-hot coals on top of the lid in order to convert it into an oven. You could tell when the bread was cooked by tapping the oven with a bit of wire. When you tapped it with a wire, and if it had a dull sound, it needed more cooking, and if it had a sharp pinging sound, it meant that it was cooked. The cook had one big advantage on his side because he was considered the most important person there; he is in the outback and too far from anywhere, and too time consuming in order to find another replacement for him. Without the cook, the whole camp would close. The camp could still continue without one of the stockmen but not without the cook.

One of the problems that occurred while I was working there, was that

I had to get up earlier than the stockman, which meant having to get up at 4.30 a.m. in the morning in order to have breakfast ready for the boys. It was also important to have breakfast ready as quickly as possible in order to meet the deadline of the stockmen, who needed to be ready to move at the break of day. For me to be successful also meant having to leave the billy full of water on the fire overnight on very low heat so that I had a head start on boiling the billy; if I did not have enough hot water when I got up, then it meant having to add a lot more cold water, and would add precious time to getting the water to boil which I had not allowed for and would require me to have to quickly speeding up the heat so I could have the breakfast made on time. An important part of my job was to make sure that I was not responsible for delaying the boys and causing them to lose valuable mustering time. My method for getting breakfast ready in the morning worked fine for a while, but then the boys started having cups of tea at night while I was sleeping, leaving me with hardly any hot water in the billy for when I got up in the morning. This made my job a lot more difficult to do, and to make matters worse, they ignored my request when I asked them to replace the water that they took out. So, one night, just before I went to bed, I noticed that nobody was watching me, which gave me a good opportunity to stop them from taking the badly needed water from my billy. I got the red-hot coals out of the campfire and placed them all around the places that the boys would be walking with their bare feet. I hadn't quite got to sleep before I could hear them yelling and screaming while they were dancing on the hot coals that I had placed there. It couldn't have worked out better; the coals had lost their red glow, so they couldn't be seen but were still hot enough to burn the boys' feet. It is a funny thing. From that day on, I said nothing about the incident, and neither did anybody else say anything about the coals, which also ended the night raids on my billy.

Working in the outback has similar rules to working on a ship at sea. At sea, the captain is isolated by water and is the one who determines how the rules for the ship are set out. This is because if someone gets out of line, you cannot tell them 'You're fired and need to go and work elsewhere', as there is nowhere for them to go. In the outback, you are working under the same rules. But instead of the captain, it is the head stockman, and instead of being at sea, you are isolated by a vast mass of land.

There is one story that keeps coming back into my memory of the time I was working on Dunbar. One day, when the stockmen were driving a herd of cattle into the holding paddock, and as one of the stockmen who at the back of the herd was trying to complete the process of putting the steers in the holding paddock. There was one steer that the stockman was not able to get through the gate. The head stockman kept on telling him to put it in the paddock. Then the stockman got off his horse and tried to physically move it in but still did not make any headway. So, when the head stockman got off his horse, I thought that he was going to give him a hand. Well, I guess he did in a way, when he broke off a branch from a tree and, instead of hitting the steer with the branch, he hit the stockman with it until he got the steer through the gate. The stockman protested by stating to the head stockman that he was hitting him instead of hitting the steer, which still made no difference to the intensity or how often he was hitting him with it, along with the zone he was targeting. I guess that was one way of doing it, because the steer got inside the paddock pretty quickly after the stockman woke up to the fact that the only way to stop being hit by the branch was by getting that last steer inside the paddock.

One day, while one of the staff from the cattle station was driving me from one campsite to another campsite in a Blitz army truck (4-wheel drive) loaded with the men's swags, their food, and cooking equipment, the truck driver went to check a large waterhole (with a perimeter of about half a kilometre or maybe a bit more) in order to see if there was a sufficient amount of water for the herd of cattle to drink. It was also the same waterhole that we had to drink from. As we approached the waterhole, the old bloke who was driving the truck mentioned that something was very odd about the scene we were viewing. At first appearance, it looked like the waterhole had a lot of short bur bushes all around it. (A bur bush is a small bush which has small nut-like seeds that are annoying and prickly, that have a nasty habit of wanting to stick to you, and that cling to almost everything they touch, such as clothing and animal fur.) It was something that was not there the last time he saw the waterhole, and it stood out as being very odd. As we got closer to the waterhole, it became obvious that it was not bur bushes we were looking at; instead it was hundreds—or more than likely, thousands—of ducks. The old man was able to identify the breed of duck as whistling ducks, and although he had lived in the outback for many decades, he still had never seen more than about 50 ducks at any one time. Another very interesting thing that took place was the fact that the ducks didn't take flight when they heard the noise from the noisy truck; furthermore, when we got out of the truck for a closer look, the ducks didn't pay all that much attention to us. As the old man pointed out with his great wisdom of nature, it was obvious that the ducks had never been shot at, and it was more than likely that they had never seen human beings before seeing us.

The thing that astounded me about the ducks was that, by having such a great success in creating such a huge flock of ducks and despite us invading their territory with such unnatural things like a noisy truck and the two of us walking amongst them, the ducks carried on by giving us just a small amount of space and carried on as if we were a few more ducks coming in to enjoy their happy times. The one thing I know for sure is that there is never ever going to be a tourist guide that is going to be able to show you that scene. There's also the fact that I was on the payroll of Dunbar Station when I saw it, which means that I even got paid to see such a wonderful event.

We had 5 Aborigines working with us at the time, and the elder who was the head of his tribe who gave me one very good piece of advice about crocodiles. There was one important thing he brought to my attention, which was the fact that at this one waterhole we were camping at, I found a great place for collecting water. This turned out to be very handy. I didn't need to get my feet wet, and all I needed to do was walk out on the large log, dip my bucket into the water, and after filling it, return to the camp. The old Aborigine man noticed that I was doing the same thing 2 to 3 times a day and told me not to do that. I thought what he was asking me was ridiculous, but at least I was smart enough to ask why not. His answer jerked me back to reality, to information I was unaware of. He explained to me that a crocodile is more likely to lie submerged in the waterhole just enough so that you cannot see it, but it can see you; it is one of the few creatures in the world that will stalk humans. The crocodile will study your behaviour and work out a way to knock you off your log and into the water, with you ending up being its dinner. Another good piece of advice that I got from the head stockman was that it is never a good idea to get between a crocodile and the water, because the water is the place where it feels safe and it is more likely to attack should you happen to be standing between it and its safety.

I remember one time when I was wise enough not to throw caution to the wind. This took place when we had arrived late at a campsite just after it had turned dark. I was feeling a bit dirty and decided to have a swim in the waterhole. As I arrived at the edge of the waterhole, I couldn't help but notice two red dots that were glowing in the water. Since I had already noticed that I had not been picking up on other important warning signs of danger, I thought it best that I checked with the truck driver about the two red dots. It's a good thing I did, because he explained to me that those two dots were the reflection in the shallow water from the dim moon light that reflected from the crocodile's eyes. This very quickly led me to believe that I was all of a sudden feeling very clean and no longer needed that swim. If it is dark and should there happen to be some light shining in the water (in this case, the moonlight) and providing that the crocodile is close enough to the surface of the water, it will create a condition where its eyes will be seen as a glowing red colour. The further apart its eyes are, the bigger the crocodile will be. By the way, that crocodile which I almost had that close encounter with was more than big enough to make me its next meal if I had insisted on having that swim.

The chance of having a day off was in the category of being few and far between, and when you had a day off in the outback and ate meat as often as we did, then going fishing in one of the large waterholes seemed to be a very good way to spend that day off. There were two types of fish that one could catch in the waterholes: Catfish is edible, but it was a low preference when it came to the fish that the boys wanted to eat. Barramundi is a much more enjoyable fish to eat. They had two methods which they would use for catching them—either by a fishing hook or by a lure, without the luxury of having a rod. They still managed to catch enough so that we all had a good feed of fish that night. I did not have any fishing gear and was not able to participate in the fishing. It was a hot day; when their lines got snagged, as they often did, and since I wasn't fishing, I decided to take on the job of diving into the waterhole and unhooking the snagged lines. Well, I did this until my old Aborigine friend told me not to do that anymore. I guess there are times when I am a slow learner, because with all the fun I was having, I thought he was wrong and reluctantly asked him why not. His answer involved pointing to where a large crocodile was, and it took me about 3–4 minutes after he pointed in the direction of where that crocodile lay waiting, before I saw it. The waterhole couldn't have been any more than about 30 feet (10 metres) across or sometimes even less when I was unhooking the boys' snagged lines. The bit that makes a crocodile so deceptive is that, at a first glance, it looks like a bit of land slightly protruding from the surface of the water, which leads you into a false sense of security that makes you ignore it; and another thing that adds to the deception is that at no time does it even make the slightest ripple in the water. The only way that I was able to identify the large crocodile was by carefully viewing the surface of the water and eventually recognising its eyes and the small ripple of its back, which was just above the waterline. It looked like my Aborigine friend had once again stopped me from becoming a crocodile's dinner.

The one thing that I have learnt from living in crocodile territory is that it does not matter whether you can see them when you are around the water, because you are now in their territory. There is a good chance that they are already there and watching you, especially when you enter the water, because they have all the advantages. If you do not take certain precautions to make yourself safe, then you may very well end up being the crocodile's dinner. The other sad part about this situation is that the crocodile does not even need to be hungry when it attacks you; after it has killed you and if it is not feeling hungry, it will hide you in the water, under the root of a tree, which is also a way of tenderising meat. So, eating you later, at a time when it does feel hungry, along with the fact that it is the preferred way to be having its meal.

Chapter 11

The Stockman in Miranda Downs Cattle Station and the Battle with the Bush Fire

Miranda Downs is a cattle station in Queensland, at the southern end of the Gulf Country, which is **58** miles (**93** kilometres) north-west of Normanton. It has an airport, which is a cleared space for small aircraft to land in, and this is one of the runways which are longer, then most of the ones that you find in the outback, as well as being in better condition. Miranda Downs is often used for bringing people in and out of its station and is sometimes the way they get their supplies when it is urgently needed; otherwise, the supplies come in via the mail truck. The station is considered small, although it is several hundreds of square kilometres in size. (I was unable to gain the details of the size of Miranda Downs through the Internet.)

I started working in Miranda Downs after I had finished working at Dunbar sometime around **1980**, although this time I was working as a stockman. I guess it must have been about **4** or **5** weeks after I started working in Miranda Downs when we experienced the need to be putting out a large bush fire which had a front of about **2** kilometres. We had just finished working that day, which was somewhere around **6** p.m. or **7** p.m., when the manager informed us that we had to go and fight the bush fire that was burning at the station. He then got all the workers inside two of his vehicles in order for us to fight the bush fire. He also had a road grader which had a blade on it that they used to drive around in front of the fire, which cleared the grass away between the unburnt grass and the burning grass in order to form a firebreak. Our job was to run behind the road grader with a wet gunny sack and whack any flame that threatened the firebreak. One of the dangers that we faced was when the fire would start on a thick, tall clump of grass about 1 - 2 meters high, called kerosene grass; the danger it presented was that it would explode into a flame of about 3 or 4 meters tall in a fraction of a second. Seeing how fast that kerosene grass reacts with fire, meant that we were in danger of being badly burnt if we got to close to it before it went up in flames, and it was something we were very wary of. We started putting out the fire at 7 p.m., and after about 15 hours, we eventually got the fire contained. The reason we accepted it being contained instead of being completely put out was the great difficulty of extinguishing the fire of the trees that were still burning, which were more than likely a long way from any unburnt grass that could restart the fire. Should it not have had enough unburnt grass clearance, we would have cleared a safety gap with the road grader so that the burning tree was no longer able to restart any more fires. After that exhausting event, we went home and headed to bed for much-needed sleep and spent the rest of the day sleeping. So, I guess that you could also say one of the jobs I have done is being a *bush fireman*.

The next day, after the fire had been put out, the manager did an enquiry and worked out what had caused the fire. It was all due to one of the stockmen, who had failed to properly extinguish a cigarette; he was dismissed from his job for smoking a commercially made cigarette. In the bush, they have a rule for people that smoke, and that is that they are not allowed to smoke cigarettes that have been commercially made. They are much more resistant to being extinguished when you are finished with them; the ones you roll and make for yourself extinguish very easily and even sometimes extinguish themselves when you don't want them to, which makes them many times less likely to start a bush fire.

Most stations in the Gulf Country have Aborigines as part of their team for mustering the cattle. The Aborigines are extremely good at tracking and are considered to be some of the best trackers in the world. One day we were out looking for some cattle that we wanted to muster so that we could get them ready to sell in the market. This team consisted of a manager/head stockman, about 5 other white Australians, 2 Aborigines, and me. In regard to the Aborigines, the oldest was the grandfather of the younger one. While riding the horses through the field and looking for the cattle, we came across a lot of trees and bushes which compelled us to travel in a single line. This presented a problem in the importance of how the line was set up, which was unfortunately formed the same way I have just outlined to you, with myself being at the back of the line, which left me in a good position to see any hand signals that may be given. The problem that existed was that the one who had by far the best knowledge of tracking was the old Aborigine man, which also meant that he should have been the one in the front of the line so that he could let the manager/head stockman know how many head of cattle had gone down some of the very faint trails that most people were unable to see (with hindsight, that would also include the manager/head stockman). If the Aborigine tracker had been placed in the front of the line and the manager/head stockman had been placed second in the line, it would have meant that the tracker would have been able to use hand signals and avoid the risk of scaring the cattle by having to talk loudly, as well as letting the manager/head stockman know where the cattle were.

Here was where the best part of the entertainment started. The old Aborigine in front of me didn't say a word, but he kept on passing out hand signals to his grandson behind him. He would hold up a certain number of fingers to indicate how many cattle had gone down the faint tracks and to indicate where the tracks were, and the manager/head stockman kept on riding straight past the tracks we should have been going down so that we could muster the cattle. This led to a disappointing thing that happened that day, because the manager/head stockman only found a small fraction of the cattle we should have collected for the muster. This left us all with the results of a poor muster and a very clear mind as to who the best tracker was.

Miranda Downs had a campsite on it called Wilson's Camp, and it was by far the best campsite on the station, apart from the homestead. It had a two-storey building on it, a big waterhole nearby, and a windmill that kept a small trough constantly full of water, and it was one of the few campsites that had some supplies sometimes stored there.

One day, when we had a day off, one of the boys became very creative with the idea of making a *bath* that had hot water in it. The only things he needed for his creation were an oxygen cutting torch and an empty 44-gallon drum (200-litre drum) which was placed on its side. He cut out the top third of it and left the two ends uncut. He then made sure that the drum was secure so it would not roll, and he proceeded to dig a hole in the ground at the centre of the drum and then half-filled the drum with water. The next thing he did was to light a fire in the hole under the drum, which ended with the stockman being able to have a good hot bath. However, it did have some minor problems to it. If you got too keen with the fuel, you could end up making the bath a lot hotter than you desired it to be (unbearable hot,) with the urgent need to add some more cold water. If you took the shortcut of putting water on the fire, you would also end up getting a heavy amount of smoke in your eyes; the smoke would occasionally still get in your eyes even without the trick of pouring water on the fire, except it was much worse when you did. The bath turned out to be a good thing, or as good as you were going to get in the bush. It was very rare to have any equipment in the bush, outside of the main camp, and as you may have noticed, the stockmen were very good at taking advantage of any equipment that they had at their disposal.

Another clever thing one of the stockmen was able to make was a whip, which he made out of a cowhide that had been tanned the year before. They also worked out a way to make alcohol by hollowing out a pumpkin and putting a lot of sugar in it. Unfortunately, it took a lot of time to mature, and we had to leave before we could determine whether or not it was successful. Who knows, it may have been all right to drink the next time someone visited the camp.

Here is a closing comment that I thought would be interesting to put in for people who have no experience with dairy or beef farms. A lot of people who have never worked on a farm have no idea what is involved in the workings of a farm, and unless they have been there, they have no chance of knowing everything that is involved, because it is so different from everybody else's world. The farms I have knowledge about are dairy farms or beef-producing farms, which very often have a good reason for having a small number of other animals on their farm, such as horses, pigs, and domestic birds (chickens). One thing I can tell you is that if a farm is going to be managed even half decently, you are going to have to spend a lot more than **60** hours a week doing it. Dairy cows do not have the weekend off, and farmers also miss out on a lot of the perks that non-farmers take for granted.

CHAPTER 12

ICI Botany: Interesting Stories of Botany and the Chemical Industries, plus Moving to Perth

Imperial Chemical Industries is better known as ICI. ICI was first established in the United Kingdom by the merger in **1926** of Great Britain's four major chemical companies, and the botany site in ICI Sydney was a place that I worked in for **8** years (**1983–1991**). The botany site was .7 of a square kilometre (**70** hectares or **173** acres) and was established in **1942**. In **1998**, ICI was bought out by Orica and was broken up into smaller sections.

I first got to know about ICI in **1983**, when I was looking for a permanent job, and I didn't even know that it existed until my brother-in-law told me that it was a good company to work for and that it paid good wages. By then, I had finished my two tours around the world and had worked many different jobs. However, this was the first time that I had worked with chemicals, and I managed to get the job with ICI as a rigger/trades assistant. I had already achieved getting *a dogman's ticket* (for a person who loads a crane with a load of building materials and directs it to where the load needs to be placed), *a scaffolder's ticket* (for a person who makes temporary platforms on the outside of high-rise buildings so the builders can work from the outside of the building), and *a rigger's ticket* (for a person who uses chain blocks, Tirfor winches, and chain blocks with lever hoists). When we were using this equipment, it was referred to as just a come-along (come-along hand wrench), along with the more primitive block and tackle, which were all used to put heavy loads in places where the crane was less suitable or not able to do the job. I got those qualifications at Mount Isa Mines in Mount Isa, Queensland, while working as part of a contracting team with Simon Carves.

When I first started working at ICI, I was living at Winston Hills, about 50 kilometres from the botany site, and decided that I needed to live much closer. So, I rented a flat in Kingsford, which was only about 5 kilometres away from ICI. After working at ICI for a few years, I was able to buy my first flat, which was a one-bedroom flat in Hillsdale. It was only about 2 kilometres away, which meant that I no longer needed to drive my car to work and now found it a better idea to walk to work.

The botany site was divided into separate factories that specialised in making different types of products. All these plants only manufactured the base products, and the whole site was required to work 24/7, apart from the administration office and the contractor's compound. The site was worked from eight different sections which consisted of, an Administration office, a plant that made Chlorine and Hydrochloric Acid, a CTC plant (the full chemical name for CTC is Carbon Tetrachloride), a Silicate plant, a Polythene plant, a Polypropylene plant, and they even had their own Power Station, which was fuelled by coal, for making electricity. There was also a Contractor's Compound that was needed for some specialised jobs, and another reason for it being there was that it may very well have been a backup for combating the problems of the many stop-work meetings and strikes that were often happening in that period.

This was also a period when the union movement was very strong, and I had to be a fully paid member of a certain union before I was allowed to start the job. They also had strict rules when it came to job classification, and it was not always easy to distinguish a clear identification that separated each job. All riggers on the site were also trades assistants and were the only ones who were allowed to have a dual role. The way that we were set apart was, whenever a rigger did some trades assistant work along with his riggers work, it was accepted. Another situation which was much harder to justify was that the union did not permit anyone to be employed as a fitter and as a welder at the same time. Part of the job description for a fitter is that they are qualified to do some small welding jobs. There are about 4 or 5 different levels that the ticket of a welder is certified by. John, the Maltese fitter, had the highest qualification on-site for welding. Yet whenever he did a welding job, he was constantly walking on eggshells (struggling to fit in) by having to ask the other welders, who were not as qualified or capable of doing the job as well as he did, and he still needed to constantly ask permission to do any welding jobs. My way of understanding this was that it was a situation where the unions' red tape was getting in the way of doing a safer job.

The union had a very strong influence in the way that the conditions of the jobs were conducted, and they were also very vigilant in the way they flexed their muscles, which was by having one person in each factory elected as a union delegate; the delegates' job was to sort out any problems that the members had with the company. The action taken after hearing the complaint was set out in steps. The first step was to get the delegate to talk to management and try to sort out any problem that the workers had with the management; if the delegate was unable to sort it out at that level, he would need to seek the approval of three workers so that he could have a stop-work meeting. Upon the approval of the meeting, the delegate would get the workers to organise the safety procedures for leaving the site and then get the members of that one factory—or if they deemed it necessary, all the members of the whole site—to the meeting. All stop-work meetings had to be held off-site, and this was for legal reasons, which also was a way of getting the company's attention. The meetings would always be held on a large grass strip just on the other side of the gate between the boundary fence and the road (this was referred to as 'going on the grass'). Once everyone had gathered, the delegate would open the meeting by expressing the grievance that they had with the company. It was then open for discussion on points for the grievance and points against the grievance, which would continue until everybody had their say on the matter. After that part of the debate was finished, as to whether or not they were going to take further action, the voting would be done in the normal manner— by raising your hand. If the vote was no, then the meeting would end, which rarely, if ever, happened. But if the vote was yes, they would get the members to verbally move a motion as to what course of disciplinary action they needed to take, which required having someone second the motion. The disciplinary action would be done by having *bans* on certain things or by going on *strike* for a period, and if the first proposal wasn't voted in, it would continue until one was accepted via the voting system. Another interesting thing that would happen at these meetings was that the union members were often reluctant, to name any of the other union members name, who was involved in the dispute and would very often substitute the terminology to being 'a certain party'.

With every story, there are two sides (no matter how flat you make a pancake, it's still going to have two sides). The union has done some good things over the course of many years, such as ensuring better safety on the job and being able to negotiate a good wage for the job which you are employed to do. On the other side of the coin, you have people within the union movement who have become obsessed with the new amount of power that they now have and who have crossed boundaries to places they should not be going to. Before the unions got a foothold on the power that they now have, the employers were in a position of being very powerful and were the ones who grossly abused their power, which created the reason why the union movement has been successful. This wrongful abuse of power, regardless of who is using it, still does not alter the fact that two wrongs do not make a right, and I firmly believe that *balance* is the key to doing what is right and that neither party should be using their extreme views of what they may be endeavouring to get away with, in order to achieve their point of being right.

Here is a story about one of the stop-work meetings that was held at Botany and one of the many reasons I consider some union movements to be abusing their use of power. On one Friday morning, the union at ICI in Botany had a stop-work meeting which was held for the whole site to go on strike for the day. The reason the meeting was held, was because of a light bulb which was faulty and was not working in one of the toilets, and left the people in the dark while they were using that toilet. When we arrived at the meeting, there was something that normally did not take place. Upon my entering the meeting place, it became obvious that 3 of the members had brought their fishing rods to the meeting. The speaker claimed that the company refused to put in a new light bulb because they did not have a replacement one on the site, and it would take about a week or more for them to get another one. When it came to having a discussion for going against the motion of going on strike for the day, I was the only one brave enough to get up and speak against it, which is not easy when you are only one out of about 130 people. My statement was that I did not believe that we needed to go on strike for this, and going by the fishing rods that some people had in their hands (where a lot of people laughed at what I had to say), I went on to say that if they wanted a day off, then they should do it another way. (They always had the option of taking one of 15 paid sick days that were collectively given to them each year, and they more than likely had some available to them.) I said, 'That I came here to work and not for the purpose of going on strike.' This created a commotion of mockery, with the combination of laughter and booing. After that, they had a vote for those in favour of going on strike for the day, followed by a vote against the motion. I was the only bloke who voted against it. One person standing behind me said that I was weak. I turned to him and calmly said that it takes a great deal of courage to stick to what you truly believe, especially when you are voting against the mob, who have already voted the other way. The only ones who are weak are sheep-minded people, who do not have the courage to vote the way that they truly believe in. Are you one of them? *Sheep-minded people*—This terminology comes from the natural things that sheep sometimes do. They can be walking, and then for no apparent reason, they start running. While running, they all of a sudden decide to jump over an imaginary object, with the rest of the sheep following them without any rational reasoning as to why they are jumping over that same imaginary object in the very same place. So, anybody who does a senseless act for no good reason is considered sheep-minded.

I later found out that in order to camouflage the sabotage for the light bulb being out of order, the light bulb was deliberately damaged, by someone wrapping the bulb in a soft cloth and banging it against a hard surface so that it did not break the glass and ended up only breaking the filament in the bulb. If the light bulb was urgently needed, the company would not have hesitated in getting a taxi to pick one up within a very short period (more than likely within an hour, more than the time it took to have the stop work meeting). The reason I am confident in making that statement is that there were also toilets nearby, which they could have used, along with the fact that with them taking longer to go to the toilet, the company would be losing out on more productive working time. The stop-work meetings were very expensive; The company had to pay for the non-production of the stop-work meeting. It was multiplied a lot more when the whole site had a stop-work meeting. The cost for the company to get a special taxi to deliver a light bulb was very small when one compares it to the company's cost for not only the stop-work meeting but even the greater expense of the day of striking. Another added cost was that they still had to pay some of the men that still needed to get paid to work without producing anything so that they could make sure everything remained safe (the cost of each plant when those six plants were operating was between $150,000 and $200,000 an hour). This all came back down to the union having no legitimate reasoning to go on strike in the first place; the only logic behind it was for the union movement to demonstrate how much power they had over the company so that *they could get anything they wanted*. In their minds, that made it all worth their while to lose the day's pay, along with being able to have a long weekend off so that they could go fishing (when you are making big money, you have the luxury of getting away with making those types of decisions).

While we are on the subject of the union movement, there was one rare occasion that I know of where the union came off being second best, which took place at the Mount Isa Mines in Mount Isa. The Mount Isa Mines are the only industry in Mount Isa, and the shops and other small industries are all dependent on Mount Isa Mines for their work, which is also extended to work created by the needs of their employees.

This is one time when the union grossly underestimated the strength of Mount Isa Mines and how far they were prepared to go with this dispute. Even though I learnt about this story sometime in 1980 while I was working as a scaffolder for Simon Carves in the Mount Isa Mines, the story took place before I started working at Mount Isa Mines. It was a time when the union was very powerful and regularly went on strike for everything and anything that they could find. And having an excuse for going on strike as well as having a good logical reason for striking was, more often than not, sadly lacking in the equation of being reasonable in what they were asking for. The real reason for most of the strikes was for the purpose of imposing the power that they had over the company. One day, the union members decided to go for a pay increase and said to the company that they were going to make this one big and, if need be, would stay out for 3 weeks. After the union had put their demands to the company, the company gave their demands a lot of thought. The company then came back to the union and said to them that they were right about 'making this one big', but this time they were going to be making it a lot bigger than they thought. The company told the union that there would be no further discussion about it and said that they were now evicting all the union members from the site for *six months*. The gates would be locked, and they would not be allowed back on-site until after that six-month period.

This took the union by surprise because this was the first time that the company had stood up to the union. The company taking this stance meant that the members of the miners' union who were now living in Mount Isa, which was a hundred kilometres—or more likely, a lot more kilometres—from anywhere they could get work, were now being forced to take a lot of time off without pay. For the first week, most of the boys, with their shallow thoughts, thought that this was a good thing. By the second week, most of them woke up to the reality of having no money. By the third week, most of them were all flat broke and were waking up to how it felt to have no money and, worse still, have no money or very little money coming in for a long time to come. The government does not pay workers when they are on strike, but I do not know how they fare when they are locked out of their workplace and are unable to go back to work. What is known is that *even if* they were able to get some government relief, it would be nowhere near as much money as what they were used to for their budget of life requirements. Most of the workers were begging and pleading with the company to let them get back to work. After the six months, when the company did let them go back to work, the company then reversed the previous demands of the union for a pay increase by paying them less than they did before the workers went on strike. They have had very few strikes since that period, and the strikes that they have now all have good, sound, logical reasoning for having the strike, along with having no desire to re-enter that battlefield again. As for the mining company, within a moderately short period, they regained all the money they had lost from the loss of production over that six-month period, and they remained a lot better off financially due to the lack of costs from the stop-work meetings and strikes that used to take place.

My employment at ICI: I first started working at ICI, in the CTC plant, for 3 years and then was transferred across the road to the silicates plant for 3 years. Later on, I went to work at the polypropylene plant for the remaining 2 years.

Safety: The good parts of working in ICI were the high wages and a very high standard of safety procedures, which were maintained throughout the whole site, especially when it came to protecting the workers. All maintenance jobs needed to be cleared with written paperwork by a qualified safety foreman, who was responsible for both the crews of the maintenance and the production workers' safety. They needed to make sure to check that all safety requirements had been met before work commenced, along with having to be held accountable should any safety problems occur between the paperwork being signed on, and till the time it was signed off.

The working management structure of the plants. Apart from the administration and the contractors' compound, all the plants on-site were managed the same way. They were divided, by using two crews to operate them: the operators and the maintenance crew, who were divided into three groups—the fitters, the trades assistants, and the riggers. I happened to be one of the riggers. When it came to the welders, where some plants had no welder, another plant might have one welder. The CTC plant had two welders. The welders were supplied by the dependence of the requirements for each plant. The contractors from the compound would do most of the welding jobs for the plants that did not have a welder, or on the odd occasion, one of the welders from one of the other plants would do it should they happen to be working overtime on that job. The contractors from the compound also did any carpentry work that needed to be done.

The CTC plant: This was set up for the purpose of upgrading the quality of the nitric acid and, more importantly, to deal with the waste products of the other plants. The main method it used for getting rid of the waste products involved breaking them down in a chemical reactor, with the main chemical used in the reactor being chlorine, which produces a lot of fumes that are very corrosive. It can wreak havoc (the damage is devastating) when it comes to the damage it can quickly do to your lungs. It also required the use of a long-distance breather while maintenance was being done on the reactor.

The reactor was mainly made of pure carbon and frequently required a lot of maintenance done on it, because of the corrosion in and around the reactor; would sometimes develop leaks. Also, the carbon was very brittle, and there was the need to take special care not to accidentally break it.

There was one interesting experience that I gained while working in the CTC plant which gave me a far better understanding of the environmental change of temperature. This happened one day when it was very hot, about 50°C. The building that we were working in had no air conditioner or fans, and it was a place where everyone in the building really felt the heat, apart from the office at the end of the building, which was air-conditioned. The reason we did not have any air conditioner in the workshop was that when we took some of the parts that we were working on with us back to the workshop for repairs, there was a chance that some chlorine may be trapped inside the part when it was being dismantled and could end up creating a severe health danger, with the chlorine severely contaminating the air in the workshop. The reason we did not have fans was the mentality that the workers had about fans, which was that the fans would only blow hot air and would make the situation worse rather than better when you turn them on when the weather is hot.

Fortunately for me, on that day there was some cool relief at hand—or so I thought. I was called into the boss's office, and as soon as I entered the office, I felt that it was very cold and wondered how they were able to stay in such a cold condition. I was in there for about 1 hour and the strange observation I made was that after a while, the temperature started to feel nice and normal. As time progressed, so did my understanding of how I was feeling the temperature, and as a matter of fact, I started feeling that it was no longer cold enough for the way I preferred it to be. Well, that was until I went back to that very hot building that I was in before going into the office. The heat now felt like it had become overwhelmingly hot and a lot more intense than it had been when I was last in it. The truth of the matter was that the temperature had not changed from the time I went into the office to the time I had returned, and the effect of my feeling so overwhelmed by the heat was created by my acclimatising to the cool temperature of the air conditioner.

The lesson I got was that one can best acclimatise to the hot temperature by making small changes to the coolness one seeks, which are the ones that leave you with the most benefits and that allow you to acclimatise to the heat. I have now clearly discovered that running from one air conditioner to another air conditioner is a long way from being your best solution for acclimatising to the heat. I also believe that when you are in a cold climate, the best way to acclimatise requires taking a similar course of action, except this time you need to make small changes to the heat you are seeking.

In regard to overtime: We were also required to work overtime for other plants when they were shut down for maintenance, and the only places where we did not work overtime were the administration office and the contractor's compound. When it came to working overtime, there were a lot of arguments of not being able to get enough of it, and the boys regularly accused each other of taking the other one's overtime. The reasons the overtime was so popular was because of the penalty rates, which were paid at double time; only the first two hours of a scheduled shift on a Saturday was when the penalty rates were paid at time and a half. They also had another good reason for wanting overtime, which was that all overtime pay, had to be a minimum of 4 hours' work, regardless of how long they worked. There was also the fact that should they be called to come back to work after they had returned home (a call-in), which required 2 hours being paid for each time they were recalled back to work, along with 4 hours for each job that they did. This sometimes meant that, through the advantage of penalty rates, they could easily end up getting more than a week's pay by doing about 3 hours' work should they happen to have done 5 jobs within 3 hours of working. The overtime that we worked had now been changed; it was now set up to be very fairly distributed. This was done by introducing three chocolate wheels: one for the fitters, one for the trades/assistants, and one for the riggers. The chocolate wheel that we had was white and had our names written on it with a marker; this was turned around by rotating the wheel one name at a time. When your name came to the top of the wheel, you now had the option of doing the overtime or letting it go to the next one on the list. The foreman was the one in charge of turning the chocolate wheel for overtime, and the chocolate wheel was always referred to as the choc wheel.

When you look at the deal the boys were getting, it would be very hard to imagine them getting a fairer—or even better—deal than what they were offered.

Remember when I told you earlier that there are two sides to every story and that no matter how flat you make a pancake, it is always going to have two sides to it? Well, here is a good example of what I was referring to. The bad side to this story is that the deal was so good that we were afraid to leave home in case we missed one of those call-ins. It was Sunday morning. ICI only had a skeleton crew after business hours for the maintenance work, which meant that the most likely time for being called back to work was from Friday afternoon till Monday morning, when there was no regular maintenance being done, therefore creating a much stronger chance for the need for the company to call someone back to work. I was afraid to leave the house, in case it would be my turn on the choc wheel for the next call-in from the company. If you were not home when they called you, they would go to the next person on the wheel. These calls needed to be on a landline, and it was not permitted for someone to be called on a mobile phone. It happened that while I was home, I had run out of milk. At this point, I was getting desperate and did not have any milk for a cup of tea that I was very much looking forward to drinking. It only took about five minutes for me to go and get some milk from the shop, and while I was gone, the company tried to ring me up for a call-in, which happened to be a very good one. That next person on the choc wheel list worked 5 hours and ended up being paid the equivalent of 2 weeks' worth of work. When I found out on Monday morning about the golden deal that I had missed out on, I then got very upset with myself for taking the luxury of being able to have some milk in my tea. The way I saw it at the time was that the milk had cost me somewhere between $960 and $1,200. The job ended up going late into the night; the men working the call-in were not able to get the minimum time off of 10 hours, which also meant that they also got paid for having the Monday off.

Many years later, when I had become much wiser and looked at what I thought was a golden deal, it now seemed nowhere near as golden as I thought it was. This great deal that I thought I had, had turned me into a prisoner in my own home, afraid of missing out on a golden deal, and now I realise that I was missing out on all the reasons I was making the money in the first place, such as a social life, which human beings so badly need in order to have a proper, functional life.

Silicate plant: Silicate is a versatile product that can be made into an adhesive agent or a lubricating agent. The silicate was manufactured in the form of both liquid and solid.

The silicate plant is a sister plant to the CTC plant, which regularly supplied the silicate plant with 2 fitters, 1 trades assistant, and 1 rigger. After a while, a small workshop was set up as a permanent base for the silicate plant to work from and was supplied with a small permanent team from the CTC plant. One fitter, named John, was Maltese and had worked there since the plant first started; he also worked with a Greek trades/assistant called Con. The other fitter was a Portuguese named Joe, and I was the New Zealander who worked with Joe as a rigger.

At that time, I had worked with well over 50 different fitters, and by far the smartest fitter that I have ever worked with was Joe. Before working at ICI, Joe was a toolmaker. Toolmakers need to work with the use of very small clearances of measurement with the jobs that they are making. Sometimes the room temperature is more than enough to change the measurement of what they are working on, and they are forced to work in an air-conditioned room so that they can work within the correct measurements of the job.

During their spare time while we were in the small workshop in the silicate plant, Joe, the fitter, and Con, the trades assistant, often spent a lot of time debating various subjects, none of which Con ever won. One day I thought Joe had put an argument to Con which I felt certain that even he had no chance of winning. The statement Joe made to Con was that the $4 watch on his wrist was better than the $200 gold watch that Con had on his wrist. (Before you continue, you may want to try and think of how a $4 watch is better than a $200 watch?)

Con felt confident that victory was now close at hand and was very confident that he had a much better watch. Joe replied, by telling Con that he could prove that he had the better watch. He then proceeded to take his watch off his wrist and threw it as hard as he possibly could on the concrete floor, and then he asked Con to pick it up, which he did. He said to Con, 'It is still working, isn't it?' After Con had picked the watch up from the floor, he had to concede that it was still working. Joe then said to Con, 'Do the same to your watch.' This turned out to be far from a fair contest. The $4 watch weighed about the same as 2 A4 paper sheets, and throwing it was equivalent to trying to damage a feather by throwing it hard to the ground; whereas Con's $200 watch weighed about 1 kilo. Throwing it was equivalent to throwing a thin glass tumbler hard to the ground. It became very obvious that, like the glass tumbler, the heavy watch would not be able to sustain the heavy damage after being subjected to such harsh treatment. I thought how smart it was of Joe to work out the one aspect where the $4 watch had the advantage over the $200 one, and regardless of which watch you used, they both kept the time with the same accuracy.

Another time, while I was working at the silicate plant with Joe, just before we started to work on the job, one of the trades assistants came over from the CTC plant in order to pass a bit of time by having a chat with Joe about the job we were about to work on. This trades assistant was considered by many to be the least knowledgeable of all the trades assistants. He then started passing on advice to Joe about the job, and to my amazement, Joe listened closely to everything he had to say. When he left and was out of sight, I turned to Joe and said, 'Why do you even bother to listen to him? He does not know what he is talking about.' Joe said, 'That is where you are wrong. There comes a time in our life when we just can't wrap our head around a problem that we are trying to find an answer to. What he is saying to you may be the very answer to your problem, and if you do not listen to him in the first place, then you have also missed out on finding the answer you are seeking.'

Joe was also very wise when it came to seeing how much attention you were paying to what he had been telling you. He set me up with a proverb (riddle) by asking me if I knew *a good definition for a wise man*. The first way to pass this test is by letting him know that you are listening, instead of running off at the mouth like I did before. This requires answering no to the question; otherwise, you will never be able to align with the wisdom of his intelligent answer. After I told him no, he said, '*A wise man is a person who knows how to throw out the garbage.*' The key to answering the proverb is understanding that garbage is anything that is not correct and that wisdom is everything that is correct. So, in effect, having knowledge about the things you need to know and rejecting it when you know it is wrong means that you are throwing it in the garbage, which sometimes requires sifting through a lot of garbage thrown your way, as well as still being able to find valuable information should it happen to come your way.

The chlorine and hydrochloric acid plant: Chlorine (which is an alkalised product) and hydrochloric acid are made from natural sea salt, which is split through the process of a high flow of electricity flowing through it, where one ends up becoming two separated products, or on another words, one becomes the by-product of the other.

There is a chemical scale by which these two solutions are measured, which is called a pH level—a measurement of the acidity or alkalinity of a solution, numerically equal to 7 for neutral solutions, increasing with alkalinity and decreasing with acidity. The pH scale that is commonly in use ranges from 0 to 14. Most people who do maintenance on swimming pools are familiar with the pH scale, which is used to control the cleaning chemicals in the pool.

Power station: The power station is fuelled by coal and supplies the whole site with electricity. It has the ability to revert to the government power grid at any time should it be deemed necessary.

Polythene plant: Polythene is a product which is black. It is used largely for good-quality piping in many sizes and can also be made in the form of a black plastic type of sheeting. This was a plant where we were invited to work overtime when their plant was shut down for maintenance repairs. Polythene is made by compressing oil with a very high pressure that ranges from 14,504 psi to 43,511 psi (pounds per square inch), depending on the quality of polythene you need to make. The pressure is so great that it needs to be done in three stages by three compressors in order to build it up to the required pressure. I was part of a small team of workers that were required to sometimes unblock a cooling system which consisted of a long set of connecting oblong pipes. The pipes were very strong and thick (the inside diameter was 2 inches or 50 millimetres, and the outside diameter was 4 inches or 100 millimetres), the ends were bolted on so that they could be taken off in order to clear the blockages which sometimes occurred, and the gasket which was used to join the pipes together was a 1-inch-thick iris gasket that had a hole in the centre of it and was made of solid stainless steel which was highly polished so that it did not leak under the very high pressure. After we took off the end of the pipe, it was important to make sure that everybody was well clear of the end of the pipe from which the product was going to be blown out off. Then we would get the operator to open the valve a little bit, wherein the product would come out at such a fast pace that you would need to put your hands over your ears because of the loud explosion it would create; it would also cause the whole pipe to freeze and turn white. After the pipe had thawed, we would refit the pipe so that the compressors could continue the normal function of making polythene. (An iris gasket is named for the resemblance that it has to the anatomy of the iris of a human eye.)

Polypropylene plant: Polypropylene is a high-quality type of plastic used in such things as safety helmets, ice cream containers, syringes, or anywhere else in which high-quality plastic is used.

Polypropylene has a catalyst of several products, and within the catalyst, there is one product used which I unfortunately cannot remember the name of. The important thing to know is that it is so flammable that as soon as it makes contact with air, it ignites and causes the product to catch on fire. Because of the problems that it could create while maintenance was being done on it, we always needed to be fitted with a very bulky fireproof suit; also, the product needed to be constantly submerged in nitrogen so that it would not catch on fire. Should it happen to accidentally catch on fire, *it would be so hot that it would quickly melt any metal that it came in contact with.* Throughout the time I worked in the polypropylene plant, the safety was maintained at such a high standard that we did not have to deal with any fires.

The first odd thing that I noticed when I transferred over to work in the polypropylene plant, was that everybody was expected to swear. It was considered cool (being favourably connected to certain group, also cool quite often means doing something dumb and stupid.) if you joined the rest of the boys by swearing. If you did not swear, then as far as they were concerned, there was no room for anyone between being cool or and someone who was outside the same swearing group as themselves, and you were considered a total misfit if you did not swear.

When I was younger, I also thought that I was cool to swearing and thought that I had my swearing completely under control. Well, I did, until I met an American professor in the Portman Hotel in London who majored in English. He was kind enough to put me on the right track when he asked me, 'Do you know why people swear?' Fortunately for me, I was brought up by a wise father. When it came to advice about information you wished to gather, his advice was 'When someone asks you a question and you wish to know the wisdom of their answer, you need to tell them that you do not know. Otherwise, you stand a good chance of not gaining the wisdom that is about to be presented to you.' So, I informed the professor that I did not know. (Sure, I had plenty of smart answers that I could have given him, but it would have still left me as ignorant as I was before he was prepared to offered me this good advice.) His answer was that, *"people who swear are out of control and lack the ability to put in the appropriate word"*—in my case, while using the only language I know. After going home that day, I carefully analysed what he had said to me, and from that answer, it became obvious that I was no longer under any delusion of the fact that I was out of control and was not even able to correctly use the only language I know. This demonstrated to me that I was presenting myself in such a bad way and that I needed to stop using this bad habit immediately. Even though it was a hard habit to break, I have since changed by improving on my education and have stopped that bad habit permanently.

So now the boys from the polypropylene plant were trying to force me back into the bad habit of swearing. They spent over a year trying every trick that they could think of—without success—to make me swear. This was until one day when I was trying to get the attention of the fitter that I was working with, and no matter what I did, I was unable to get his attention in order to pass on an important message. We were in the workshop at this time, and desperate to get his attention, I decided that I would use two swear words, with the thought that it would gain his attention. This worked far better than I could have ever imagined. There were about 20 people in the workshop, and to my amazement, by using these two swear words which instantly stopped everybody in the workshop dead in their tracks. The whole place went completely silent for about a minute or two, until one person said to me that I had just sworn. I turned to him and confirmed that I had. I guess that the boys had thought that they had won the swearing battle with me. Well, that was the one and only time that I did swear, and no, they did not win any battle. I believe that I was the winner of that battle, because not only did I gain the attention of that one fitter, but I also gained the attention of the whole workshop for a short period and was in full control of what I was doing.

The thing that surprised me was the massive effect that is created when you very rarely do something. When you do that one rare thing for one time only, it then works out to be a very powerful tool to use. I know that had I ever sworn in front of them again, it would have been nowhere near as effective as the first time that I swore.

It wasn't until I was in Polypropylene before I was able to saved up $10,000, although I still needed to borrow another $30,000 so that I could buy my first flat. At the time all I was able to afford was a one-bedroom flat. The real estate agent that I went to showed me a one-bedroom flat which was very close to ICI and informed me that the selling price was $40,000. I then gave the agent a counter offer of $38,000 in the hope that the investor would come back with another counter offer of $39,000. The investor stayed firm with his offer of $40,000, and since he was not prepared to budge, neither was I.

With hindsight, along with the fact that this was the beginning of the first big property boom that has continued for over several decades, as one is judging the property market, you would have to concede that the investor had all the advantages heading his way. Although it did require waiting for a period when he would be able to get many more times the price that he was currently asking for, the closer he got to waiting up to a year and a half, the greater his reward would be. Fortunately for me, the investor was impatient and went with the option of putting it up for auction, and as far as I can ascertain, he was not willing to wait for anyone and was in a hurry to sell it. The real estate agent came to me just before it was ready to go on auction and asked if I was still interested and if I was still prepared to make a bid for it at the auction. I informed him that I was already seriously looking at another flat which was not quite what I had in mind and believed that it was the one that I would be settling for. The real estate agent then asked me if I would attend the auction so that I could see how much it went for. I agreed to attend the auction, and when the big day came, I sat amongst the people at the auction. The agent came over to me and asked me how much I was prepared to offer for that flat I had first looked at, which was now about to go on auction. I told him that I was not really interested, although if I could get it for the price that I first offered for it ($38,000), I might make a bid for it. The auction started and nobody was prepared to make a bid, so I got a bit cheeky and offered a bid of $34,000. Then another bidder joined the auction, who I strongly suspected was a real estate agent who was there for the sole purpose of raising the price and who had no intention of buying the property. The bids were continued by the same person in increments of $1,000, so they made a bid of $35,000. Then my bids kept coming at a very slow pace, indicating that I was reluctant to continue, so I made a bid of $36,000. Since the bidding was going so slowly, the auctioneer decided to change the bids to increments of $500, so my next bid was $36,500 and his next bid was $37,000. The auctioneer got nervous about whether the bidding would continue, so he reduced the bidding increments to $250. So, my next bid was $37,250, then it was brought up to $37,500. I then very reluctantly went to $37,750. Now before we proceed further, let's have a look at what was offered. The real estate agent was confident that I would go as high as $38,000 but was in great doubt as to whether or not I was prepared to go past $38,000. Should he put in another bid, he would be making me go past that golden figure of $38,000. The auction was then closed under the reserved price. I was asked to come back into the office, where they haggling for higher price, my offer of $37,750 stayed firm, and was accepted for the sale. I considered that I had done very well by getting this flat for such a low price when you take into consideration that I really didn't have anything close to being as good when you take in the price and it having the closest and most favourable location.

After I bought the flat, the boys at work often talked about the way the housing prices kept going up at a very fast rate. I did not pay as much attention to what they were telling me, because the figures seemed too high to be true, and I thought maybe they were playing a game amongst themselves to see who could come up with the better price in the housing market to making a game of mockery to the great deal I got with my flat. This went on for about six months. I thought that it was about time to put a stop to it, so I offered them what I considered to be a ridiculous price of $50,000 for my flat and told them that I was prepared to sell it to them. One of the boys took me up on that offer and said, 'How soon are you prepared to sell it? Because those flats are now worth about $80,000.' So, I went and checked with various real estates and found out that the market really was moving that fast.

After doing more research, I found their figures to be true, and the prices had even exceeded what they were telling me. I went on to learn that my flat, after about 11 months, was now worth about $100,000 and that a three-bedroom brick house in Perth was only worth about $80,000.

Going to Perth: It so happened that I had a friend in Perth that I had met on the Fair Star Cruiser about a year before who had invited me to come over and stay with them in Perth. I also had a cousin living in Perth who was in the real estate business, although we would have been about 8 years old when we were last in contact with each other. I decided to give my cousin a ring and asked her if it was all right for me to come over and see her, because I was looking at the prospects of buying a house over there and finding out a bit more about Perth before I committed to the idea, and told her that I would be staying at my friend's place while I was over there. She informed me that she was looking forward to seeing me. So, I decided to take 3 weeks' holiday from work and went to visit my cousin in order to find out for myself how easy it was to get work over there and to gain a better understanding of the housing market in Perth. I also had the expectation of being able to talk to someone who I believe that I could trust, and I could rely on her to have knowledge about Perth, especially since she was a real estate agent who had been living in Perth for about 20 years. I was 44 years of age at the time and had been around the world twice, and while travelling around the world, I was able to get a job any time that I needed one. This also included jobs, wherein I had had very little experience in that field of work at the time and where most people would not have expected me to achieve a successful application. My cousin said that she did not think that I would have much of a problem getting a job in Perth and that since she was in the real estate business, she would line me up with a good house when I got over there.

When I returned to ICI after having my holidays, I was excited about the prospect of being able to exchange the one-bedroom flat that I had in Sydney for a three-bedroom brick house in Perth, as well as being able to have a good deposit for a flat. All I needed in order to make it successful was a steady job that paid a moderately good wage. This great offer that Perth had going for it also showed great prospects for me getting a good head start in my life. So, I terminated my job in ICI and sold my flat for a very good price of $120,000 and then loaded up my car and trailer for Perth. The distance from Sydney to Perth is approximately 4,000 kilometres. I considered it too far to drive by car all the way over there, so I drove as far as Adelaide and put my car and trailer on the back of the train and continued the remainder of my journey to Perth in the luxury of a train.

So far, my dream of financially gaining a better position in my life was on track. I had bought a nice three-bedroom brick house for $80,000, and going by what my cousin had told me I considered it to be in a good area. I had also borrowed $20,000 and bought a two-bedroom flat for $40,000. I thought that I had been very conservative with the way I had spent my money and that I had left myself with plenty of reserve cash for anything that might go wrong.

As we go through life, we often discover that the journey of our life is not going to be a success-only journey and that there are things that can go wrong for various reasons. More often than not, we are presented with a thing called a red flag. Sometimes there are several red flags to watch out for. A red flag is a warning sign that allows us to recognise when something is going wrong. For example, you may have a friend that is always the perfect gentleman, and one day, he loses his temper and slams the door in your face, which is out of character for him to do. The red flag that you need to watch out for is how often is this part of his history which is going to be part of his normal behaviour. This raises the following questions: Is this new friend still worth being with? What other surprises does he have waiting for you? The red flag is the warning sign; you need to make a decision as to whether this is a one-off thing and not worth worrying about or whether it is an example of something which is just the start of the pattern of similar behaviour and is a window of behaviour which is going to get much worse? Maybe this is a time when you need to start viewing the possibility of what the future holds in store for you, and maybe you are considering if it is still worthwhile staying with this friend or if you should wait for further evidence before you make that decision. Red flags may present themselves in many events in our lives. Like everything in our lives, it requires having a balance attached to it. The more we are emotionally involved in this person or thing, then the more likelihood there is of us not being able to recognise the red flag. On the other side of the coin, we may be too objective, wherein we might start raising red flags that do not really exist and venture along the line of being overcautious, with the result being that we missed out on something good in our lives.

After I spent a couple of weeks in Perth, it became very obvious that getting a job there for a reasonable wage was not going to be an easy goal to achieve (like I was led to believe), especially since the only skills I had were considered to be labouring skills. The other thing that went against me was that I was over forty years of age; since there was a big surplus of young people who were unskilled workers, the employers considered that anyone over forty who wanted to do a labourer's job was not worth taking on for employment. This was backed up by my neighbour who was a union delegate for a large company and who was trying to get me a job as a rigger. After a lot of his hard work by trying to fit me in for the job, the boss eventually had a private chat with him and said that I was too old for the job and that I was not going to be a successful applicant for a rigger's job or any other labouring job.

After a few more weeks, I managed to get a job as a brickie's labourer; I had already done brickie's labouring work in Sydney for a much higher wage, where I worked for a guaranteed 40 hours a week. In Perth, the best wage that I could get for being a brickie's labourer was about $12 an hour. It got much worse than that because of the few hours of work one would accumulate over the week. Rain delays would cause a lot of lost time, which would reduce one's weekly hours to about 20 hours a week and sometimes even a lot less. The money I was making each week was not enough to support myself, and this included the money which I was getting from the rented flat. I was also unable to find another job that could pay me a reasonable wage to live on. I don't drink, I don't smoke, I do not go out at night, I do not gamble. I am very conservative with the way I spend my money; yet the income was so low that I was unable to live on it.

However, it wasn't all bad. I managed to have a good time with my girlfriend in Perth, and my mother came over from New Zealand to visit me for two weeks, while my girlfriend was here. Who I met up with just before I left Sydney, and who stayed with me for four weeks while my mother was here for two weeks, this was the highlight to the time I spent in Perth.

Even though I had a good reserve of cash to start off with, it dwindled away at a fast rate, and the lack of finance for living started catching up with me. I had to sell my flat and, a few weeks later, had to move back to Sydney and rent out the house that I had in Perth.

All this real estate work was done through my cousin. I even got the last job of renting out my place done with her, wherein she told me that I would get special treatment if I opted for the higher graded rate for managing the property, which I was silly enough to accept.

When I went back to Sydney, and managed to make arrangements for being able to stay with my girlfriend. This made the transition of moving back to Sydney much easier.

The red flags that I so blindly missed. I was told that getting a job would not be a problem. The bit left out was 'if you have a trade to work from' and 'if you are not considered to be too old'. I was also not informed, that there were a big surplus of young people looking for work who stood a far better chance of getting a labours job than I did at my age. And being past the undesirable age of more than 40 was the reason for not getting the job

The buying and selling of my flat and house were nothing special; there were many real estate agents who could have done just as well, if not a lot better.

The buying of my house turned out not to be a good deal. This time it was not necessarily my cousin's fault, although if she had been good with her homework, she might have known about the government wanting to do a so-called good deed by taking the Aborigines out of their settlements and mixing them into dominantly white suburbs in Perth, with mine being one of them. This devalued my house by about $20,000 and made the Aborigines a bit like fish out of water, with it not working out for either party.

The last thing my cousin did before I returned to Sydney was when she supposedly rented out my house with this special deal that she offered me, which was also the most expensive that she had to offer. I say supposedly special, because any other package deal that she may have had to offer me could not be worse than the one I got. It took 3 weeks for her to get a tenant. The other thing that I considered a bad deal was that when I had been living in that house which the tenant was living in for about a year, the tree was perfect and did not need pruning, but then after I left and went back to Sydney, the tree all of a sudden was dangerous and needed to be severely pruned. I was left with a bill of $700. After 4 weeks, the tenants stopped paying the rent and got away with 5 weeks of unpaid rent before we were able to evict them, along with us paying a $500 bill for getting rid of the rubbish. I ended up having to sell the house for about $60,000 ($20,000 less than I bought it for), which was mainly due to the Aborigines moving into the area.

This bad experience was something that I needed to be responsible for, because I was the one making the decisions and also the one that missed all the red flags. I could have had enough information if I had paid more attention to the red flags that showed her lack of ability to forecast things like opportunities in the job market and the housing market, as well as her not being good at rental management.

I remained in Sydney and have managed to get back on my feet financially. Mainly due to my age, I am not able to finance another property, and I have learnt my lesson about recognising a red flag when I see one, and more importantly, acting on it when it occurs. Emotion is an important part of life; however, it always needs to be balanced with rational objectivity. These extremes can equal the knowledge of a book when someone explains all the things that can go wrong while working from those two extremes.

CHAPTER 13

My 11 Year Career in Ajax which was brought by APS Chemicals

In 1992, I left Perth, where over the period of approximately twelve months, I was now forced to go back to Sydney, and to a place where I would be able to gain some sort of employment that would support me with a moderate style of living. I started off in Perth with a sum of about $200,000 and had high expectations of turning the real estate business into a way of sustaining my financial needs for the rest of my life. I would have succeeded if I had been able to get a permanent job of 40 hours a week, and I also would have needed to be paid a reasonable wage. Unfortunately, it did not happen. A few other things also went wrong, wherein a big bulk of the money eroded away, and it turned out to be the most disappointing part in the journey of my life thus far.

However, a good bit of fortune did happen to venture my way. I met my girlfriend before I had gone to Perth, and she was living in Sydney. We had maintained a romantic relationship by way of the phone while I was in Perth.

As soon as I got back to Sydney, good fortune started turning my way. My girlfriend offered to let me stay in her flat, and I was very familiar with the suburbs that I use to live in, in the past, and it is much easier to establishing a job when one is familiar with the area one lives in.

This arrangement lasted for a few months, wherein I was able to gain a job of casual employment from Skilled Engineering. It was also a time for me to move out and live on my own. The reason for the short stay was that the relationship was based on two different agendas. Her agenda was one which was based on the gratification of sex, and my agenda was based on the need for a permanent partner in my life. And when you are at the age of about 45 and seeking a permanent partner in your life, where I am inclined to believe that you do not have the luxury of letting a few more years drift by.

After a few weeks, I found that the working hours with Skilled Engineering was unreliable for being able to supply me with enough working hours in the week, and on average, I worked about 16 hours a week. However, I was able to improve my financial situation by gaining employment from another company, called Drake, which did the same type of work as Skilled Engineering. Skilled Engineering and Drake do not own any company or manufacture anything; instead they just supply various companies with people who they hire out to temporarily cover the workload for people who work in different companies when required, such as when someone is sick, on holidays, or filling in a temporary position for someone who is about to be permanently employed to a new position.

The first job I got when I got back to Sydney was a casual job with Skilled Engineering. While working for Skilled Engineering, I found some of the most interesting machinery that I have ever seen or worked on, which was at Kellogg's botany plant, where I was employed as a rigger/ tradesman assistant for the maintenance of the machinery. Kellogg's had many interesting machines, although there were three machines wherein, I found the conceptions of their working requirements to be very interesting. This unusual machinery was also where I sometimes needed to work.

Before I start to tell you about these three fascinating and wonderful machines, I would like to enlighten you on a story about one of the permanent employees from the maintenance crew in Kellogg's. The story starts when I was talking to the person from the maintenance crew about a machine that I refer to as #1. Machine, which is the one that makes Special K breakfast cereal. That permanent worker of Kellogg's had been there for a few years, and to my amazement, he had an extraordinary lack of understanding to physics, particularly when it came to the powerful strength of gravity.

I was sitting at the place where we all sat for lunch, and I attempted to share my enthusiasm about the extraordinary way in which the food of Special K travelled up the ten-foot (3-metre) spiral. It was mystifying because there was no obvious logical reasoning which could justify the way in which food was able to travel up that spiral. If one did not know better, the most logical explanation would be that it was being done by a magic trick. The lack of intelligence from his reply was equally extraordinary. He said to me, '*That is nothing.* They also have another spiral where the food goes down.' I guess it was about time that someone woke him up to the fact that gravity makes it many times more difficult for the food to travel up the spiral, as opposed to getting it to go down. My response to him was 'Dummy! Having the food go 10 feet down the spiral is the natural way that it wants to travel, and if you give the spiral a good kick with your foot, then the food stands a good chance of going down without any further assistance. Now try giving that same spiral a kick with your foot and make it go 10 feet up the spiral. Have you ever heard of gravity?'

#1. **Machine**—This was where they made Special K breakfast cereal, and it was mystifying to watch the productive procedures of the food travel *up a spiral* with no air or any other noticeable way that would explain how the food was travelling up the spiral. The gaps between the parts of the spiral were open, which would allow someone to be able to stand at the side of the spiral and see the food travelling up the spiral. The spiral was about 4 feet (1.4 metres) across and had about a 6-inch (150-millimetre) lip on the edge of the spiral which stopped the food from falling off it. The spiral took the food up about 10 feet (3 metres) to the next floor. One might find it interesting to work out how this machinery worked, and you will find the answers, along with answers about the other two machines, further down the next page.

#2. **Machine**—I can't remember the name of that product, but I believe that it was shredded wheat. Not that it is important anyway, because the interesting part is how the machinery worked. The conveyor belt travelled along only one direction, and there was also another conveyor, a double-threaded screw conveyor, which was situated across and over the top of the first conveyor belt. Inside the two threads of the screw conveyor was a knuckle which locked into one of the threads. The conveyor had a product that would fall from it and would go across the conveyor belt below and would pour backwards and forwards across the belt. The screw of the screw conveyor always travelled in the same direction. The knuckle was locked into one of the screwed threads, which meant the only journey it could travel along was that of one thread. The screw continually turned the same way, yet when that knuckle in the thread of the screw when it reached the end of its journey, would return in the opposite direction each time it came to the end of the thread. While viewing the way in which the screw was operating, which appeared to be very mystifying while watching it work. How do you think it did that?

#3. **Machine**—This had small boxes of breakfast cereals, such as muesli, cornflakes, etc. These products are very often presented for breakfast in motels and some hotels. These are packaged in small cartons filled with breakfast cereal that travel along a conveyor which is driven by air at about 60 kilometres an hour or more. I do not know the exact speed it was going, but it was very fast. It was a case of 'seeing is believing'.

These are the answers to the way the three extraordinary machines worked:

1. The energy that caused the Special K breakfast cereal to move up the spiral was driven by two large vibrating cylinders that were mounted at the base of the spiral at a 45-degree angle, which produced a very small vibration. This vibration was barely noticeable to the naked eye unless one was paying meticulous (very close) attention to the movement of the screw, which gave the appearance that the screw was not moving and showed no signs of the energy that was making the food go up the spiral. So, it appeared as if the food was going up there by some magical trick.

2. The conveyor screw had a *double thread*, wherein one thread turned clockwise and the other thread turned anticlockwise, and is the key reason for the need of the double thread. I think this analogy might prove to be a better way of explaining the action of the conveyor screw: Picture a handheld screwdriver that you use for screwing metal screws into timber. Or maybe you are more likely to be familiar with it by remembering a tradesman who worked with a handheld screwdriver. This is a special screwdriver used in a handheld operation, which was designed to quickly turn the metal screw in or out of timber. The way this special screwdriver works is by the pumping action of pushing the screwdriver (when used vertically) up and down or (when used horizontally) in and out. On the shaft of the screwdriver is a double-sided thread

which works with a knuckle moving on one thread at a time. The way you changed the direction was by changing the setting of a button, which was either pushed up or down; each time you pushed the button up or down, you would be aligning it with one thread that would take you one direction, and the other thread would take you the opposite direction. The conveyor screw in Kellogg's dropped down to the other thread each time it reached the end of its journey on the screw at both ends. (It was another place where gravity came into play.)

3. The breakfast cereals travelled a long journey that changed in many directions. It has a long a deep grooved conveyor which was laden with small cartons of breakfast cereals and is driven by a controlled flow of very fast air along the channel of the groove in the conveyor. The journey of breakfast cereals along the conveyor was so incredibly fast that it would take a little while after seeing it to be able to register the capability of the speed in which the cartons were travelling.

(This part of the article is not going to make very good reading for my former colleague from Kellogg's who was having trouble with the conception to the power of gravity, because #1. Machine and #2. Machine require respecting the rules of gravity.)

I held this job for a few weeks and was the replacement of their permit worker, who was on holiday. After that, I continued doing the work that Skilled Engineering provided me with. Unfortunately, the working hours that I got from Skilled Engineering were far from being enough to sustain a decent standard of living. This led to the need for another job, with a company called Drake, which did similar jobs to the ones I had with Skilled Engineering. The jobs were working in a warehouse, cleaning, and packing various products. However, there was one job that I was given that turned out to be very beneficial for enhancing my career. The job I am referring to is packing chemicals for a company called Ajax Chemicals in Auburn.

As good fortune would have it, Drake had an agreement with Ajax. If one of their workers stayed in the job for six weeks, Drake was prepared to release that person over to Ajax so that they could end up working there permanently.

I passed the requirements for working permanently at Ajax, and continued working on packing of chemicals for a short while, where I later got transferred to the maintenance side of the factory. I guess this was one time where my maintenance skills landed me with a much more interesting job, plus a small wage increase. I worked for Ajax for six years.

Ajax Chemicals in Auburn was a chemical factory that consisted of the following:

1. **Ammonia Plant**

   Ammonia is a poisonous gas with a very strong, unpleasant odour. Ajax did not manufacture the ammonia; instead they bought it in bulk and repacked it into 20-litre cubed containers and 200-litre drums. Ammonia was also sold in different strengths: 25% and 30%. Part of the operations of the ammonia plant was to condense 25% ammonia into 30% ammonia. The strength to the effect that the gases would create from the 30% ammonia is roughly double that of 25% ammonia. Well, at least that is the case when you are trapped into breathing its toxic gas. Ammonia is usually very heavily diluted when it is put out for the public to use and is a safe product to use when the proper safety procedure has been adhered to. While I was working in the factory of the ammonia plant, on most of the occasions when the gas was detected, it was in a concentrated form, and it was easy to recognise the gas. It will very quickly let you know of its presence by the strong smell, and you will quickly experience great difficulty in breathing. It will also have some severe effects on the rest of your anatomy should you continue to stay in the environment of the gas fumes, and the speed in which you pick up the damage of this poisonous gas will largely depend on the strength of the gas you are breathing and how long you are exposed to it. The bad side effects include breathing difficulties, sore throat, swelling of the throat, severe pain in the throat and lungs, or burning in the nose, in the eyes, on the lips, or on the tongue. More severe signs include blood in the stool, stomach pain, and vomiting, and given enough exposure to this poisonous gas will eventually cause damage to the brain. When left long enough to develop into severe problems, any one of those symptoms can have the ability to cause permanent damage, with the possibility of the poisonous gas leading to someone being killed. I worked on that site for six years, and over that period, there was no one on that site who was seriously injured from the gas, which goes to show that the safety procedures in the factory were correctly adhered to.

2. **Distillery Plant**

The distillery plant was used for distilling hydrochloric acid and nitric acid. The distillery plant had three vessels for the hydrochloric acid and one vessel for the nitric acid, and there was also a warehouse attached to the plant for the distilled products. The purpose of boiling the acid was to upgrade its quality. When the acid was boiled, it came with the likelihood of some dangerous occurrences that could go wrong if it was not being closely supervised. It was a very good case of 'an ounce of prevention is better than a pound of cure', and the safest way to prevent something going wrong was to have very close supervision of the distillery vessels at all times while it was operating.

3. **Repacking Plant:**

Repacking of Liquid Products, Most of Them Being Corrosive.

I can't remember all the products that were repacked in that part of the factory, although the ones I do remember repacking were Bond Crete, hydrochloride acid, and sodium hydroxide, which is sometimes referred to as a liquid form of caustic soda which is an alkaline-based product. (Caustic soda is made up of a solid form of crystals.) There was also one product they made, called Bycol: Bycol which is a product that is used for improving the workability of mortar between bricks. The repacking plant also had a warehouse next to it.

4. **Finechem Pharmaceutical**

This was the place where they repacked the pharmaceutical products that came in bulk. One of the problems with repacking was that it required a lot of patience in having to weigh very small weights very accurately. This also came with the burden where one of the biggest parts of the job was the constant need to keep everything spotlessly clean.

5. **Chemical Laboratory**

All the products that came into the laboratory were tested for the quality of the manufactured products, and sometimes they upgrading the quality of those products. Before unloading a tanker truck of product, it would be tested for its quality as well as having the product retesting it once it had been unloaded into the storage vessel. The testing in the laboratory sustained the quality that was needed to ensure the constant high standard of all the products. Furthermore, this was also an important reason why most of the customers chose Ajax for their chemicals. The chemists also had one other important job that they did, and that was that when the company brought in some of the products that they sold, as well as their own products, the chemists would test them for a certificate of analysis.

6. **Liquid Flammable Products**

The flammable products were such things like kerosene, turpentine, acetone, etc. The main job was repacking flammable products into smaller packaging, as well as upgrading the product. The biggest concern in the plant was making sure no fires started up, for obvious reasons, and the only forklift that was allowed in the building was a flameproof one. The company even went to the extent of banning the use of all mobile phones while in the flammable section of the plant.

7. **A Warehouse for Poisonous Goods**

This warehouse was only used for storing 200-litre drums of poisonous goods.

8. **Hydrofluoric Acid**

Hydrofluoric acid is a nasty and dangerous product due to the fact that it does not give you any signs of burning or any other sign that shows something is wrong when it first makes contact with your skin. If you do not notice it getting on your skin, it will take quite a few hours or maybe a day or two to show some red lines near the place where it was spilt on your skin, and it will still not produce any sort of pain. The pain kicks in much further in time, should it not be properly treated. Hydrofluoric acid has a very weak corrosive action on the skin. However, it has a very strong corrosive effect on the calcium in your blood and bones. If you have a strong enough dose, and given enough time, it will eat all the calcium in your body. The problem can get even more depressing when you know that once it develops to a certain point, there is no way of eluding certain death. I was told of a case where someone had hydrofluoric acid spilt on them, and they were not aware of it until a few days later, when the hydrofluoric acid had progressed past the point of them being able to save the bones in their body; they ended up dead. The only antidote to this problem is being injected with a lot of calcium. Ajax treated this product with a lot of respect, and so did I. It was also repacked in a special section of the factory.

9. **Two Acid Plants**

The two acid plants were in two different places on the site.

10. **Maintenance Workshop**

At the side of the maintenance workshop was an open pit which decontaminated waste water.

11. **First-Aid Office**

12. **An Administration Office**

My job ended after that six-year term with Ajax because it was bought out by a company called APS, the Seven Hills branch. This was also the last branch of the Ajax companies, to exist. Part of the deal when APS bought out Ajax was that all the equipment, along with all the men who worked there, were transferred to Seven Hills; this included all the workers' entitlements, such as sick pay and annual leave, and their term of employment was added to their service record. APS is a big company, and the abbreviation for *APS* stands for 'Asia Pacific Specialty Chemicals'. I guess that should APS be correctly abbreviated, then it would have a *C* added on (APSC). But since I am not part of the company that makes that decision, we need to settle for the way the authorities of the APS company have stated it. APS is also on the stock exchange and trades under the name of Nuplex. The APS company consists of 6 different branches: 2 in Sydney, 1 in Queensland, 1 in Victoria, 1 in Papua New Guinea, and 1 in New Zealand.

APS at Seven Hills:

The APS site at Seven Hills was at least 3 times as big as the site in Ajax. APS was ½ a kilometre long and was a bit less than ⅛ of a kilometre across. When I got to Seven Hills, my job was changed over to being an acid plant operator. I was also in charge of unloading the tanker trucks into the storage vessels, and once every three weeks, I loaded a truck with phosphoric acid. This proved to be an interesting job where I got a higher wage. I also spent a large part of my time in APS working as a safety officer for the acid plant division. The factory at Seven Hills had a staff of about 130 people.

The workers always got a good start when they went to work, because the site was not on flat ground, and from the front of the site to the back of the site was a moderate downhill slope. However, it did not pay to get overenthusiastic about the pleasing journey you had going down the slope, because somewhere down the track, one had to walk back up it. The entrance to the site had a car park on either side of the private road, and the first place one needed to go through when using a vehicle which was authorised on the site was through the gatehouse entrance, which also had a bypass section used for weighing the trucks on the weighbridge. The weighbridge would provide the gatekeeper with the weight of the truck both when it was arriving on the site and when it was leaving the site, and by subtracting the different weights, one was able to calculate the amount of product that was either coming into the factory or going out.

The factories that were on the site at Seven Hills were divided into three rows. The trucks drove between the rows while travelling around the site and when they proceeded from the gatehouse at the entrance.

Left row of factories:

1. **The Administration Office.**
2. **Nappi Sand**—This is an additive used for washing the clothes and is added with powdered soap in the washing machine for the purpose of removing stains and making the washing cleaner. This was quite a big factory where they worked shift work.
3. **Solvents Plant**—Even though Nappi Sand was the bigger part of the solvent plant, there was a division which was considered a separate plant, where the other domestic solvent products were made.
4. **Chemist Laboratory**—By supplying a certificate of analysis, the chemist played a very important role in regard to the successful sales of all the products that were made or sold on the site and also for the products that were upgraded to a high grade. There were many tests which were required to be done before and during the time any of the products were made. When any of the products that came into the factory from the bulk tanker truck, then the product would be required to be tested, before it was unloaded from the truck, and it would also be retested when it was unloaded

into the storage vessel. Whenever a wholesaler company buys dangerous goods, it is important to rely on goods to be having a good consistency with the quality of there product, especially when it is of a high grade or has been made into a higher grade. I know one product whose basic procedure required testing 4 times and sometimes even more when the test would fail the standard requirement; it would continue to be modified and retested until it reached the required standard for the customer. All the products needed to pass a certain standard or were reworked until they met the required standard.

5. **Finechem Laboratory**—This was situated on the first floor the one above the ground floor. Finechem is the place where they chemically made artificial additives, such as chocolate flavouring and strawberry flavouring, as well as many other food additives.

6. **Finechem Factory**—This was situated on the ground floor, beside the laboratory. This was the place where they repacked pharmaceutical products.

7. **Finechem Warehouse**—This was situated next door to the Finechem factory, and it was a warehouse where all the high-graded products were stored, such as high-graded acid, pharmaceuticals, and the base products that are used in pharmaceutical products. (From Nappi Sand to the end of Finechem warehouse is one continuous building which is separated by thick concreate walls.)

8. **Epoxy Plant**—This was a 5-storey plant where they made epoxy, and the product was stored on-site in a nearby warehouse. The control room was on the fifth floor, and it was very good exercise for anyone who needed to go there, regardless of whether or not they enjoyed the 5-story journey to and from the control room.

9. **Concrete Recycled-Water Basin**—This was an open water basin which was used for treating the waste water on the site. After the waste water was treated, it would be reused in making some of the products that would be suitable for the water being used, as well as in washing down some of the factory floors.

10. **Acid Plant**—The acid plant had large vessels which were loaded up by a tanker trucks, and the vessels ranged from about 30,000 litres to 10,000 litres. There was one bay that had two large 33% hydrochloric acid tanks. One was used for commercial acid, and the other was used for making a higher grade of hydrochloric acid

in the distillery. Sometimes they used the distillery not only for increasing the grade of the acid but also for increasing the strength of the acid up to 36%, which was of a high grade. The second bay had two sulphuric acid tanks (one was large and contained 98% sulphuric acid, and the small one contained 70% sulphuric acid), as well as a large tank that contained formaldehyde. The third bay contained a large tank of 70% nitric acid and two smaller tanks of 75% phosphoric acid. We also repacked 2.5-litre glass bottles out of 200-litre drums of lactic acid, acetic acid, hydrobromic acid, and formic acid, and we packed quite a lot of bottles of perchloric acid. In a different part of the factory, there were three big mixers wherein we mixed two different acids—35% sulphuric acid, which is used for battery acid—and in the second one, we mixed two different acids to make one type of acid, called blended acid. We also had a special vessel where we made 9% nitric acid, which is used for developing analogue photos. The only other job that we did in the acid plant was to make some very high-graded purified water.

11. **Cleaning Bay**—To the right of the acid plant, at the bottom of the site, was a special bay which was mainly used for cleaning recyclable 15-litre hydrochloric cubes. We also cleaned 1,000-litre dangerous-goods containers, which were referred to as jumbos, along with some of the trucks. The waste water was diverted back to the recycling water basin.

(The acid plant and the cleaning bay were at the end of the site, which had a small bit of vacant land that led to the boundary fence.)

Middle row of factories, starting at the bottom of the slope:

12. **First-Aid Building.**
13. **Oils and Fats.**
14. **Esters: Esters** was the place where they made a food product. I am not sure what it was, but I believe that it had something to do with grains. The one thing that I found strange in Esters was that the food needed to be blessed by the rabbi.
15. **The Lunchroom.**
16. **The Planners' Office**—The people here planned the weekly workload for the various factories. This was also the office space

for the manager and three supervisors of the various factories on the site.

17. **Liquid Flammables**—This was the place where they repacked and upgraded some of the products, and it was also used as a warehouse for liquid flammables.
18. **Maintenance Workshop.**
19. **Organics Plant.**

Right row of factories, starting at the top of the slope:

20. **Main Warehouse.**
21. **Three Warehouses**—The three warehouses were next to each other and only had wire mesh fences that identified them as warehouses. The products were all packed in 200-litre drums.
22. **Solid Flammables Warehouse**—This was at the end of the site, which had a small bit of vacant land that led to the boundary fence.

The last time that I was at the site of APS in Seven Hills was back in the year 2007. Recalling the layout of the site and remembering all the products was quite a chore, and there are probably some details that have been left out. It is now 2017, and APS has been closed down permanently for 10 years, which made it very difficult for me to reconstruct the past. The Ajax site was also a big challenge when it came to remembering the history; it closed down in 1998 (19 years ago), whereupon the old buildings were replaced with new buildings.

There was one event that happened while I was working for APS, in the acid plant, and this incident was no fault of the company. It happened in my last year of working for APS. I suffered a stroke and lost half of my eyesight in both eyes. However, the story did have a good ending, because I managed to get my eyesight back again. The full details of that story are explained in the article 'My Medical Achievements Where Others Have Failed'.

The job at APS came to an end on 30/3/2007, whereupon the whole site was closed down and subdivided into small sections. I believe that the company was closed down for financial reasons and that the company made a lot of money through the sales of the property, which had been subdivided. I did all right financially, but I was 59 years of age and would have much preferred to have stayed on for another six years, until I retired.

One of the things that I have noticed in life (especially in the field of manual labour) is that once you get past a certain age, the older you get, the harder it is to regain employment. Nearly everybody was made redundant, and some got transferred to different places. I got **64** weeks' redundancy pay for my **13** years of service, along with sick leave and holidays.

Summary of Ajax and APS

Ajax was in the city of Sydney, in Auburn. I started working in Ajax in **1994** and was informed in **1998** that all the workers on-site—along with the materials on the site of Auburn, where we got the accreditation of maintaining the service record that we had accumulated, along with other entitlements we had established while working with Ajax—and were transferred to APS in Seven Hills. The information that we were not told was that when we left the site, all the buildings were levelled to the ground and replaced with a complex of small industrial buildings. I was not able to get any information on the Internet regarding the closing of Ajax in Auburn, and it appears APS sold the site to another developer.

In regard to APS, well, we were well informed of what happened when it was closed down in **2007**. All the buildings were taken down, and the site was broken into smaller sections; the company honoured all the entitlements that we were entitled to. When I look back at the things that stood out to me while being in the two factories, I would have to say that one was when I had a heart attack while I was in Ajax and the other one was when I had a stroke in APS. Neither the heart attack nor the stroke had any connection to why I had the heart attack or the stroke, while I was working for those companies, and there was many a good time had by the staff working in both Ajax and APS.

Having that large pay-out from APS turned out to be very useful for my financial needs. However, unfortunately, my age proved to be a large stumbling block that prevented me from getting back into the workforce as an employee with full-time work. In the past, I was always very proud of being able to have travelled around the world twice, and always being able to get work when I needed to start a new job, and up to this point in time, getting through the journey of my life by always finding a way to support myself by working for a living. I was not pleased with having to swallow my pride and going on social security benefits for the first time in my life. The global financial crisis also made a heavy impact on my being able to gain employment. I spent a lot of time trying to seek employment for about three years. However, the employment situation changed for the better when I grew a bit of wisdom by working out that I did not need to have someone supply me with work, because I already had enough skills to create my own set of working skills for employment.

I decided that it was about time that I started using the skills that I already had, since I had learnt the skills from the many jobs that I had done in my lifetime. The one job that stood out the most to me was the one of a *handyman*. Well, I kind of kicked myself about it later, thinking that it was something which I should have thought of much sooner. All of my life, I have always enjoyed doing handyman's work. I first started doing handyman's work as a young child on the farm, and later, when I left home, I extended my skills to my family and friends. I had also accumulated a vast amount of knowledge from the many different jobs I had done along the journey of my life; I believe that it is fair to say that I have done somewhere between 20 to 30 different types of jobs. That included mostly labouring jobs, along with carpentry work and plumbing skills, which I believe made me a very good candidate for being a handyman. The only thing I was missing to become a professional handyman was the manageable business planning that would make my goal successful.

For me to be successful as a professional handyman, also meant doing a lot of research in my marketing plan which would make my goal successful. The first thing I worked on was the type of jobs that I was going to be doing. The jobs that I was prepared to do while being a professional handyman were painting, carpentry work, plumbing, maintenance work, lawn mowing, and gardening. In order to establish an hourly rate which would be fair and acceptable and would take into account all the hidden cost involved in doing the different jobs, such as lost time between jobs, lost time loading and unloading my car, cost of travelling with the car, cost of maintenance of equipment, cost of replacement of worn equipment and tools, advertisement cost, cost of doing paperwork needed for the business, and cost of doing my tax return with H&R Block. Considering the customers' perspective, I needed to keep the cost low enough so that the customers would want my services as well as being able to afford them.

I thought of a flat rate of $30, which excluded the cost of quotes, call-out fees, and the travel to the job. I could have also charged $5 for every ten minutes that I went past the hours worked, but I decided that collecting that extra $5 was not worth it because it would cause more stress than it was worth. I also did not charge the customer for the time I spent talking to them, and I take pride in knowing that I always went past the time that I charged them, which would create a more peaceful environment for both the customer and myself.

When it came to the top of my Priority list, I decided that it was important to make the job enjoyable for both the client and myself by talking to them and letting them understand the job better, as well as letting them have a better chance of understanding my character and getting to know who I really am. The one thing that I did with every customer (so far, that was 165 customers) was to tell them that I wore many hats (did many different jobs) but concerned myself with two things only, and that was *doing a good job and making the customer happy.*

In regard to advertising, I found the local papers too expensive and found that I got a lot more people to respond to my adverts by making and printing my own flyers, as well as putting the flyers into letter boxes. Over roughly a three-year period, I put out about 12,000 flyers, and the response one gets from flyers is very low. If one gets a 2 per cent response, it is considered to be good, and even getting that low response only means that someone will ring you up along, with no guarantee that you are going to get business from them. The best way to gain their business is by how well you treat them; gaining more business from the customers you have worked with will depend on their satisfaction with the business that you did for them. Doing handyman's work is a job which I have always enjoyed doing and which worked well for me, and now that I have got past my retirement age of 65, I am now tapering it off and am semi-retired. At present, I only have four lawn jobs that I do when they are required to be done, and the majority of the work that I do now is that of a writer.

I know that since I have dyslexia, writing a book is ten times harder for me than for those who do not have dyslexia. On average, I would spend about 40 hours a week or more writing, although the majority of that time would be spent in the role of a teacher who has a mammoth job of sorting out the fragmented information that I have in my head, correcting the grammatical errors that I fail to recognise at the time that I am working, and putting in the most appropriate word required, and above all, making sure that my work is grammatically correct. I take on the roles of teacher and pupil at the same time. Being a teacher while writing requires doing a lot of research; I need to spend a lot of time working with several dictionaries and being on the computer, along with bouncing back and forth between the role of teacher to pupil. I also spend many hours checking and rechecking mistakes that I find each time I revise while continuing that journey of bouncing back and forth between the two roles. Fortunately for me, I am not afraid of doing a lot of work, and now, as an adult, I am most grateful to my parents, who gave me a lot of work to do as a child. I am now in the position of seeing hard work as a natural and easy thing to do, and it has turned into a strong point in my journey of life. I am also blessed in seeing the challenges of life as a good thing to pursue, and I have no intention of slowing down in the near future. The more work one does, the more alive they are, and I am in no hurry to achieve the goal of being permanently shut down.

CHAPTER 14

Brian's View of Dyslexia through Many Years of Study

Before I get started on writing about dyslexia, I think it is important that you understand what dyslexia is; otherwise, everything I am about to write is not going to make much sense. There are a lot of people who I have talked to who claim to know what dyslexia is, yet very few of them give the same explanation or are able to complete the important details, including doctors, who also come up with different explanations of what dyslexia is. My understanding of the different definitions is that the source of their explanation is explained by the symptoms, which are all more than likely to be correct. This is because their answer is not where the problem derives from. Dyslexia is a problem that comes from the overuse of signals in the creative side of the brain. When many people are working on creating something, it stands to reason that there will be many different ways that they come up with their creative ways of thinking.

Here is a description of dyslexia. The area where dyslexia is most noticeable is sometimes in the reading, although it is more likely to be detected in the writing, which can also extend to mathematics. Here's why. When someone with dyslexia is exercising their reading and writing, they are inevitably spending an excessive amount of time working with the right hemisphere of the brain (the right side of the brain, which is the creative side). Meanwhile, a normal person without dyslexia works a lot more with the left hemisphere of the brain (the left side of the brain), which is the direct side. There are two ways we gather information: directly and creatively. Direct information: to except thoughts and ideas, without change or facts that we accept as being correct and instantly ready to use for our own benefit. Creative information is new information that we bring into our thoughts in the form of new ideas or by modifying some information that we have received.

The left hemisphere of the brain is used for direct information, like the spelling of *cat*. After you know the right sequence of the three letters, there is nothing to add or subtract from the information received. On the other hand, people with dyslexia, who overuse the right hemisphere of their brain for reading and writing, will inevitably run into the difficulty for the needing to change the word in some way so that it can be creative. Their brain is deeply locked in the creative side of their thoughts, so when they go to spell *cat*, they still look for something to create. Since the word *cat* has been directly given to them correctly, then they are no longer able to create anything, so they need to do something that creates, such as putting in extra letters, substituting one letter for another letter, taking out some of the letters that already exist, or even changing the colour of the word. So, they can continue being creative, the letters that spell *cat* are going to be buried somewhere in all that altered information that they have created. I used the word *cat* for simplicity's sake, because sorting out how to spell *cat* is something someone with dyslexia would try to sort out in the early stages of their life. They are capable of working with the left hemisphere of the brain and do work from the left hemisphere, but they have a lot of trouble getting there when required to do so. That is not a conscious decision they make; instead it comes from the subconscious. In short, they are not able to control the part of the brain that determines where they work from, and they are left with the mission of trying to solve a problem that has already been solved, which comes back to overusing the right hemisphere (the creative side) of the brain.

Dyslexia does not always present itself in exactly the same way. For example, one might have trouble with mathematics, while another does well with it. One thing you can depend on with dyslexia is that you are always going to be struggling when it comes to reading out loud, and it is a lot more dominant in writing. The reason it is so much more dominant in writing is that writing requires being a lot more creative by knowing how to spell the words and having to know all the grammatical rules for constructing written material. By the way, if someone with dyslexia is having a problem with mathematics, it is an extension of the problem that they have with their reading and writing, which is because of the overuse of the right hemisphere of the brain that has a different way of accessing information than the left hemisphere. While the brain is working in the right hemisphere for information that is processed and which may be coming to us in the form of an image, should that image be in the form of letters or figures, then a lot of extra information that will be given to us will be in a fragmented state. I also believe that the biggest obstacle we have to face is sorting out the fragmented information that we have in our thoughts; when dyslexic people try to defragment information in a hurry, the only thing they achieve is to leave themselves with a bigger chunk of information which is in a fragmented state. The bigger the hurry, the more fragmented it will be; metaphorically, it is a bit like trying to sort out lots of small pieces of a large jigsaw puzzle really fast. On the other hand, people without dyslexia mainly use the left hemisphere to access their reading and writing. Going on the evidence of what I see, the left hemisphere of the brain gets the information directly and *does not need* to sift through extra images of information and relies heavily on that information being correct in the first place. The people without dyslexia do not have to concern themselves with information being added to their memory or replaced or taken out of their memory, with the result of them receiving it many times faster and also far more accurately, should it be correct in the first place. Let's face it, anything that has been completed correctly does not need to be recreated or changed in any way whatsoever. It does not matter if you are only just reviewing the information; it's still going to take a lot longer than someone who was prepared to accept the direct information.

I have dyslexia and find this piece of information to be important due to the fact that I quite often have a different way of understanding reading and writing. I'll rephrase it in a different way. The right hemisphere is the creative side. When someone with dyslexia is looking to come up with an answer, they are very often locked in the right hemisphere; they will see this as a normal function for them at that point, although most people can change quickly between the two hemispheres. The sad fact is that you cannot work from the left hemisphere and the right hemisphere at the same time, and the upside is that most of us do have the ability to switch from one hemisphere to the other very quickly. Obviously, not all people can. The simple answer as to why someone has dyslexia is that they are overusing the right hemisphere of the brain when they should be using a lot more of the left hemisphere. So much for the simplified answer, because here is where things get even more complicated. The act of working in the left or right hemisphere has a lot more to do with the subconscious than it does with the conscious part of the brain. An analogy for it is that it is a bit like lifting your hand in the air even though you have no idea how you worked each muscle to be able to do it. This also means that you would not be able to fill in all the details accurately enough so that you could write a manual with precise details in it which would show the timing of how each and every muscle worked, in order for that action to take place.

The *Oxford English Dictionary*'s definition of *subconscious* is this: 'Of those activities of the mind that we are not aware of; concerning the part of the mind of which one is not fully aware but which influences one's actions and feelings'.

This piece of information deals with the *subconscious* part of the brain, which gives a lot of information for the benefit of the conscious part of the brain. The conscious part of the brain can often find it difficult to fill in the finer details of understanding the active job of the subconscious and the chain reaction of the finer details of how the events in our body take place. Another important thing that makes things even trickier when we are dealing with the subconscious is that the conscious mind has a very poor communication that links the two of them. The communication from the subconscious has a lot more to do with piecing the evidence of the facts together than it does with having a clear picture to deal with. Maybe this analogy will make it clearer as to explaining how the subconscious works. Take a *simple thing like standing up and putting one hand on top of your head*, and then try to imagine the subconscious role in this event, especially all the things it needs to do. Also, while doing this exercise, be sure to add all the finer details, such as how each and every muscle in the whole body needs to be working. In case you did not know, there are somewhere between **656** to **850** muscles in the body, depending on how you distinguish what a muscle is. It also gets a lot tougher than that; you need to bear in mind that you know, through the output of this exercise, when the muscle needs to contract or when the muscle needs to expand, as well as how much pressure to take away or add on, with the right precision of timing with the energy needed. This also applies to the action of counterbalancing your weight so you don't end up falling over when you stand up and put your hand on your head. Now try to *imagine if you did* have a good connection of communication with your subconscious—how much time it would take to perform this simple movement, and let's not leave out how awkward it would be to perform.

This is what the subconscious does for us. Aren't you glad that you do not have to contend with that heavy workload for what we now take for granted as a simple exercise? Let's be grateful that Mother Nature has given us a free pass on that one. I hope that you can now see from that exercise how poor the communication is between the conscious and the subconscious part of the brain. Despite the poor communication, we still have a reasonable idea of what is going on with our subconscious, and you can see that it is the *evidence of the action* which is the major part of our understanding of the subconscious.

When it comes to human anatomy, while looking for the best leads to facts and evidence of how the subconscious works, I find that the best detectives for this part of our knowledge are the scientists who tell us about our anatomy through the various tests they do. One such test is an MRI scan, which can tell you what part of the brain is active through various activities it does. Also, there are X-rays, CT (computerised tomography) scans, ultrasounds, operations, and autopsies, which give us valuable information. There are also many other instruments that have been able to assist us with getting evidence about the brain and the rest of our anatomy and that have been used throughout the passing years. All of this testing needs to be worked through the cooperation of a human being. The individual human being also has the ability to work out some of the evidence and the facts that machinery is not capable of finding out.

One thing that I feel I need to point out is the method I employ while presenting my evaluations, which is to simplify as much as I possibly can while the message continues to retain all the important information which needs to be easily understood. I would rather leave something out that may be required to be put in later than to put in something that would need to be deleted later. I am also very much aware that there is a lot more to the brain structure than just the left and right hemispheres; however, to go deeper into that field only serves to make it more confusing and contributes very little value to the final outcome of what I am presenting.

The best understanding I have of my dyslexia is this: More often than not, I could have extra letters thrown into the mix so that I can stay creative, but I could also substitute some of the letters or take some of the letters out. To be "creative," means that you have to do something different; otherwise, it is not creative. Another thing that needs to be taken into consideration is that when someone is creative, it also means that their creativity can be shown in many different ways, such as going to the point of changing the colour or something else (although the changing of colours does not happen with me). There is no clear answer to it. All one can do is follow the facts and evidence of what you personally know. I believe that each person that has dyslexia may have different ways that they create, which is also influenced by how far they are prepared to battle with their problems or how far they are prepared to sit back and be the victim. In order to advance in life, you will always need to do some creating; otherwise, you are only going to have an intelligence level that is not much better than one of a parrot.

Even though I have dyslexia, I cannot really say when I got it, but for the first 60 years of my life, I didn't even know that I had it. So, the answer of when I got it has to be somewhere between just before I was born (I inherited it) or when I was on the way to becoming five, which is my best estimation of when it took place. It was when I started school at the age of five when the pieces of evidence started showing that I had some of the signs of having dyslexia, and if you believe in the theory that one has it before they notice the signs, then you will need to accept the theory that it started before I was five. Going back to my early days as a child, I remember always putting a lot of effort into trying to learn to read and write and having great difficulty in keeping up with the lessons with my fellow peers, along with being constantly confused with the information which was in my head and what part of the knowledge I needed to learn as well as what part of the knowledge needed to be disregarded. To make things even worse, I was unaware that some of it even needed to be disregarded. I also found it strange that I was forever trying to figure out why I was putting in such a major effort and still coming up with such poor results, and unfortunately, I always ran with the assumption that everyone else was learning their lessons the same way I was (all the history behind me now clearly shows that it was not the case).

Something I found useful at school was that I was quite often able to come up with answers (messages transferred from the subconscious to the conscious part of the brain) to some of the problems that other students were not able to come up with answers to. This demonstrated to me that even in that early stage of life, I knew that I had quite a lot of knowledge, which happened to be my creative knowledge and also was one of my strengths. My weakness was my not being able to use as much direct information as I needed to use from the brain, which was what my fellow peers were naturally doing. I found it mystifying that, for some unknown reason, I was having a lot of trouble presenting the understanding of my knowledge clearly to anybody else except myself and that it would take me a long time to come up with a lot of the answers that my fellow peers came up with very quickly. They were also able to find the lesson a lot easier to follow. I guess that stems from my inability to accept the importance of some of the direct knowledge which I should have been able to directly accept (and would have, had I not had dyslexia).

One of the problems I had as a child was that I did not know about the dyslexic thing either, during that period in my life. I was not much better off than the teachers when it came to the things that I did not know about dyslexia, and there was the fact that the teachers did not want to look into something that they still had no knowledge of. One thing that clearly stood out was that I was constantly putting in maximum effort in my reading, writing, and mathematics, as well as always working hard at trying to learn the lesson. Yet I was very often unable to understand a lot of the things that the teacher was trying to tell me, and I had a big problem when it came to conveying the message that I had in my head to the teacher—or anyone else for that matter. Another thing that added to the difficulty was my being a child and having a brain that was less than half-developed to work with.

However, some of the hardest challenges I had to confront while I was at school was my not being capable of understanding what they were trying to teach me and being constantly locked in a deeper version of understanding the lesson while the teachers were teaching everyone the lesson in a simplified way or one may want to refer to it as a shallower—version. The method the teachers mainly used while teaching was to give some information on a subject, skip a bit, give some more information, skip some more, and then go back and join the rest of the information together. It is important at this point to understand that I was a child that did not have a fully developed brain and was struggling to understand what was going on. The problem I had was that *when I did not understand what was being presented, I was not able to proceed further into the lesson* and was left at that point where I did not understand the second part of what I was being taught, meant that I was not able to proceed to the third part of what they were trying to teach me. The consequence of that led me to being confused when the three lessons were joint together. I was left to constantly play catch-up, while my fellow peers found it easy to keep up with the lesson because of their different way of understanding the lesson.

This left me in conflict with the teachers. They failed to understand that I was not trying to be difficult but was being left behind, with my brain not allowing me to proceed further. If the teacher had filled the gap of what I was not being told instead of bouncing to the third part, then I would have been able to proceed like the rest of my peers. I am fully aware that someone without dyslexia would more than likely see it as just me being stubborn—like the teachers did. However, to be stubborn means that you have control of the decision you are making and that you are deliberately making a different decision so that you can have your own way of doing it. The reason we have dyslexia is that we are *out of control* with our creativity, along with the side effects that accompanies it, which leaves us continually needing to know how and why; this is the main reason for our being dyslexic. The thing the teachers failed to do was supply a logical and rational answer to the very important question *of why* I would put in such a big effort to do it differently (I guess they never will while they fail to recognize the huge effort I am putting into learning.) 'He just wants to be stubborn' is not an answer, and even though the teachers were unaware of it, I still had an even bigger problem that I needed to deal with. That was my being buried in a lot of confusing information that had been deeply fragmented in my head. (Being stubborn was a long way from where I wanted to be; I desperately wanted to seek some way that I could get through the lesson which I was trying to learn.)

Some of the unhelpful comments I received were 'You are not very bright' and 'You are never going to be smart enough'. Another one that used to chew me up a lot was when one of the teachers I was working with put in my report card that I was not making much of an effort to learn the lessons. This came amongst the many other unfounded negative comments they gave me. How would they know! They were not the one with the mammoth battle that I had in my head, and if I was going to make any sort of progress, I needed to look beyond the undesirable insults that were administered in vast quantities. I found that it was imperative to make learning my top priority. The most powerful tool I had to work with in order for me to successfully learn the lessons was not a tangible tool; instead it was the need to be considered *normal* by the standard of my fellow peers and was also the very thing which stopped me from quitting and fuelled my desire to continue.

One of the problems dyslexic people have is that they gather a lot of extra information which they do not need at the time while they are working on reading and writing; they wouldn't have to contend with this if they were able to spend more time working from the left hemisphere instead of the right, which they have a strong tendency to lock themselves into. I am aware of that now since I have done an intensive study on dyslexia. I have come to the conclusion that more often than not we do not have a choice to which hemisphere we go too, the dyslexic's natural instinct is to go to the right hemisphere and that the people who are not dyslexic, process their information in a different way. This became very obvious much later in my life. When I look back many decades later, when I was aware that I had dyslexia, it allowed me to see how the other kids had already got the answer and why I was left being the one that was considered to be holding everybody in the class back—or at least, that was what the teachers kept on telling me. Even though the teachers are right when they say that you must always have some way to work out each and every thing you do, it would have made a huge difference if the teachers had been able to understand that I had so much fragmented information in my head that I was unable to always fill in all the gaps of how I got the answer right. I guess that I should not complain, because it took me about sixty years to fully work it out.

Another interesting fact is that having all that unwanted information can sometimes work out to be a good thing, because sometimes, for no reason that I can explain, a correct answer that I would be seeking would come out of nowhere and present itself. Now if you find that weird, then you are going to find this second part harder to understand. The answer would always be correct, and the reason I say that, is that when I had received similar answers in the past, it was always correct; I had no reason to believe that anything had changed (why would it?). Yet I would still be left with no way of explaining how I got my answer. This turned out to be less than helpful for the teacher, who was unaware that I was gathering big chunks of information from the right hemisphere of the brain while I was reading and writing and had no way of explaining how I did it. Meanwhile, the teacher and the students had their information coming in a neat little package (directly), without any extras. This represents the clearest understanding that I have of it, which is extra information that is stored in the brain which sometimes can come back into the memory with an answer that I am seeking at an unpredictable time (usually when given enough time and when I badly need it, although it is not always guaranteed to be reliable when it comes time to present itself). The bonus that comes with that package is that it nearly always comes in a form that is *not* fragmented, or at worst, lightly fragmented. This gives me the ability to bridge a huge gap in the improvement of the quality of my work. I am not certain that all the extra information is presented with great accuracy, although it is the best answer, I can think of that fills the void that allowed me to move up three or four grades and left me with the side effect of being very inconsistent in the quality of the work that I passed on to the teachers. Yeah, I know, here we go again with the teachers giving me that famous speech! How did you work it out? I believe that if the teacher was as young as me and had dyslexia, then that teacher wouldn't have known how to explain the way they found their answer either.

The teachers were no help in bridging the gap of my dyslexic problem. However, we need to bear in mind how different the methods were used for teaching in those days (1952–1963) when one compares to the methods and understanding that they have of teaching today; most importantly, they had no idea what dyslexia was. This also meant they did not know that I was gathering a lot of additional information that I didn't need or want in regard to my reading and writing, and even I, was a long way from being certain what I was supposed to be gathering or what I should have been disregarding. However, after a while, by following the evidence, I was able to work out that there were some parts of the information that I had that were not required, which then required the need for some form of sorting. This still did not wake me up to the fact that I was getting my information in a different way than everybody else, and the thing that made it worse was that the teachers were still hell-bent on believing that everybody gathered information about reading and writing in the same way they did. They were the teachers with fully developed brains, so shouldn't they have been the ones to figure it out? My brain at the time was many years away from being fully developed (the brain is fully developed when we are 25 years of age). Unfortunately for me, the story kept getting even worse. In that era and as far as I am now able to understand, in their rules of teaching, there was no flexibility in the teaching methods which were allowed to be used, regardless of prevailing circumstances. However, this decision was passed on from another teacher of a higher ranking than the ones I was working with, and that is the best understanding I have of it. So even when I was capable of working out another way to get past the post, it would be rejected, and I would be told to do it the way I was taught. Should you eliminate the dyslexic factor, then you would have to say that they are right, because they are the teacher, not me. But it was clear to see that in order for me to do better, something needed to change.

The teachers weren't necessarily bad teachers, because at the time, dyslexia was totally misunderstood and was not recognised as a problem that needed to be addressed. However, I believe that the teachers should have recognised that something was not quite right with my ability to learn, and they should have done some sort of investigation. Well, I guess they did in a way, except that, for the bigger part, they got it back to front, saying that I was lazy, with a bad attitude of not wanting to comply with the lesson. There was a lot of evidence around to show that I was not lazy and that I worked hard, despite the fact that we were working on two different pages (alignment of understanding of thought). A good example of how I was able to work with the pattern of thoughts that I had available to me are now easier to explain. When it came to one of the ways I would work out one of my mathematical problems. In this case, it was my times table up to 12, which I had to learn—and yes, I did get it! I knew that the times table was important to learn, but trying to learn all those numbers became very overwhelming, to the point that it seemed senseless to try and register all that information. The reason I say that, is that when I would try to remember all the information that I had in the right hemisphere, which was all I had available to me at the time—Well, I think it may be easier if I first show the difference of how someone learns the 12 times table from the left hemisphere of the brain, as opposed to how someone learns it from the right hemisphere. In this case, I can only show you the experience I had with it as a young boy of about 8 or 9.

Someone learning the 12 times table from the left hemisphere only needs to learn 144 sets of numbers that are correctly presented. When you are learning it from the right hemisphere, you are presented with a lot more numbers—maybe about 900 or more—which are more than likely to be coming from a state of fragmented information. Then you need to transfer those numbers into a defragmented state, as well as working with it being more than likely to have no set gaps between the numbers which need to be converted into the correct sequence. Let's give a little example of what I am talking about: $92171281454===\times\times\times$. So, if you look closely and with a bit of imagination, you will see the answer to what I am looking for, which is in that jumbled mess: $12 \times 12 = 144$. This is only one of the 144 sets of numbers which I was required to remember (the line of numbers that I have just presented is not necessarily an accurate description of what I had in my head but is my best example of a thought which I believe I would have had at that time). Look at the numbers which I have just visualised that were floating in my head; well, that was only just a small segment of what I still needed to acquire and was still short of forming another **143** sets of numbers. When I look back and refer to all those studies I did on dyslexia, the one thing I do know for sure is that I am receiving the information from the right hemisphere, which throws in extra information. It is not like someone who receives it from the left hemisphere in a neat package of **144** sets of numbers. At the time, while I was trying to sort it out as a child, it would not have been clearly present to me in my thoughts, and it is my belief that the scrambled version was what I had been trying to understand at the time. When I think about remembering those **144** sets of numbers, I find myself visualising a mammoth collection of fragmented information floating around in my head, as well as having to contend with the majority of the information being structured from the subconscious and hoping that it would not have missing parts of information which were needed for sorting out that fragmented mess. Another thing that was taken away was a lot of my confidence, because of the enormity of what I had to deal with, and since I was also struggling with a lot of simpler things, it led me to believe that this task would end up becoming far too big and that I would never be able to complete it.

So not being one for quitting and still having a very creative mind; I manage to work out a method where I only had to learn **three** out of the twelve-times table. I found that the **two, five** and **ten**-times tables were real easy numbers to work with, with the two-times table, all I needed to do was add two more on to the previous answer, and also found the five and the ten-times tables were equally as easy to multiply. When it came to doing my eight-times table, I would multiply by ten and then minus two for each time I multiplied. For example, 3 x 8 would = 30 – 6 = 24 or with the seven times table I would us multiples of five. For example, 5 x 7 would = 25 + 10 = 35 So, as you can see with my method I only needed to learn three out of the twelve multiplying tables which would allow me to go far beyond the twelve-times table, for example, one could use this method on your 20-times tables or any other one you may wish to use it on (not that I would have known that when I was struggling at school.)

The problem with my new formula for learning the twelve-times table was twofold: First of all, the teacher wanted us to verbally recite the times tables that we learnt. This blew my method right out of the window because the teacher insisted that I verbally recite all the times tables, and since I was only able to recite hardly any of the times tables, I lost all credibility of working within their structure. (Talk about not giving a guy a bit of slack.) I felt that I was being buried deep in my studies, despite putting in immense effort to comply through the only way I knew, and let's face it, a bit of diversity would have come in very handy. I am aware that my method was nowhere near as quick as the first method that the teachers supplied me with. However, it did allow me to gain all the answer for the 12 sets of tables that were required to be learnt. Another thing that should have been taken into account is that I would have been the *only young child* in that class who was capable of working out a different method of doing the times tables. I believe that the teachers should have been able to pick up on the fact that it was a lot harder to do what I was doing than to do the task they were asking me to do, had I been able to work a lot more from the left hemisphere of the brain and to be able to remember all that direct information.

One would have thought a good teacher would have been able to work out that something was not right and would have tried to find out what it was, or at the very least, would not have gone around saying I was lazy. There was nothing lazy about what I did, and another thing is, that most children around the age of 8 or 9 are not very good at creating new workable ideas. I guess the teachers were only interested in grabbing hold of the easiest answer, which required leaving out a lot of the facts in order for it to remain right. Unfortunately, I was trapped into having to work out things in my own way due to my lack of understanding of what I was being taught, and most of the time, I would usually work out a way to find the answers. The one thing which would have been a lot more helpful is if they had left out that pet saying of theirs: 'That's not the way to do it. Do it again, the proper way.' I guess if you look more closely at what I have just said, you would have to say that most of the time, I needed to be the teacher and the pupil at the same time, who worked out of the curriculum that the teacher presented me with. This was not a voluntary choice that I made; instead it was the hardest way to do the lesson and was very often the only option I had left. My driving force for wanting to continue learning came from an urgent desire to be *normal in the same way as the rest of my peers.*

One of the most gratifying things I have found in the results of the studies that I have done with dyslexia is the understanding of why I found it so much harder to find out what was going on while trying to learn at school, as well as why the other students for most of the time were able to follow the lesson faster and with a better understanding of it. Another important issue for me was trying to find out why the teachers did not understand all the hard work I kept on putting into my reading and writing, as well as my mathematics. Despite the downside to dyslexia, it also has an upside attached to it. While I was learning at school—although this didn't happen often—the teacher would present a problem to the class, who would find that task very difficult to understand, and I would find it really easy to do. However, it wasn't all victory, because in the back of my mind, a bit of doubt would creep in, and I would wonder if I got it wrong, since I was the one who was more likely to find the lesson difficult to learn. Yet with a moderate degree of certainty, I knew that I was right, because it was the same answer the teacher would give to the class. I guess that must have been when they would try to visualise something that they needed to create. At the time, it was unbeknown to me that they were now entering my world of understanding (the right hemisphere of the brain). No wonder I found that part easy; this was something that I had a lot more time practising with. I know that a lot of the time, when the teacher would show us something, I would quickly get lost when trying to follow the exercise that they were presenting. This was one of those times when I would unknowingly revert to looking for the big picture that would give me my best chance of comprehending all that they were trying to teach me, because to keep asking questions that the rest of the students understood and I didn't, was something the teacher would not accept. I would be considered to be deliberately disrupting the class.

I know that I said gathering all that information was a good thing. Well, unfortunately, that is not entirely true. There were times when an answer would just come floating into my head while I was learning at school, and the thing that put a damper on that much-needed information was that it was never accepted that all you needed to do was produce the correct answer. You also needed to show how you constructed the answer; even when I did get the answers right, I was still told to do it again because I did not do it their way. Another thing that eluded being in my favour was that the teachers were not able to understand that I was not *authentically capable* of knowing how to understand a lot of the lessons that they were trying to teach me. This left me deeply mystified as to what rational theory

I was supposed to be working from. I was also working out of a mountain of confusion that continually served to severely diminish my ability to work through the lessons. We still haven't got to the worst part yet. When I got all those answers which I believe had come from the extra information that I was continually gathering, well, even that created a problem, because I could not explain how the standard and the quality of my work suddenly jumped up quite a few grades. The reward I would get from the teachers for that great effort would be them saying 'You must have cheated'. This hurt me very deeply because of my upbringing and the shame that it represented. The only thing I could do when I was falsely accused of cheating was allow myself a brief period to blank off all my thoughts in order to get over the extreme hurt I was feeling. This is the one thing I strongly believe the teachers did wrong. They could have at least done an assessment on me to check and give me *a chance*, to see if I really was cheating, before they accused me of it. I highlight *a chance* because my guess is that even if they had done an assessment on me, there was no guarantee that the assessment would have come up with the true result, especially given their way of thinking and the consistent, rigid way they dealt with their method of teaching. However, I would much rather that they had taken that chance than not have taken it at all, because it would have demonstrated that they were trying to understand, and in my book, that would have represented a form of encouragement or a possibility of providing some sort of light at the end of the tunnel.

The biggest problem the teachers presented me with was their lack of understanding of the communication from the way I understood the lesson. I found myself frequently being locked into accessing my reading and writing from the right hemisphere of the brain, while the teacher mainly understood reading and writing from a better position, which is from the left hemisphere of the brain. The left hemisphere of the brain is a place that I most certainly needed to spend a lot more time in. Regardless of their understanding of me, had they put a similar effort into wanting to fill the gap of communication, they would have stopped running with the accusations of me being lazy and one who cheats and lies. There was a lot of evidence to support the reverse of what they were saying, and more importantly, it hurt to be told those things. The teachers never took the time to assess whether their accusations were true or false. Had they properly done so, they could have eliminated their old theories, and we could have been working along a different path than the one we were working on.

I know they had no way of knowing how strict my father was about anyone lying or cheating and the heavy effect that it had on me. I also know that saying I am lazy is a thing that my father was able to easily see through; he would have known that it was definitely not true. When I was at home, I was very dedicated and quick to do any job that I was required to do, and the jobs were always completed. Besides, we lived on a dairy and poultry farm, where there was an endless amount of work that always needed to be done. So, the lack of evidence of my being lazy did not line up with what they were saying. However, lying and cheating are bad habits that can creep back in and a place where my father would have been giving the teachers the benefit of the doubt and this is notwithstanding the consideration to the punishment my father would have given me when I either lied or cheated. It was *not* by hitting me physically, which is something that I would have found more preferable, but it was withdrawing from me emotionally. By that, I mean that I might as well have been a chair or some other object in regard to the attention he would give me, and that would last up to about three weeks, depending on what I was considered to have done wrong. So, when the teacher accused me of lying or cheating, unbeknown to them, they couldn't have done more damage to me than if they had hit me with a large batten, because the emotional damage was far more devastating to me. My only defence was to shut down my thinking for a short period. My Dad was also not to blame for what he did; they were the only tools (techniques) that he knew of at the time to control the situation.

One of the things my father taught me when it came to handling stress was, when someone is giving you a hard time, wear it sweet and give it hard when it is your turn to reverse the situation. I modified that to 'wear it sweet and look for the best way you can get around it'. It may very well be giving someone a hard time sometimes, but that certainly was by no means a first option. Here's another thing: saying I was trying to disrupt the lesson was far from accurate. A much more accurate account of it would be that I was trying to find another way of having the lesson presented to me and in a way that I could understand it. But then I guess that with me having that isolated way of thinking, it was just as isolated as thinking the teachers would come around to backing off having to prove everything I did and to having an understanding of the fact that their way was never going to help me succeed. In order to learn, you first need to understand what you are being told about in the lesson. In my case, it would very often revert to the fact that I was left no other option than to work on having to constantly build bridges from what I did understand to what I didn't understand.

I did not know that I had dyslexia till the age of about 60 and did not start the evaluation of my studies of dyslexia until after becoming 60 years of age. This was by no means an easy subject to research, especially when it came to revisiting what happened several decades ago. However, the irony of doing that research is that the hard time which I was given over that period has made it so much easier for me to remember it all. Because when it comes to storing long-term memory, the easiest memories to remember are the times you found something very interesting or unusual, and let's not forget to include the two more dominant ones: the good times and the bad times.

My thoughts on what I have assembled about dyslexia come from several sources, some from books that have given me facts I was unaware of. Another interesting thing I found in some of the books were problems and solutions that I have encountered in my own life's journey and that I already knew and understood the answers too. A lot of the books kept on referring to children who have dyslexia and who deal with most of the problems that I have already sorted out. A big part of my study was done on the evaluation of what was happening between my conscious mind and my subconscious. Some of the important facts that I discovered while studying the books about dyslexia were about being able to change the road map of the brain and its ability to be very flexible to change. One of the books referred to it as 'the plastic brain'. Some of the illustrations in that book gave an extraordinary demonstration of events from problems like stroke and schizophrenia. Unfortunately, not a lot was discussed on dyslexia, although it did open the window to let me know that it is possible to remap the brain and correct a lot of the problems that dyslexia presents. Another interesting book that I read showed me about the function of the two hemispheres (right and left); this book also did not go into any depth about the brain, other than referring to the two hemispheres. I got a big breakthrough from one of the books that I was studying, which gave me great assistance in managing my dyslexia problem. It showed me how to force myself to work from the left hemisphere while reading and writing, which is one of the major keys to managing dyslexia.

The answer is *to read out loud*. This exercise can only be performed out of the left hemisphere of the brain. So when someone without dyslexia sees that answer, they would be forgiven if they naturally thought that the solution was a very simple one, whereas it would give a dyslexic person a lot of joy and excitement because of the perception of its simplicity and the belief that the only requirement of the exercise that they need to deal with is to read out loud, especially since it holds an important key to correcting a lifelong problem. Well, unfortunately, "it is not", and the side effect creates a monster of fear that comes out of the field of the unknown, along with the fact that it took about 60 years before I started to work on reading out loud. The gap of fear that is created is due to the fact that the left hemisphere almost stayed stagnant in regard to gaining more knowledge of grammar over those years, and the right hemisphere gained knowledge about grammar at a fast rate over the same period, thus expanding the gap of grammatical knowledge between the two hemispheres as the years passed.

The gap of grammatical knowledge between the two hemispheres has created a monster of fear within me, which has been created through the decades that drifted by with me not knowing that I had dyslexia and which was most certainly a big contributing fact to the fear I was feeling. In the case of someone who has been dyslexic for a long time, not reading out loud means that they are guaranteed to have a big gap in the understanding of grammatical knowledge between the two hemispheres, and my first experiment of reading out loud was done through a very strong intensity of fear. This fear factor is something that very slowly decreases when I read out loud.

Sure, I had read out loud when I was younger, which was many years earlier when I was a child and beyond (excluding the last 6 years of my life). Or did I really read out loud when I was younger? My belief is that when I was younger, it was perceived that I was reading out loud, but in reality, all I was doing, for the purpose of avoiding the fear factor, amounted to reading the words without wanting to understand what I was reading. This is the reason I consider the reading out loud which I did in the early years as invalid. The first time I considered myself to have read out loud was when I was 60 years of age, at a writers' club in Sydney. It was my job to read out the article I had written so the rest of the group could analyse it and give advice about improving what I had written. I felt that the fear of reading it out loud was too much for me. I did attempt to read my article, but the fear I was feeling led me to the embarrassing situation of having to ask someone to read for me.

It is very scary when you have a lot of knowledge about grammar in the right hemisphere and so little in the left hemisphere. As soon as you start reading out loud, while you are venturing through the left hemisphere, you are confronted with a big portion of all the grammatical knowledge that you had in the right hemisphere which has now suddenly all gone; you have no idea at that particular time as to whether you will ever regain that knowledge or maybe just get some of it back, and you don't know what else you have lost besides the things you are now aware of losing. As soon as you stop reading out loud, you instantly revert to the right hemisphere, where you once had all the knowledge and from which you are now trying to retrieve the lost information. It gets worse: All that knowledge that you are now working with is deeply fragmented, along with being very confusing, which greatly adds to the fear factor. Until you defragment the knowledge in your head in the correct sequence, you will still not know what knowledge you have regained and how you might regain from the important knowledge that you once had.

One of the first things you think about is 'Look what reading out loud has done to me'. This comes with a strong belief that you are now self-destructing with your grammar by reading out loud and that your knowledge of grammar is going backwards at an alarming rate, as well as a firm belief that reading out loud is taking all that knowledge away from you and that there is a possibility that you may never retrieve all the lost information. So, is it any wonder that it creates a strong urge to discontinue reading out loud? You have that big load of uncertainty hanging over your head, along with a huge amount of destruction and an unequivocal belief of what will happen (a feeling of certainty that it will happen).

The variables of the degree to which the fear affects you are largely governed by how low the amount of knowledge is that you have in the left hemisphere compared to the greatly increasing amount of grammatical knowledge that you have in the right hemisphere, and the span of time it would take you to be able to regain all that knowledge. We still haven't even got back on the path we started on in the first place. This makes me wonder, how bad can reading out loud really get?

Getting a successful result also relies on the fact that you haven't quit and made yourself the victim by disconnecting yourself and letting everybody else think for you. When you choose the role of a victim, it certainly is going to change who you end up becoming. It also changes the size of the gap of grammatical knowledge you have between the two hemispheres. Let's face it, if you quit, then you have accepted the worst possible outcome; you no longer have a good reason to be in fear of losing something very valuable to you. Why would you? You are now the victim and are relying on everybody else to think for you; if they won't think for you, then neither will you.

Here is an example of the big gap between the two hemispheres from my earlier years of life and how it affected me. This part of my life's story starts when I was 22 years of age, while I was doing my two working tours around the world, which took about 10 years to complete. A big part of the fun of travelling around the world is writing back to family and friends to let them know how you are getting on and to tell them of the great new adventures that you are having. In my case, the dyslexia proved to be very embarrassing when I would try to write a letter. I had plenty of great words in my head which would have been very useful in constructing a good letter. One of the major problems that I needed to get past was the bad diction that I had in my speech (not saying the words properly), which was the major cause of my inability to spell a lot of the words that I wanted to use. As for that old saying 'Look it up in the dictionary', well, that works just fine if you already know how to spell the first 3 or 4 letters of the word that you want to use. Otherwise, you almost have Buckley's chance of finding the word in the dictionary. The standard of the letters I was writing were equivalent to that of a 7-year-old, and to make matters even worse, they had a lot of minor grammatical errors, even if you put the spelling issue aside for a moment. The embarrassment of the quality of my letters hurts even more when you know that the majority of the time, I should have been able to get past the many minor grammatical errors that I was making, especially since, when the errors were pointed out to me, I knew almost all the answers, as well as how and why I made them. The problem was that I was not picking up on those mistakes. Had I got past that hurdle, my standard of writing would have been equivalent to someone who does well in grammar and has just completed secondary school.

The example I have just given is an instance from one of the many difficult periods of adventures that I have had in my life, and hopefully it explains some of the reasons for the fear that lurks in the gap between the two hemispheres.

There is another part of the reason for having a fear of reading out loud. I believe this analogy is easier for most readers to relate to, and this requires a simple experiment. The example is for someone who is right-handed (use the opposite of the hand mentioned in the instructions if you are naturally left-handed). It can only work providing you are not already ambidextrous (able to write with both hands). The experiment requires writing a two-page letter using only the left hand. Sure, you know what is needed to be done. It is just something that you are a long way from being comfortable with, as you lack the experience of writing with that hand. The left hand has the same muscles as the right hand. It is just that the subconscious has not been programmed to do that task with the left hand and is coming up short in having a clear understanding of the signals needed while performing that task. The difference of whether you write with the left hand or the right hand does not change the fact that you can still perform that task, regardless of which hand you use, and it leaves you not having much to lose in switching to the other hand. The reason that I suggested writing two pages is that if you only write a couple of lines, you will be a long way from feeling the hopelessness of failing to meet the expectation that you have in the other hand, that you use to write with, which leaves you with a fear of uncertainty. When someone with dyslexia forces themselves to read out loud and work from the left hemisphere, a place they are not used to naturally working from, it means that reading out loud is always going to present some fear to them until they get the balance right in the two hemispheres and that they most certainly have a lot more to lose when they feel that something is a little bit different.

I believe that I have worked out what I do when reading silently, and that is that I would snap-read the paragraph by plucking out a certain group of words and piecing the rest of the information together by filling in the empty gaps of the picture in my head instead of reading what is written down on the paper. I can't guarantee that piece of information is completely correct, but that is the best understanding I have of it.

There are other things that can be done to combat the problems of dyslexia, and this is one I call the ruler method, which is less stressful than reading out loud. This is done by placing a ruler over the second line of the text and, as you read, taking the ruler down the lines, one line at a time. This method will enable you to mainly work out of the left hemisphere and also allows you to quickly revert to the right hemisphere for changes that may be required; it also prevents you from grouping your words together in your head instead of reading what is written down.

Another thing that I have just learnt recently and, at first reading it, did not believe that it applied to me, which is that some dyslexia people, sometimes read from right to left, despite the fact that a page is designed to be read from left to right. Yet while doing further studies on another one of the exercises, I found out what I was doing. In this case, I was trying to find a certain phrase that I thought was in a book that I had previously read. After going through about 40 or 50 pages, I noticed that something was not quite right, and I slowed down and paid particular attention to what I was doing. Well, at first, I didn't want to believe that it was true, that I was reading right to left, but the longer I read, the more obvious it became that I was. This got even worse, because when I did it quickly, I also found myself cheating by starting halfway across the page while reading right to left; so, all the text on the right side of the page had been missed. To correct it, I need to be sure to read the first word on the left of the page more slowly and to be certain that I'm reading it correctly, left to right. The good part is that this only happens when I am racing through what I am reading and is the only time that I recall it happening to me. Another common mistake that dyslexic people make is not recognising a word which is there or putting in a word and believing that it is in there, as well as other minor mistakes. Yet when the mistakes are pointed out by someone who they believe knows what they are talking about, they can clearly see the mistake and why it is wrong. So, you would have to say that the answer was there to them the whole time; it was just that they did not pick up on it.

The reason I pay so much attention to the detail of whether something is right or wrong is not for the purpose of beating myself up about it. It is because you are never going to change something you consider to be right, should it be wrong, until you accept that it is wrong. Also, if you do not acknowledge when you have done something wrong, then the sad thing is that the default is always going to be the wrong thing you did in the first place; thus you will still consider yourself right even when you are wrong (you cannot change what you do not acknowledge.)

An interesting thing I have found which I relate to dyslexia—and I have also read it in the books—is that very often, a lot of the extra benefits that I got from the creative side of the brain have come from my dreams, as have most of my inventions. These thoughts usually happen after a lot of deep thought from the previous day that then manifests in my dreams. However, the downside is a bit of the case that beggars can't be choosers, which means writing down the valuable information as soon as it becomes available, regardless of the time and even though you may not find it appropriate, should that happen in the early hours of the morning. The thing that keeps you honest is that there is no guarantee of the reliability of you being able to retrieve all the details at a later point in time, when it would have been more convenient to do so. It may end up with you only remembering a small part or not remembering it at all. If you come up with a new idea the next day, it may cause you to forget the previous idea or, at best, take a long time to retrieve some of it—or with more wishful thinking, to retrieve all of it.

On Saturday, 5/10/1996, at age 49, I ended up in hospital with a heart attack, and I also returned to hospital five times with an irregular heartbeat (arrhythmia, or to be more precise, in my case, atrial fibrillations). This gave me a wake-up call, because of the way my life had been heading. There was a very real possibility that a lot of the physical activities I was able to do were going to be taken away from me, and at the time, just after I got out of hospital when I had the heart attack, I was reduced to having roughly 10 per cent of the physical capacity that I had before the heart attack. At first, I was only capable of walking about 20 steps before needing to rest for a while in order to recover the energy that I had just used up. As time progressed, so did the distances I could cover before needing recovery time, which ended up becoming much further apart. The most concerning thing at the time was how much of my physical capacity I would be able to regain. At best, I knew that there would be some physical restriction that was going to occur, even if you only took into account that some of the muscles around the heart had died, never to return. So, the trick here now was to work out ways to minimise the physical loss. With that in mind, I urgently needed to get a complete understanding of what my options were and to address the worst possible circumstances which could transpire. The first thing that came to mind was me losing a big chunk of my physical abilities. The other concerning point that needed to be taken into consideration was that when you reach my age, you will naturally age and gradually lose some of that physical ability that you once had. As a result of that, it now became very important for me to be able to read and write with a good understanding of grammar, because I believed that there was a possibility of it being the only option I had left available to me. With that in mind and within a short period, I went back to learning reading and writing at a vigorous pace, similar to the one I had at school, and as time progressed, so did the pace that I was working at to improve my grammar.

Fortunately for me—and now I am referring to a couple of years before I had my heart attack—I had a good friend who told me about the great advantages of a Word Processor in regard to how good it was when it came to showing you how to spell any given word. Listening to him, you would have thought that it was God's gift to spelling (the very thing that I so desperately needed for my spelling). So, I bought a word processor for the purpose of being able to spell words that I needed to use when writing letters to family or friends. Now I felt confident, after listening to all that good advice, that I would be able to use all the rich vocabulary that I had in my head, and I believed that I would now be able to spell the words that I could not spell before. The problems I had before getting the Word Processor, was by not knowing how to spell or being able to find the words which I was looking for in the dictionary. It's a funny thing with those dictionaries; if you are not able to find the first two or three letters of the word you are looking for, then you are in a lot of trouble as to whether you are ever going to be able to find the word in the dictionary at all. For example, with the word *especially*, I would look under "*a*" for the first letter, instead of "e". This was one of the many reasons that there was no question in my mind that, in that period, I was definitely only capable of writing in the grammatical standard of a seven-year-old. However, if I were able to write with all the information I had in my head, my grammatical standard would extend a great many times closer to being of a far higher standard.

I gave the Word Processor a heavy workload to do—or as I liked to refer to it since I bought the computer, is the dinosaur of computers—and unfortunately, the Word Processor did not always run smoothly. In my case, it ended up presenting me with a few problems of its own. The only memory it had was a floppy disk, which was very primitive and fell short of expectations when it came to storing memory, as well as being very slow when it came to extracting memory from the written text with today's standards. Regrettably, it was not the answer to all my dreams of writing that I thought it would be. The upside to it is that it made a considerable improvement in my ability of spelling. However, as my demands for a higher quality of grammar evolved, so did some of the frustrating problems that I had before I bought it, such as when I would unknowingly put in a wrong homophone, or homograph, etc.

In the early stages of learning grammar with the Word Processor, I used to compile my own dictionary, and the words that I would use were the ones that took up to fifteen minutes or more to find. Then I would write down the meaning from the dictionary and transfer it into my word processor in alphabetical order. In order to give you an idea of the amount of work I needed to put into learning, well, this should help. I ended up with a bit over three hundred words, with their meanings, and spent hundreds of hours writing it. I was kind of proud of all the hard work that I had done, so I sent a copy of it, with all the pages of my dictionary, to my Mum in New Zealand. Oh yes, Mum did let me know how excited she was to receive it, all for the wrong reasons. If I remember correctly, there were 64 pages of it, and it was sent in a big envelope. Now here is the part she got really excited about. The envelope was intercepted by ASIO (Australia Security Intelligence Organisation), and Mum was asked whether this was some kind of secret message that she was receiving. It didn't take too long to let them know that this was not the case. I guess that ASIO had a hard time believing that someone would spend such an excessive amount of time writing a dictionary when they clearly already had one (my dictionary had the meanings written from other dictionaries). Obviously, they were not familiar with the determination of someone with dyslexia who wanted to learn grammar. I shouldn't complain, because I didn't fully understand the dyslexic thing either at the time.

The Word Processor ended up not being able to handle the workload, and it started taking just as long, if not longer, to find a word through the Word Processor than it did to find it in one of my many dictionaries. So, then I was left with no other option than to buy a computer to continue my work. This also created another problem which was caused by the Word Processor and the computer not being too friendly towards each other (they were not compatible for transferring memory). At first, I was annoyed because rewriting the whole thing was a big job that would take a few hundred hours to do and was something that I was not looking forward to doing. So, I put it off for a while, hoping to find a way around the problem. But as good fortune would have it, it turned out to be a good thing, because I found a new way of finding the words that I could not spell. At first, I did not realise that I had advanced enough that I did not need to go back to compiling my own dictionary any more. I am now able to find all the words I need to spell, one way or another. I mainly search through the thesaurus (dictionary,) or another dictionary which I had on the computer and quite often I would go through the check list of over

2,000 words in it which I have created in a folder with spreadsheets, I also have **25** other dictionaries that I own.

I also use the computer's spell check, but I do it a bit different than most people. Most people are not willing to find out what they need to do to spell the word correctly before looking at the suggestion of the spell check. They use the suggestion of the spell check in a parrot-like fashion, failing to understand where they went wrong or what they need to do in order to not keep on repeating the same mistakes that they are almost doomed to make in the future; the lesson has been lost because they are only concerned that the word is correctly presented. I find it strange when I hear people say that the spell check on the computer is a bad thing. When people stop using the spell check in the computer in a parrot-like fashion and revert back to the way that it was intended to be used—as a learning tool—then it will go back to being the great learning tool that it can be when used correctly.

As soon as I see a red line under a word, I will check to see if I can find a way to correct it before looking for the suggestion (double-clicking on a single word highlights it and allows you to spell check, one word at a time), and if I still can't work it out, I'll look for the suggestions it supplies and take the time to work out the reason I wasn't able to correct it. Also, if it has a green line or a blue line under the text, I will try to correct it first before checking with the computer. I do the same thing on some of the rare times I am fortunate to have someone grade my papers. I look to see what I did wrong. What is the most common mistake? What is it that I need to watch out for? And what do I need to do in order to stop repeating the same errors? Where there is a will, there is a way. When it comes to using the computer and using spell check properly, the trick is to learn why you made the spelling error, how you need to correct it, and what you can do to prevent it from happening again. Another big advantage that I get from the computer is that when I click on the speaker, it will give me the verbal sound of any word that I use with the spell check, as well as any word I highlight with the current file I am working with, via the thesaurus.

Another thing that needs to be addressed in regard to improving my grammar is the glaring fact that not a lot has changed in regard to improving my reading and writing between the time I had left school to the time I had my heart attack (a period of **33** years). This was due to the fact that I had put very little effort into learning grammar in that period. So now the heart attack had put a new spin on my wanting to intensify the upgrading of my grammar in order for me to be in a better position to work as a writer. Since the time of my heart attack, I have started putting in a lot of hard work in my learning to read and write, which is now improving at a fast pace, and I am finding that the study I am doing of grammar is resulting in me making fewer mistakes; the mistakes are also, now drifting into becoming of a more minor nature. I still need to keep working hard on a lot of defragmentation in the text that needs to be sorted out from the thoughts in my head.

Some things *I didn't do* while taking on this enormous task of greatly improving my grammar were things like trying to look into the future and seeing how hard it was going to be. When trying to achieve a goal with a long-term solution in mind—like in my case, correcting my grammar—and knowing that it is at least doable, I usually find that the best way to deal with it is by concentrating solely on the important mission at hand and not allowing myself the luxury of indulging in the semantics that could end up derailing my goal, such as: Is it going to take a very long time to learn? Is it going to be too hard to do? Is it going to be worth all the time that it will take? And there are a bunch of other semantics that you could also add in. That would have only left me, at best, greatly diminishing my chances of success. The other things I spent a lot of time concentrating on were the tools I needed to acquire in order to make this mission successful. When I say *tools*, I am not referring to a pick and a shovel. The tools I am referring to are things like dictionaries, the things I need to learn, the way I am going to proceed in my learning, the method I need to adopt, etc. At the time I started it, I still had a lot to learn about the management of dyslexia. The other thing that weighed heavily on my mind was that I needed to do a lot better and improve my standard of grammar, because at this stage, my grammar still needed a serious upgrade, especially knowing that I have the capability of working at a far higher level.

A problem that would occur while I was trying to improve my grammar would be that I would incorrectly spell a word, which was by far my biggest problem and which was compounded by me not pronouncing a lot of the words properly. Another heavy problem that existed was that I would put in a different word than the one I intended on putting in, such as a homophone (a word that has the same sound as another word but is spelt differently) or a homograph (a word that has the same spelling but a different meaning). I would miss a word and not read the word even though it is there, and I would put in a word that is only in my head and, when reading it, believe that it is there. Also, there were a lot of other mistakes. I would mix up the tenses (the future, the present, and the past) and the 1st, 2nd, and 3rd person in my written speech, as well as forgetting to put the suffix in some words or put the wrong suffix. I found that the best way of overcoming these problems is to leave the work I am doing alone for a while and then, after maybe half an hour or possibly after a few hours, to come back and read it, not using the words I have in my head but the ones that are written down. Unfortunately, that is more easily said than done for me.

I have now been using the method of reading out loud with my written work for about 7 years. As opposed to the early years, where I was using the act of reading out loud as a masquerade, because in earlier years, I was not prepared to understand what I was reading due to the fear I was feeling; this is the reason that I have classified my earlier attempts of reading out loud as invalid. It may seem strange to others who do not have this problem of fear that I have, which comes over me even when I am alone and nobody else is able to hear me reading out loud (most of my written work is done when I am alone in my office). The reason for reading out loud being less successful for me than it could have been is that, after reading out loud for a short while, I would gradually find myself drifting back to reading silently. My understanding of my doing that is because of the fear of losing the advantages that I have developed over the last 60 years, and more often than not, I have elected for the safer option of repeatedly rechecking my written work. However, that method does have a bad side effect, which is that it extracts a mountain of time when I am working on it. For example, in my earlier days, while working on multiple pages of an article, on average one page could take up to 8 hours or even a few hours more when I would recheck my work (this time span includes taking time off to free my thoughts between the different checks), and each time I would find mistakes in it that I did not find in the previous checks. Sure, the mistakes were there the whole time while I was doing my previous checks. With a majority of the mistakes, I would have fully understood what they were should someone have pointed them out to me, but even spending all those hours rechecking did not guarantee that my work was correct. Some of the many reasons I was not picking up on the mistakes was that I could be reading the same place in the paragraph many times and would still keep putting in a word or leaving out a word that is only in my head and not what is written down. I have also found that slowing the pace of my reading gives me a better understanding of what is written, as opposed to what I often use to do, which is to work from what I have in my head. As far as I know, there is only one way of being sure that you are working from the left hemisphere and that is by reading out loud. However, that can also leave you in a state of declining from the high standard of work that you have already obtained; it puts you back into the loop of the right hemisphere, which adds in a lot of information that needs to be sorted out. The left hemisphere lets you accept information as being correct because it is *direct information*, and it has the possibility of not being correct in the first place, along with the end of the loop left at having to work the balance of where I need to be working from. The upside to it all is that I am improving at a fast rate, and now a page of rechecking usually takes no more than about an hour, or even less than an hour if it is a simple page. My work has progressed into being far more accurate and quicker to correct, and I take shorter and fewer breaks than I did before, while checking my written work.

A thing that I have included in this section of my article is the improvement that can happen when you do realise you have dyslexia and take the right approach to correcting your problem. However, it is important to understand that this is not a black-and-white situation, because there are some things you need to change and some things that you need to hold on to which give someone with dyslexia an edge on life; dyslexic's work excessively from the creative side of the brain, which can give them some great advantages. But this is also their downfall as well, because they are left with a lot of information that needs sorting, which is fragmented and leaves them with the difficult task of transferring that mixed-up message, as well as some times the inability to recognise where their mistake was made, even though they can clearly recognise it once it has been pointed out to them. This problem is very time-consuming and very frustrating. There are often times when I review what I have written a few days later and find myself venturing into a field of more mistakes that still exist in the work that I have just done. This is not the only way I do my editing. I also work with various dictionaries and have made up a special checklist to find and correct the things I have done wrong. It's a slow way of editing my mistakes, but the important part, especially when I am correcting my own work, is that I need to be dedicated enough to continue pursuing this immense task and, even more importantly, to accept that it is doable as well as worthwhile to pursue the best I possibly can for the results.

My Summary

Due to the complexity of the article I have just written, I feel it is important to unfold and conclude some of the facts which I have accumulated in the intensive studies that I did on dyslexia. There are three important topics I wish to clarify, along with a few more minor topics.

- Why I have a different way of thinking than people without dyslexia.
- What gave me a strong driving force to get past the many—and might I add, massive—hurdles that most people would have given up on.
- Why dyslexics have a different demeanour that gives them some advantages and also why they have some disadvantages that characterises them with dyslexia. This also goes along with the prospects of the results of either having a positive attitude or having a negative attitude—and let's not rule out being somewhere in between.

The answer to the 1ˢᵗ question. The reason I have a different way of thinking is that while I am reading to myself, as well as when I am writing, it leads me to spend a lot more time working out of the creative side of the brain, which gives me a greater depth of reasoning and thought, which allows me to see and understand things differently than someone who does not have dyslexia. When you are working mainly out of the left hemisphere, you are relying on that information being correct in the first place, and it does not allow any room for modification should the modification need to take place. Direct information is without any alteration, and created information comes with alteration or new ideas.

When one works from the creative side of the brain, there are side effects that occur: One is that you are creating a lot of new information and remembering all that new information while you are working with it and understanding how you are going to use it, along with sorting out what information needs to be kept, what needs to be put aside, or what needs to be disregarded. The most disruptive one is the need to defragment the additional information that you have in your head. It is a lot easier to work from verbal information that comes from the left hemisphere than it is to create a lot of new information.

The thing about dyslexia, when it comes to identifying it, is that it is not a black-and-white subject to deal with. The thing that blurs the boundaries is the degree to which you have dyslexia. Let's refer to what it really is. It is overusing the right hemisphere (the creative side) of the brain, which ends up creating problems in your reading and writing and can also extend to mathematics. If you were able to shift to the left hemisphere (the direct side of the brain) a lot more when you needed too, then you would not have dyslexia in the first place. There are times when you should be in the left hemisphere of the brain, and that is when you *clearly* have the correct information to work with. However, there lies the problem, within those 7 letters! *Clearly*—whether the gathered information is *clearly* right or *clearly* wrong or somewhere in between. This adds to the confusion as to whether you should be working out of the direct side of the brain. Let's face it, if you go back into history far enough, then you will find that there were people of high authority who used to insist that *the world is flat*, and anyone who challenged that theory or disputed the fact would find themselves in very serious trouble. The world being flat was direct information you were expected to accept (in reference from the medieval era). I believe that I have made my case as to why it is not always clear to accept direct information. Sometimes the decision to accept direct information does not always come from the conscious part of the brain; it more often than not comes from the subconscious part of the brain, to which we do *not* have a lot of control of.

Here comes the mysterious part: what I believe happens to all those unwanted alphabetical letters which have been put in my memory. The only certain thing I can tell you about it is that I have lived in that battlefield for a very long time, and I still do not have a clear picture of what is happening in the subconscious. As usual, all we can do is investigate the facts and evidence that we have available.

The answer to the 2ⁿᵈ question. What gave a child between the ages of 8 and 9, who was working with a brain which was a long way from being fully developed, the strong driving force which allowed him to be able to invent another way of learning the 12-times table? The reason was, I was unable to learn through the method that the teachers were teaching me, and providing I didn't quit, as well as continued to proceed along the only way that I was capable of understanding the lesson. There was also a reality that needed to be dealt with, and that was that, in my mind, I believed that there was no way I was ever going to memorise all those numbers the way they were trying to teach me, which was because of my different way of thinking.

I believe that the teachers could have sorted out a more successful way of teaching me, and even when you take into account the fact that they did not know about dyslexia, that does not change the fact that they should have been able to strive for a workable way to get their student to succeed; I believe that it was part of their job to do so. This also meant that they should have asked themselves a few questions, such as why I wanted to use a different method for doing my twelve-times tables, and why I worked so hard to do it differently. This would have also required them to give answers that could have been worked out through rational reasoning based on the facts and evidence, which would have at least proved that I was not lazy and which would have given them a better basis to be working their answers from. If you accept the concept that we had the same way of thinking, then you would have to concede that they had a better method with the 12-times tables than the one I had just created. Another thing that needed to be addressed was why I would want to take on this heavy workload which I was self-imposing. Furthermore, the thing that made matters worse was the mentality from the way that the teachers worked with their idea's, which gave them permission to throw in a lot of comments that were humiliating and most discouraging. These were often thrown my way, such as when I was told to do the work that I had just done *again* even though I got the answer right in the first place, as well as when I was told a lot of things which were not true, like how I was lazy, did not want to comply with the lesson, and was cheating. A very destructive thing was that I was considered to be asking too many unnecessary questions, and from the teachers' point of view, I was *purposely* and *deliberately* continuing to disrupt the class (the teachers had a habit of using two different words with the same meaning so that if you did not understand the first word, you would understand the second one). When it came to being successful then it did not matter that they were wrong, because their wrong point of view was never going to change anything that would enable me to succeed in getting through my education. It was my modifications which I created from the lessons that gave me the gap for learning or being left out by failing to learn. This also required the need to stay very vigilant in spite of the fact that they were the ones in charge. This was the only platform I had to work from.

Looking back at all the studies I have done on dyslexia leads me to believe that asking a lot of questions would have given me one of the best chances that I had available to me in order for me to rely on working from the left hemisphere a lot more. Most of the changes I have made that require me to work out of the left hemisphere have come about by me asking other people, as well as the questions I ask myself, which received satisfying answers to the grammatical work I was doing. So rather than discouraging me from asking questions, the teacher should have been encouraging me to ask questions, especially given the fact that I was trying hard to learn and that it held one of the keys to my inability to work more from the left hemisphere, a place I so often needed to be.

Even though neither the teachers nor I knew about the problems of dyslexia, someone with a fully developed brain—in this case, the teacher—should have realised that what they were doing left them creating less-than-satisfactory results and that it would have been a lot more professional if they had worked on evaluating the potential of my abilities. However, that would have required them to recognise that I was not lazy, along with a few other obvious facts that needed to be recognised. This also created a chain reaction, such as my parents getting an inaccurate evaluation of how I was doing at school, which led to more unfair and unwanted comments that contributed to impairing my desire to learn.

That very strong driving force I had within me had a very simple explanation to it. In my case, it was a strong desire that came from within, where I wanted to be perceived as "*normal*", and even though I didn't know it at the time, this quest that I was seeking, proved to be a powerful tool that worked in my favour. The real enemy I needed to be battling with was my inability to understand what the teacher was trying to teach me and the great difficulty I had in trying to convey the messages that I had in my head over to the teacher or anyone else for that matter, and also having to deal with the confusion of regarding what information I had in my head or the information that I did not need to be using—and let's not leave out all the humiliation the teachers threw at me.

One of the nasty things my peers would constantly do for good measure was relentlessly tease me and repeatedly call me 'red hair, long nose' up to 50 or 60 times (within about a 10 – 15-minute period) in a rhythmical and in a repetitive series. This was something that I had almost no control of, because I was not prepared to take it to the level of violence. My father taught me that the smarter person talks his way out of a battle, and the person who deals with their battles by physically fighting their way through will either be ignorant in the field they are working in or they are too frustrated at that point of time and will not be able to access the information that they need. This battle of teasing me that my peers where giving me was a relentless one, that served to try and push me further out of the range of being normal. The things that my peers endeavoured to gain from all that teasing was to have entertainment at my expense and to have a false sense of power which made them feel good about themselves (the reason I stated a false sense of power is because on their own they have very little power and rely very heavy on there numbers.)

There was still another continuous battle that I had to contend with, and that was the one from the people who were closes to me, who often told me that I was never going to ever be bright at anything. This left me battling with the thin threads to being *normal*, which lay lurking in sight. Although I did not fully understand it at the time, the one advantage for avoiding the role of quitting. Which is evident to me now, is that both my parents were well conversed in the art of being strong-willed and domineering. They were also very often able to achieve goals that you would not think possible. I still had two options left open to me. Seeing it as being too hard to achieve, and quit. The second option required to do what I do best, and that was to battle on and achieving that important quest to be normal.

Not everybody who has dyslexia, has the advantage of having two dominating parents. This leaves the dyslexics that don't have a strong driving force within them with the probability of not being able to get past the hurdles that they need to face. They will more than likely want to look for the so-called easy option of being the victim who lies back to wait and see what someone else will do for them, and if someone will not do something for them, neither will they. I much prefer the journey to be normal, although the battlefields change as you progress along that journey of wanting to be normal. I work on the theory that the bigger the battle, the greater the glory should you win, and the bigger the loss should you lose. This throws the desire to stay a victim in the first place right out the window and leaves me with the outcome of being able to continue improving the quality of my life.

The answer to the **3**rd *question.* My understanding of dyslexia and the advantages I believe we have through a deeper understanding to most things we do in our lives. We very often analyse the events that occur in our daily lives by frequently challenging the logic and rationality of the information we receive. This usually leads us to the path of only accepting logical reasoning and very often rejecting ideas that do not fall into that precondition of logic, and then we usually go on to creating different ideas that we believe need changing or to think that maybe the idea needs modifying from the direct information that we received in the first place. This does not rule out the fact that we often stay with the original situation that we first had because it does not need changing. This also relies on one's attitude, whether they have a tendency to quit or whether they consider it to be worthwhile following through with a new bit of information. The two different options are obviously going to eventuate with the two different decisions leading to two different paths in their life's journey.

So, the key to successful results is the balance between the left and right hemispheres. It may appear to be a simple choice to change the balance of the two hemispheres. However, finding the balance is quite often complicated, and it can be difficult to find where that balance needs to lie. Since I have done my intensive studies on dyslexia, I have worked out a code for how I understand most things in life. It is what I call my ABC, which are **attitude, balance,** and **choices**. These three things have the *balance* of power to change the result of almost everything you do. For example, when one is trying to learn something new, and should that person resort to sabotaging the lesson by saying '*I can't do it*' to the thing that they have been instructed to do and going on the theory of them being very capable of doing it, leads back to an attitude of taking the role of a victim, which allows them to excuse not doing that exercise. A good understanding of the word Can't; "*can't* means you don't want to do it". This now sets up one's *attitude* for a formula of failure. Someone saying 'I can't' also translates to the fact that they are unteachable while they carry on with the belief of can't, because they have now achieved the success of a very easy goal of '*I can't do it*'. But if you discuss the aspects of your difficulties to the same problem and learn why or how you did not understand at that time, then your *attitude* is now set up for at least a part of the formula to succeed. If you concentrate your thoughts on only one insignificant part of a problem, then your *balance* in solving it is going to be taken away. Your *choices* are always going to be very heavily influenced by your *attitude* and *balance*, which you work from and which are what lead you to the *choices* you make.

The disadvantages dyslexics have, involve us not always being clearly understood because of our deeper and creative way of thinking, which leaves the people who have shallow thoughts not able to understand us. However, this is the easier side of what we need to deal with. The tougher side of the equation is that we gather a lot of thoughts and pieces of information that we may never utilise, and this creates fragmented information that constantly requires sorting out. For the benefit of the person who is not dyslexic, try to envision a time in your life when you have several inventive ideas in your head at the same time, and then try to envision trying to pass on just one of those messages while you have the other ones floating around in your head. This is what I am referring to when I say *fragmented*; all the mixed-up messages you have in your head also intensifies the possibility of not passing on the intended message and of making mistakes. This occurs because you are not always sure that you have always recognised the things that you do or do not require, even though more often than not, when someone points out a mistake to you, you are able to fully understand the mistake and how and why it went wrong. At this point, I am referring to what is being read from what I have written. Some people with dyslexia give up and put it into the 'too hard' basket, and some have a more positive attitude that proceeds with whatever motivates them to proceed in sorting out that relentless task. Obviously, the two different attitudes are going to make a big difference in the results, and this is the major reason you cannot go around with the perception that everybody with dyslexia are the same, along with the fact that there are many different ways of creating.

While reviewing the study of my dyslexia during the period while I was at school, and after weighing all the evidence up many years later. I found myself having a big advantage due to the special lesson I was getting at the time with my education. The lesson I am referring to is one that revolves around the complications of having dyslexia and the fact that neither the teachers nor I was aware of what dyslexia was. This also meant that the teacher was teaching me the lesson one way and I was understanding the lesson another way. The reason for this was that I was not capable of understanding the way the lesson was being presented to me. This left me with only one other option, which was to try and fill in the gaps between the things I did not understand and bridge the gap to the things that I did understand. It also meant having to be the pupil and the teacher at the same time, which is not an easy role to perform, especially when you are a child. As if things were not bad enough, I also had to endure the ridicule that diminished my chances of getting through the lessons, such as being told to do it again even though I got it right the first time, just because I did not do it the way they taught me to do it;

telling me I was lazy when the evidence clearly showed that I was not lazy; telling me I was cheating when I most definitely wasn't; telling me that I would never be smart enough; and giving me a host of other degrading comments. Even though the teacher's lessons were hard to achieve, with me having to perform two roles at the same time and having to get past all the humiliating techniques that they would throw my way, it also created a way for me to raise my level of endurance in learning to a very high level. Another advantage was having parents who were strong-minded, which also continued raising my endurance to a higher level. As tough as that may seem, after coming out of years of ongoing troublesome lessons from the teachers and now that I have left school and gone out into the workforce, well, all the lessons that I need to learn now seem insignificant compared to what I had gone through in the past. Most importantly, it has given me the confidence which allows me to get past those many tough hurdles that I don't believe I would have got through without the tough teaching that the teachers gave me (it took the quitter, or my want to stay a victim, out of me and brought me into the field of being a battler).

I cannot recall another time in my life when I got such great results and when everyone involved was unaware of the actual lesson that was taking place. With the wisdom of hindsight on my side, along with the advantage of the understanding of how this special lesson took place, it now makes it very rewarding to know that all that hardship I endured is giving me some great advantages. As usual, with my grammar, it still has more than its fair share of self-made booby traps (minor errors that keep reoccurring in my reading and writing). It is OK because I am used to dealing with it. It happens to be part of the package that comes with dyslexia.

My different way of thinking often throws my pattern of thought out of alignment with the way other people who do not have dyslexia think, and I regularly need to be wary to respecting the way in which they choose to deal with their thoughts. This quite often means that I need to make some modifications with my response for two good reasons: that person may not want to know about the subject in any other way, and I am also capable of making mistakes and not recognising the fact that I have.

It is not necessary to see a mistake as always being a bad thing. It all depends on how you respond to it after you have recognised that it is a mistake. I remember a wise man once told me, 'The person who never made a mistake never made a goddam thing.' This leads me to the understanding that a mistake is not necessarily a bad thing and is also not something that I vigorously seek to make. Making a mistake does demonstrate that I am not stagnant when it comes to learning. The thing that needs to be avoided is making the same mistake twice, and something which is far more devastating is making the same mistake for a third time. Mistakes can be a good thing if something is learnt from them, whereas the luxury of the mistake being a good thing, expires when you keep on repeating it. The thing that needs to be concentrated on is to look for the correction or what is needed so that it can be modified and to revisit it for more accurate results. Another thing I do is look for the worst thing that can transpire from the result as well as the best thing that can transpire from the result, and find out where the balance needs to be that gets me my best results.

There is something else I would like to clarify in regard to the way the teachers taught me. The teachers did not accept the knowledge that I was not always capable of learning the way that they were teaching me and that I was forced into having to do my lessons differently because it was the only way I knew how to do them. Their attitude was to see me as someone who was stubborn and always wanted my own way. This was a quick and simple answer they would grab hold of, and it lacked rational reasoning to it. The way I saw it was that the teachers considered it important for them to always be right so that they could sustain their command of authority. They also required having everything taught the same way, without any alterations, and left no room for flexibility, should there be some unrevealing circumstances that they may have needed to deal with. My parents always backed the teachers and had no idea what dyslexic was either. This made learning a very hard thing to do; it also made me very tough, having to battle all the adults in my life. This special lesson was not an easy one to do, although it did give me a huge advantage in being tough when it came to learning. To quit or take the victim's role would have meant that all the learning that I had achieved would backfire in my face and that everything that I was being accused of—such as that I would never be any good at anything or that I would never amount to anything—would now be true, and I really would have ended up being the so-called victim (I see it as the self-inflicted victim). There was another role to take, other than the victim's role, which was the one I took—the battler's one.

Tidying up fragmented information in my head is an ongoing assignment that I feel needs to be constantly worked on. I am a firm believer that valuable information needs to be passed on for the greater benefit of society, yet if I am unable to pass that message on to anyone other than myself, then all that valuable information is wasted, along with all the hard work spent developing it. One of the main reasons for writing my autobiography is to pass on valuable information and to share the exciting adventures of my life. Being able to vastly improve my grammar is a goal which is most important to me. When I look back through the eyes of my youth, at the time when I had bad grammatical skills. I am now finding by improving my grammar that it has gone from being a lot of hard work to being an exciting challenge; this comes along with the brighter side of knowing that my grammar is continuing to improve at a rapid pace.

Something that needs to be remembered about someone who has dyslexia is that they do not only work out of one hemisphere of the brain, and people without dyslexia also don't only work out of one hemisphere; people with and without dyslexia work out of the two hemispheres. The most important thing to work out is where the balance needs to be. So when someone with dyslexia looks through the uncertainty of the entangled mess that they have to work with, it is justifiable that that someone reading out loud who has dyslexia will have a great fear of losing all the advantages that they have gained over many years, especially since it can end up making a huge change in the journey of their life which will inevitably strongly affect the rest of their life.

The only thing I am aware of that can successfully get me past the post from what I have already achieved is finding the balance to getting my best results while I am doing my reading and writing through the left and right hemispheres and realising the value of respect that needs to be paid to each hemisphere. This requires spending the right amount of time in the right hemisphere so that I can continue putting in creative thoughts for writing and being able to understand the bigger picture when I am reading something complex. However, I am now directing my thoughts a lot more to the left hemisphere and work more along the theory that the more I read everything out loud, the more I am guaranteed to be correcting the balance to where it needs to be, providing I do not overdo it.

There is a thing I believe the teachers could have and should have done, although this would have required them to get out of that rigid box which they had locked themselves into, along with maintaining the credit for themselves to always be perceived as right. When I started asking questions about the things I did not understand, for which they quite often did not have answers, rather than examine the true reason I was asking so many questions, they would divert by taking the attention away from what needed to be addressed in my studies. This led to the teachers saying that I was asking too many questions for the purpose of being annoying and deliberately disrupting the class. How convenient that was for them since they often failed to provide an answer to what I needed to know. Then the question would be diverted around, with me being accused of wanting to make trouble by disrupting the class through the method of asking too many questions.

I believe that when a teacher is educating a pupil—not just the majority of the pupils but each and every one of them, where the pupils need to have their education continually evaluated through the evidence of improvement along the journey of the pupil's schooling. If they are not showing a satisfactory amount of improvement or are showing difficulty in being able to achieve what they need to be learning, then I believe the teacher needs to work out why and how that is happening, providing they are showing a *glimmer* of hope of wanting to learn. Even when they are not showing a glimmer of hope, I believe it is still the teacher's job to work out why the child is not showing that glimmer of hope and to try to work out what is needed to be done in order to get them back on the right track. Only then can you say that the teacher is teaching all the students and not just the ones who are easy for them to teach. The thing I am disappointed with is that they constantly take the easy option of throwing labels from things which many of the other students have done in the past, as opposed to evaluating the work I was doing. Let's have a look at the evidence that I am referring to. This wrong piece of evidence, with the facts following it, will best explain it: 'He is lazy and does not want to apply himself.' So, at that time, I was about 8 years old, yet I was able to work out another way of working my multiplication tables up to the 12 times table by only learning three out of the twelve through multiplying, adding, and subtracting. I believe that the teachers who were teaching me should have known that the first way that they presented my times tables to me would have been easier and quicker if I was capable of working from the left hemisphere while I was learning from that exercise and that my method of doing it took a lot longer to do, as well as having to do a lot of hard work in order to achieve it. This piece of evidence clearly shows that I am not lazy, because it did take a lot of work for me to work it out. If the teacher had asked any one of my fellow peers to do a similar task, I firmly believe that they would not have been able to come up with an answer, especially when they did not know whether there was a possibility of being able to produce a different workable formula.

So if the teacher had worked as hard to find evidence as to why I did not do as well as my fellow students, as they did on being rigid with their fixed ideas, then they could have worked out that I was not lazy and that they needed to start trying to work out why I had spent such a huge amount of time working out a new system for doing my 12-times table when they clearly had an easier and better one already presented to me before I started. In retrospect, the irony of it all is that the teacher needed to work more out of the right hemisphere for more creative ideas for me to do better, and I needed to work a lot more out of the left hemisphere for direct ideas so that I could do better with my grammar.

In regard to the 12-times table, and where I was able to create a new formula, that I needed for learning was difficult to create. This difficulty of forming a new formula was compounded by the fact that I was only a child of about 8 to 9 years old, in the era of the 1950s, a period when nobody in the educational system had any understanding about the problem of dyslexia until a few decades later. However, for the reader that may wish to go deeper into the journey which I travelled as a child, it is possible for you to work out each and every one of the times tables that I formulated by *adding*, *subtracting*, and *multiplying*, should you choose to go down that journey. It is not necessary to do the exercise, because it is only for the reader who wishes to have a deeper understanding of the experience of that child. I was neither victim nor perpetrator. I was just a boy who wanted to be normal and to be able to get through the things I needed to learn at school in a world of having nobody that understood me, and even I was a long way from fully understanding at the time that I was learning things in a different way.

There are some compelling reasons I did not put in all the details to the formula I created for the 12-times table and left out some of the finer details. The reason is that once all the details are put in, the person reading the formula would be more than likely to work under the assumption and genuine belief that this new formula was easy to create. Most things are easy to do once you have seen how it is done. Since I have encrypted the full answer in there, should the reader who wants to read it through the thoughts that require a deeper and fuller understanding of it. Who would need to be able to work out how I did each of the 12-times tables? It may be tougher than you think it is, but there are some advantages you have which I did not have. For you to be completely successful in recreating a new formula, that would mean not having the key information supplied to you to start with, such as the knowledge that there is a workable formula to proceed with in the first place. Your motivation is always going to be of a great concern when you are not sure that it is even possible to be doing the same job in a different way. The reader is also more than likely to be working out of a brain which is a lot more developed than that of the 8-year-old child who successfully created it. Another advantage the reader has is being given all the key details for the things which are needed to reproduce the formula or one similar to it. Another important factor which cannot be ignored is that this all needs to be worked out within a short time frame.

So, should you find this mission of learning the 12-times table in a different way a bit tough to understand, then give a thought to the young child who had to dance through all those obstacles which were thrown his way and how he still made it through. I did not put the formula that I created in, so that you would see me as a victim. Even as a child, I chose not to be the victim. I believe that I would not have even understood much about what a victim was in that period of my life. My overriding choice would have been more to the theme of wanting to be normal, which meant successfully learning the lessons that needed to be done. Being the victim means you quit, and all that valuable knowledge will be lost. The reason I explained about the hard times I experienced in my life is that I am endeavouring to demonstrate how the battle was worth it in the end, even though it may not appear to have been the case at the time. The default is to quit or to partially quit in some way, which will more likely end up with you believing that it is the easier option to take at that time. Well, that may be so if you are prepared to take out the heavy price tag that you'll end up paying through the rest of your life's journey. The main reason I did not give all the details to the formula of the 12 times table was to throw in a challenge and, even more importantly, to make sure that the authentic value of the story is retained, as well as to ensure that the story is not devalued without a just cause.

So not being one for quitting and still having a very creative mind, I managed to work out a method wherein I only had to learn *three* out of the twelve-times tables. I found that the *two, five,* and *ten* times tables were really easy numbers to work with. With the two times table, all I needed to do was add two more to the previous answer, when it came to doing my *eight*-times table, I would multiply them by *ten* and then minus two for each time I multiplied. For example, 3 × 8 would be 30 – 6 = 24. With the *seven* times table, I would use multiples of *five*. For example, 5 × 7 would be 25 + 10 = 35. So, as you can see, my method only needed three out of the twelve multiplying tables which I was required to learn.

Something the teachers could have done, had they known, was to force me to read out loud, without throwing all the humiliation techniques they would use on me. Well, let's face it, belting someone over the head while they are putting maximum effort into learning the lesson with a humiliating technique is going to have a stronger tendency to make them want to shut their minds off to further abusive thoughts so that they no longer have to feel the pain of the humiliating techniques. So, if you take away the humiliation, then their mind can be set free; they can be productive and understand the importance of learning the exercise through a way that they are capable of doing it. Going on my knowledge and what I have now learnt about dyslexia, reading out loud would have been a really uncomfortable place for me to be in. However, being uncomfortable in reading out loud would have been something that I needed to do in order to do a better job of improving my education in grammar, and it would have helped me get better control of my dyslexia.

The one thing that would have made it worse would be if I were to have been treated as a victim. Because then it would have amounted to me wasting a lot of time on being 'poor me the victim' instead of working on what needed to be worked on. If I had taken the backward step of being the victim, then the after-effect would have more than likely ended with me becoming greatly retarded from the strength I needed to be able to retain that strong determination of development over the years and is also important for the need to maintain a quicker learning ability that gets me past the difficult situations. Let's face it, determination is one of the pluses that I was able to develop from dyslexia, providing I had used it in a positive way; if I hadn't, then that would have weakened the goal's to my success. Without that strong will of determination, my progress would have been even a lot slower, maybe even to the point that I would have become stagnant or had an even stronger chance of coming to the point of giving up altogether, which is contributed to the consequences of being overwhelmed by that excessive fragmented information I had floating in my head which I had to constantly deal with. Sometimes the option that first appears to be the easiest one available to us will more often than not have a far greater price tag to it than we can imagine. One thing I believe that I have learnt in life is that victims are poor—in every sense of the word, in most cases. So even though we are all victims from time to time, what counts is how long you are prepared to stay the victim and how hard you work to avoid staying the victim so you can end up with a richer outcome in life.

Another important thing that needs to be recognised is that there are two ways we gather information: directly and creatively. The direct information are thoughts, ideas, or facts that we accept as correct and instantly ready to use for our own benefit. Creative information is new information that we are bringing into our thoughts or that come from modifying some information that we have received.

People without dyslexia are more than likely to think that all someone who has dyslexia needs to do is work a lot more out of the left hemisphere and their problem will be solved. As simple as that solution may seem, it is riddled with unsolved problems. The first thing that needs to be taken into account is the understanding of where the balance needs to lie and how much more one needs to be going into the left hemisphere for direct information. When does it come to the point that you are overusing the left hemisphere and it ends up becoming more destructive than it is useful? The right hemisphere is still needed for creative material, yet when it is overused, it creates a host of other problems, along with having to deal with the uncertainty of the balance between the two hemispheres while reading or writing to the knowledge you had in the right hemisphere to when you force yourself to be working out of the left hemisphere.

Reading out loud is one of the key factors in managing my dyslexia and presents a very difficult problem to sort out, because of the side effect that accompanies it while even reading it from my own material. The most obvious point to address is when I am forced to work from the left hemisphere, which only deals with direct information. In my case it leaves a big void in the information that I have in the right hemisphere and inevitably sends me back to seeking all the additional knowledge that I have stored in the right hemisphere. This will reactivate the loop to reworking the balance between the hemispheres, and trying to regain the missing information, as well as sorting out a lot of fragmented information and also being left with the trick of being able to decipher it accurately, not only for oneself, but also to be far more accurate for someone else. Otherwise, the message I have in my head is greatly devalued by being useful to anybody except myself. There is a very big question mark as to where that balance needs to be, and it requires being able to work out the requirements of establishing the boundaries for it. Besides, there are also other concerning things I need to work on while I am doing self-editing, such as being able to recognise when I have made a mistake (I am now making some great improvements in being able to recognise them), as well as continually improving my ability to spell. I still have fear while reading out loud, where I may still be losing some of the knowledge which has taken me decades to achieve. However, I have now got the advantage of having been able to greatly reduce a large portion of the gap that I first had with the two hemispheres since I first started to read out loud. I have spent about six years working with reading out loud and still find that I need to be very vigilant of not overstepping the boundaries of the balance required between the left and right hemispheres, especially the left hemisphere, because there is still no guarantee that if I do not use the right hemisphere enough, I will end up losing the creative advantage that I already have. The good part is that the more I work on writing, the less time it takes to self-correct, and I am finding fewer mistakes that need sorting out. The fun part for me is that the standard of my grammar is definitely heading in a steep upward direction. I guess now is a good time to indulge in the semantics that I didn't care to pay much attention to when I first started, and why not! I can now see that this is very much doable, and it is definitely, and clearly worth all the work I have put into it. I will gladly keep on doing it. The fun part is now creeping into the writing big time and has drifted out of the category of appearing to be very difficult and into the category of being a great challenge.

After doing a lot of careful studying into the viewing the part of unwillingly reverted into reading right to left instead of left to right. I have found, that it comes down to reading at a slower pace and making sure to read the first word on the left side of the page, on each and every line. The good part is that I am no longer having that problem, because I have now continued to make the necessary adjustments that are required.

My rational reasoning for being prepared to make so many changes with my thoughts and ideas are not only due to the fragmentation I have in my head, although it does play a big part in my thought process. The other side to that thought process involves analysing the ideas from facts and evidence to things that I find make logical sense, and if it does not make logical sense, then I have a strong tendency to dismiss it.

I also steer clear of answers that do not line up to produce rational answers or some sort of substantial reasoning for the answers (such as being lucky or 'It magically happened') or a lot of the 'just' answers ('It just happened that way', 'It is just how it is', 'It's just old age', etc.). I am also a firm believer in the saying 'Nothing comes from nothing, nothing ever could'. So, I would rather put in my best educated evaluation than quit and stay with nothing, or if I do not come up with an answer that I believe is close to what it should be, maybe I will put it on hold until a suitable answer can be found. If I cannot find a suitable answer, then I need to settle for the fact that I don't know the answer.

The reason for my writing this next paragraph is that the reader can have a better understanding of how someone with dyslexia who evaluates it through a deeper pattern of thought, as opposed to someone who thinks in a shallow way. This story demonstrates what happens to someone who has shallow thoughts and does not answer a certain question because they fear that they will be left feeling foolish about asking the question. When someone is there who is able to supply them with the correct answer and when that person is afraid of asking it in case, they look foolish. Then they ended up being more foolish and remaining ignorant about the answer they first went about seeking. Here is a true story about the wrong reasoning for feeling foolish.

This event happened in one of the places where I used to work. There were 130 people who worked in that factory, which was going through the process of a change of company ownership. The current company owner arranged a meeting for the executives of the new company. A meeting was set up for the purpose of setting out the new conditions that the employees would be under when the changeover took place. Nearly everyone attended the executives' meeting, and there were a lot of people in that meeting who were nervous about asking questions due to the fact that they thought that they might appear foolish by not knowing the answer to what they believed a smart person should already know. I remember asking three important questions that needed answering. After the meeting was finished and the executives had left, a couple of my friends said to me that those were the questions that they were too scared to ask, and they continued to say, 'Didn't you feel foolish having to ask those questions?' The truth to the question of feeling foolish was that yes, I did feel a bit guilty about not having an answer to those questions, and maybe I should have known the answers. However, by not asking those questions meant that I would have avoided gaining wisdom and, would have created the foolishness which was feared in the first place.

My intellectual ability of learning grammar has greatly improved, with the majority of it being through the many hundreds of hours I spent working on improving my grammar, which has gone from being the equivalent of a seven-year-old's to that of someone who has just finished secondary school and who is doing well in grammar, should you be able to read past a declining, disarray of minor errors that have a tendency to reoccur every so often. Since my learning of grammar is ongoing, I am finding that my mistakes are dissipating at a fast rate with each article that I write. I have also compiled a folder with various methods to use for my checklist, which has a list from different types of spreadsheets. This starts with over **2,180** frequently misspelt words (a list which keeps gradually increasing), **41** pages of homophones, **16** pages of homographs, etc. The exciting part is that while I am working hard on grammar, I am left with the feeling of working with a fast pace of achievement and joy. When I look back to, say, **40** years ago and see where I was with my grammar and compare it to where I am now, then that bridge of improvement in my grammar looks like it would have been inconceivable to achieve; I would have lacked a way of ever seeing that it is possible to be able to bridge that gap. So, is it any wonder that I feel that I have been very well rewarded for my efforts, which continues to go on improving.

I have added a few extra stories into this article with the hope of giving the reader a better understanding of my different way of thinking and of the way that my life's journey has taken me.

The answer of where I need to be heading with my dyslexia relies on my being able to get the best results that I can, from what I work with in the two hemispheres, and even though I have been overusing the right hemisphere (the creative side), where I have got a lot of great results in my life's journey, I still need to work more out of the left hemisphere so that I can sort out the remaining grammatical errors that keep invading the ongoing written work. The good news about my reading out loud is that a great part of the fear that I first had a few years ago has now been greatly reduced. It is also rewarding to know that the grammatical errors in my work are reducing at a fast rate due to the vast amount of study that I do. I am now semi-retired, which allows me the luxury of being able to do a lot of grammatical study. The balance of management between the two hemispheres is the key to where I believe I need to be heading, and I need to be wary of the fact that I do not want to lose the advantages that I have gained in having dyslexia for so many years (1952–2014 and beyond).

It has now been a few years since I have set up the formulation of dyslexia, along with my personal journey of history while writing the chapter about dyslexia, and normally that would be where the article would have finished before being ready to write it. However, there was something that has compelled me to change my mind which happened when I was watching the Dr Phil show recently. The thing that I found confusing was that his statement at that time appeared to be wrong from my point of view. This clearly was not the case, because Dr Phil works with an experienced team of people who thoroughly check such important details before it goes on air. So, the thing that needed to be accomplished was what I was doing wrong. The subject he was discussing was the use of body language. When it comes to body language, and when one is trying to determine whether someone is telling the truth, you look to see which side of the head their eyes are looking at. If they are looking at the side of the brain where one collects direct information, then it is fair to assume that they are telling the truth; if they are looking at the creative side of the brain, then there is a good chance that they are not telling the truth, or it could be that they are checking to make sure that the details of their statement is correct.

Throughout my article, I have repeatedly stated that the direct information is in the left hemisphere and that the creative information is in the right hemisphere, which is correct. However, at first I found it very confusing when Dr Phil said that when you check to see if someone is not telling the truth, then you check to see if they are looking to the left. The part I got confused about was a part that I had completely forgotten about, and it is that the brain transfers information to the visual side (the eyes), which is not straight across, although it is the natural way that most people would expect. Instead it is transferred diagonally. Therefore, it is understandable that one may be fooled into believing that one of those statements is incorrect, when, in fact, they are both correct.

While writing my articles, I consider it important to try and strive for accuracy and to avoid misleading my readers. I feel that it is important that I do not confuse the readers with the material that I have written. One never knows whether the reader might use some of the material from my article and link it to something else that they may be writing about for their own project, whether it be written or verbal.

Chapter 15

My Medical Achievements
Where I have Succeeded and
where Others Have Failed

In writing this article about my medical problems, I am in two minds, and for the bigger part, being my 1ˢᵗ thought, there is valuable information in the article that shows why we do not need to always continue being the victim when it comes to medical problems that we are facing. Now here's the thing: I am fully aware of the fact that when we first get a medical problem, we are a victim. However, once we have identified the problem and have worked out what is causing the problem, we are usually able to work out a course of action or a way in which we wish to solve it.

Doctors are always very useful, and also, there are other medical professionals, such as acupuncturists, hypnotherapists, and physiotherapists. There are also medical procedures and tests that can give you accurate information *which is important to know*, and there are, more often than not, things we can do for ourselves. When I say that, I am not referring to a magic pill or an operation that will give a magic fix. Although don't get me wrong, there are times when you need to take a pill. I have also had a life-saving operation; when I had my appendix removed, and I firmly believe that when your appendix is in a bad state, it is the only course of action you can take if you like the idea of living. There are also other times when it is wise for you to take a tablet or have an operation in order to keep yourself in good health.

In regard to taking pills, well, I take a pill every day called Coumadin, which is better known by another tablet that has the same medical benefit, called warfarin (warfarin is the generic name,) Warfarin is sometimes used for rat poison, and that is because rats have little resistance to haemorrhaging. Humans have a moderate tolerance for haemorrhaging. The main difference between rats and humans taking warfarin is that rats are deliberately given an overdose of it, which is purposely set up to make their blood too thin in order to prevent their chance of surviving. The reason humans take warfarin, which also makes our blood thinner than normal, which is to prevent things like stroke and other diseases that can kill you or severely disrupt your health and to take advantage of using the thinner blood that slows the blood's ability to clot. Unlike the humble rat, we have regular INR blood tests done to make sure that our blood is not made too thin so we do not end up haemorrhaging. If we allow the blood to go back to being too thick, then we lose the added protection we need from certain illnesses that have bad results, such as stroke, heart attack, and other thrombotic diseases.

Now to the second part that I find concerning, which also comes with a note of caution. When it comes to sorting out medical problems, well, there is no safe haven to be working from, especially when it comes to wanting to work out things you can do for yourself. One of the biggest obstacles that one has to overcome is the fact that human beings have a habit of wanting to always be right even when they are wrong, and they will very often go to extraordinary (excessive) lengths in order for them to remain within the position of being right, even when the evidence and the facts show different results from which they are acting on. The more someone tries to ignore the facts and evidence, the more they turn into a person who is referred to as a right-fighter. In this case, I am concerned about a person who would try to work out their medical problem using the same method as me and who is a right-fighter.

My definition of a right-fighter is someone who puts being right ahead of everything else; getting a workable result is something that *gets buried* under the theory of their having to always be right. Being what one considers to be right because it is convenient for them is nowhere near as important as making or doing something that is workable from the facts and the evidence, which they have available for being right. If you find that last sentence to be a little confusing, well, this is what it means! Sometimes we think we are right when we are not, and this usually results in us throwing away any inconvenient answer that does not fit our expectations of being right or not requiring the answers to be rational or logical within our justification of being right. So, if we go on what works, based on the facts and evidence, as opposed to what we would like to think is right, then what we are really seeking has a far better chance of achieving a good result when we follow the facts and evidence that is available.

When I think of the right-fighter, I can't help thinking of what a mess they can end up in. When sometimes their first answer is wrong, and since they are a right-fighter, they are very often prepared to distort the logical reasoning of the evidence and facts just so they can stay with their own opinion of being right.

At this point, I would like to take the opportunity to tell you a little story which I have titled 'The Death of a Right-Fighter'. This is about a married couple named Ethel and Ron, who had been lifelong soulmates for a long time and who unquestionably loved each other very much. Ethel was someone who was normally good-hearted and considered herself always right, along with being quick in voicing her opinions, with very little or no thought of the effect that it may have on anybody except herself or anything around her. On the other hand, Ron was a much more caring person who had a deep love for Ethel, and his biggest concern was making Ethel happy. More often than not, he would substitute her thoughts and ideas for his own, regardless of whether she was right or wrong. As he saw it, 'Why not, if it would make her happy?'

One day, Ethel and Ron were walking down the street and decided that they needed to go across the road. A little further down the road was a pedestrian crossing with no traffic lights to direct them across it. Now here was where a concerning problem lay ahead of them. There was a big tall truck, parked illegally on the right-hand side of the pedestrian crossing; it was blocking their view of the right-hand side of the oncoming traffic. Ethel said to Ron, 'Come on, Ron, let's go across. They have to stop for us because we are walking across a pedestrian crossing, and we have the right of way.' This was one of the rare times when Ron disagreed with her and said, 'No! I think we need to find a better way to get across safely.' But before he could finish his sentence and say what he needed to say, Ethel charged across the intersection and got hit by a car that was coming down the road; where she and the driver that hit her were unable to see each other before the point of impact.

The result was that the car had no chance of stopping when someone suddenly appeared in front of it. Ron was left distraught by the fact that he had lost his beloved and now departed Ethel. Now he would never be able to go on any more walks with her—or do anything else with her for that matter, and as you may have noticed, he let her have the last say, of the last completed sentence, before she was killed while being right, the way a right-fighter always wants it to be. Unfortunately, in this case, she was _**dead** right_.

I do believe that when you depart from this world, there is not much satisfaction in discussing your case of being right with the angels or the devil, whichever the case may be; because whether you are right or wrong, dead is dead, and there is no coming back.

If you have trouble understanding it, ask Ron. I am sure he can fill you in on the sad, intimate details of how he must be feeling by now. After all, the only mistake he made was enabling Ethel to be a right-fighter and not pointing out soon enough the dangers that can occur because of it. Well, that last statement is not really true when you look at it more closely and when you follow good rational thinking that adds up to logical reasoning, because then you can't even blame him for that, when you address the fact that Ethel was a fully mature woman who needed to be completely responsible for her own actions and that Ron was not her keeper and was in no way responsible for her actions. You may have noticed that her righteous actions had left Ron with a lot of grief and sorrow that he did not deserve; he was left to deal with the loss of Ethel, the one that he loved and adored so much.

This is just one illustration of what can happen to someone who works out of the character of a right-fighter. The secret of wanting to stop being a right-fighter only requires two changes. The first one requires breaking away from the fear that you always need to be right. Being wrong about something is not necessarily a bad thing, provided something is learnt from it, and it plays a big part in the way we learn or improve on what we are doing. However, it is bad to make the same mistake twice and very bad to make the same mistake for a third time.

The second requirement for preventing yourself from being a right-fighter is that you cannot change what you do not acknowledge. So, if you are wrong and if you are not prepared to acknowledge it, then the default is that you will continue to believe you are right. What needs to be worked out is what is right, and what needs to be changed, and how to prevent making the same mistake again. It is not wise to seek making a mistake, but should it come your way, then the wise thing to do is to turn the mistake into a learning tool, and you will end up happier and wiser in the future.

I remember what a wise man once said to me. 'It is OK to make a mistake once. It is not OK to make the same mistake twice, and God help you if I catch you making the same mistake for a third time.'

I do not have an answer for everything, and the only things I can tell you are the achievements I have accomplished through being in tune with my body and thoughts. My belief is that the body talks to you when you are in trouble, and the trick here is to learn what it is saying. I guess it is almost the same thing that you have to do with babies who are unable to talk. It is important to be flexible should you choose to work on your own experiments and follow the evidence of what is happening along the way. Results are the things that count. Everything else may need to be modified or re-examined or, if necessary, worked from a different perspective.

Here is a list of the solutions to most of the medical problems that I have had through the course of my life, such as a severe case of *sweating hands and feet* (the sweating has now completely stopped), *spurs* (a hooked bone at the base of both heels; these are now both gone), *heart attack*, *arrhythmia* (irregular heartbeat), *stroke* (completely losing half of my eyesight in both eyes and then getting it all back again), *gout*, and *dental plaque* on my teeth.

Sweaty hands and feet. The first medical problem I was able to contain was one that developed as far back as I can remember, which would have been when I was about four or five. Who knows, it may have started before that period. But the one thing I am sure about, is that I did have a lot of trouble with my hands and feet sweating profusely (a hell of a lot). I do not have an accurate account of the amount of sweat I was losing when I was having trouble with it, but I believe that in 1 hour, I would have gone through about half a cupful to three-quarters of a cupful of sweat; and I believe it to be a good estimation of the sweat that I was losing.

Whenever I went to someone's place for a visit, I would often get a bit nervous, and this had a bad habit of starting up a case of sweaty hands and feet. It had the sweat reacting a bit like a tap which was fully turned on from the sweat glands, and as a consequence, it left me with a huge amount of sweat dripping from the hands and feet. It was like the hands and feet were trying to have a competition as to who could produce the most sweat at the expense of my embarrassment.

My mother believed that she had good intentions when we went to visit someone, and in her mind, by trying to constantly justify the point of announcing that I always had trouble with my hands and feet sweating. However, instead of helping the situation, it had the reverse effect, which left me annoyed at her raising such a private and embarrassing matter, which had now been brought to everyone's attention. This added attention was something that I would have much preferred to have been left out and put into the case of 'the less people who knew about it, the better'. Furthermore, if she had skipped the event of announcing about the sweaty hands and feet, then there is a good chance that the sweating episode might never have taken place. The announcement was guaranteed to cause me to tense up and trigger the sweating of my hands and feet, and if they were not sweating before that announcement, then they certainly were after it.

I guess that I shouldn't complain, because she did her best to try and fix the problem by sending me to several doctors. Their solution to the problem was, one would say that I needed to take more salt, and another one would say I should use less salt. When I was about 30 years of age, I managed to work out that the thing which triggered the sweating problem had nothing to do with salt, and I can prove it. However, the doctors did have a point, and that was that sweating creates the side effect of using a large amount of salt while all that sweating is taking place.

This is still reverting back to the time when I was 30 years of age and was when I saw an advert about acupuncture; I knew very little about it at the time. The only thing I knew about acupuncture was what I was told—that it is supposedly very good and has something to do with having a lot of needles being stuck into you. At this stage, I was very serious about wanting to get rid of this extremely embarrassing problem that I had been enduring for such a long time. Acupuncture was something that I had never tried before, coupled with my strong urge to resolve this problem, led me to be open to the fact that there was not much value in running around and complaining about the embarrassment of the problem when there was a possibility of being able to do something about it.

What I needed to do was find something that would give me a good opportunity to resolve the sweating problem. I remember that first day when I went to see the acupuncturist. With the benefit of hindsight, I have to say that I went there with a very bad attitude with my way of thinking, which was that it was not going to change anything, but at least I had tried everything I could. As it turned out, that day my hands and feet were producing a lot of sweat, and with the needles, he stopped the sweating dead in its tracks. Unfortunately, it only lasted for about a fortnight, and then the sweating would come back again. Each consultation cost $40, and this continued for about 7 sessions. After the seventh session, he said to me, 'Do you want to know what is causing your hands and feet to sweat so much?' Obviously, the answer was yes. However, the thing that did surprise me was his answer, which required such a simple solution and was something that I could do for myself. The answer was that I was not breathing enough oxygen. Now this was something I knew I could do, and I was truly excited about it, although he did not supply me with all the things that I needed to do in order to properly sort the problem out.

Whenever someone is stressed with tension, one of the first things they do is shorten their breathing pattern, which means that the body is getting less oxygen when it needs more. The stress can then be triggered by a chain reaction of events and is the body's warning signal about the need for more oxygen. I believe, from the evidence that I have collected, that the body does not only use the sweat in our bodies for cooling, but it also uses it as a warning sign of a lack of oxygen. By the way, after learning of this new-found information, the next time I found myself having sweaty hands and feet to which I found a good place to test out my new breathing exercise. If it could pass this test, then it could pass any test. This was at the table tennis tournaments where I competed and which took place each Friday night; it was also a place where I always had trouble with the sweating. To my delight, the deep breathing exercises worked within a couple of minutes of me doing the exercise, and the sweating of the hands and feet had completely stopped.

Increasing the amount of air, I breathed appeared to have been a simple problem to solve, and in the short term, it was. So, as I kept the short-term review in mind, every time the symptoms of the sweating problem occurred, all I needed to do were some deep breathing exercises, and it would resolve the sweating problem. Unfortunately, you are still only dealing with the short-term problem, and this solution does not do a good job of addressing the long-term problem, which is that your body keeps on reverting to the old breathing pattern of not supplying enough oxygen to your body to maintain a healthy condition. By far, the majority of our breathing is done through the involuntary muscles, and most of the time, we are not aware that we are breathing, thanks to the involuntary muscles. But we still have the ability to do our breathing through the voluntary muscles that allow us to override the involuntary pattern of breathing, and by repeatedly doing so, we can change the breathing pattern. This may still seem like a simple solution, but the problem is that the involuntary muscles have been working that pattern for so long that when you stop paying attention to your breathing for a long period (maybe the period is a few hours, a few weeks, a few months, or a few years), it eventually ends up going back to its old pattern again. If you change the pattern to the new pattern often enough, it will eventually spend more time responding to the new programme, and it is less likely for nervous tension to reactivate the situation of the old pattern of breathing to come back again.

Now that I have stopped the sweating of my hands and feet, the nervous tension is no longer applicable; I have now got back to having full control of the sweating problem that I used to have, and should anyone still be foolish enough to want to keep on embarrassing me by accusing me of still having that problem, then I have the ability to discredit their statement. An important lesson that I learnt from my father is that there is no point in getting upset when someone else is wrong about a statement being made about you, because it is now their problem; they are the ones who are wrong, and it is much better to rejoice about what you have got right, where you can leave all that stress behind you. Getting rid of that stress has a much higher value than being right or wrong, and getting a result is the most important thing to remember.

The longer the involuntary muscles have stayed within the old pattern, the more likely it is to return again. It's a bit like any old bad habit that you may have had for a long time. But even though the old pattern is resistant to change, I know that I am slowly winning the battle of changing it to a new pattern. Over the course of recent years, I have spent several hundreds of times working on changing the breathing pattern, which is constantly improving. I still need to work on improving my breathing pattern every so often for other problems that are created by the bad breathing habit (a lack of oxygen). When I look back at the situation of the sweaty hands and feet, some forty years further down the track, I feel pleased and contented that it is still working for me, and I have now eliminated the problem with the sweaty hands and feet.

Hepatitis A. This is an inflammation of the liver which is contagious and comes from an infectious virus. Symptoms of hepatitis A include having a mild pain in the entire part of the lower half of your back, and a problem which is a lot more devastating is that you are left feeling very weak.

First of all, hepatitis A is something that I had not even heard of before I contracted it, and I was taken by surprise to learn what it was and what it could do to me. The first piece of evidence that came to light was a mild pain in the lower back and it started off by feeling weaker than normal, and this proved to be a bad combination of problems to be working with. The reason is that the doctors, after hearing about a bad back and feeling weak, would only think that you are looking for a certificate so that you could have some time off work. Worse still, the doctors would lock themselves into that position and would not move from it. I guess the reason for that was that when I went to the surgery, I appeared to look perfectly healthy, and finding what was really wrong was not something that they were prepared to look into, although a simple blood test would have gone a long way into sorting out that problem.

The symptoms were a constant feeling of weakness and minor lower back pain. I went to several doctors about the problem, and none of them took me seriously; each one would offer me a work certificate and ask me how much time I needed to take off from work. The truth was that I was not looking to see how much time I could get off work. I was looking to see what was causing this abnormal problem. This problem lasted for a few weeks and continued to get worse and the most obvious symptom, was that I was constantly getting weaker. So, I decided to ditch the doctors (the general practitioners) and went to the Prince of Wales Hospital in Randwick.

At the Prince of Wales Hospital, I was given a blood test. I sat there and waited for the results, and from the results, it was confirmed that I had a severe case of hepatitis A, which is very contagious. The hospital was very quick in warning me about hepatitis A being very contagious, but unfortunately, they failed to present a lot of details which I needed to know. I was scared of letting any of my friends come near me, in fear of them catching this terrible disease. I was also feeling very weak and lived alone, and apart from the need to get a lot of rest, I was at a loss in knowing what to do. Other than that, I had to regularly go and get a blood test in order to see how I was progressing with this terrible disease. With every other medical problem that I previously had, I was able to fight it, but this one required me to succumb to it. Not being able to fight back made me feel very helpless, along with being extremely weak and left with a feeling that I had almost no control of the situation. I also felt very lonely in having to isolate myself from my friends in order to stop them from catching this horrible disease that I was suffering from. When I look back at all the health problems that I have had, I consider this one to be the worst. After about six weeks, I became well enough to go back to work.

One thing that happens when one has hepatitis A—and this is in accordance with medical records that I read—is that after 1 year, it is OK to resume drinking alcohol. Unfortunately for me, I got a rare strain of hepatitis A that prevents me from ever being able to take even a very small amount of alcohol, and I found out the hard way when it came to learning about my no longer being able to consume alcohol. Unfortunately for me, after the year was up, I tried two glasses of beer, and I found that the alcohol had created a return to severe liver problems again. This created the same symptoms that I had when I first had severe problems with hepatitis A, although the liver did return to functioning normally after I spent two days resting in bed. The story gets worse. After about another year since that time I tried alcohol, I had three cough lollies which contained a very small amount of alcohol in them. This proved to be not as safe as I believed it would be. One would have thought that because we are able to buy cough lollies over the counter to soothe a sore throat, they would be safe. However, this guarantee of safety no longer applies to me since I have developed a strong allergy to alcohol, and this statement is backed up by the symptoms I received, after taking the cough lollies, which was by spending three days resting in bed with severe liver problems.

The symptoms I get with the severe liver problems are that the lower part of my back aches all over and I am left feeling very weak—to the point that sometimes the energy needed just to make the bed becomes a major effort and I am forced to take a rest and split the making of the bed into two separate jobs. As desirable as it is to fight the condition of being weak, the fastest way to recovery is to rest rather than fight it; if you put up too much resistance against being weak, you stand a strong chance of doing a lot of damage to the liver and making the situation worse, along with a very strong chance of doing permanent damage to the liver due to the liver's weakened condition and inability to cope with the workload that it has.

I went and had a consultation with a liver specialist, who informed me that I had developed a severe allergy to alcohol taken internally after contracting a rare strain of hepatitis A. He also confirmed the importance of having to stay well clear of taking alcohol internally, and it is a strict rule that I have adhered to ever since. Staying free of alcohol requires me to be very vigilant when someone else is cooking the food that I eat, because I don't know if alcohol is one of the ingredients; and there is always a possibility that someone has used alcohol in cooking. It is also wise to be vigilant by staying clear of anything else that is harmful to the liver. After all, the liver is the source which the problem derives from in the first place. Something I have found to be unusual and proves that I am not allergic to alcohol when taken externally, is when I have an alcohol swab in the area where they are going to inject me with a needle, and end up by having no further problems after they used the swab.

In **1990**, at the age of **43**, I contracted hepatitis A. I am now **66** years old, and when I look back at my medical history and look at the problems that I have had—such as spurs in both my heels, a heart attack, arrhythmia, stroke, and gout—as surprising as it may appear to someone who has not gone through all these problems, the one which I found to be the worst to have was hepatitis A. Since my heart attack was severe and had the biggest chance of killing me, one would naturally think that, that was the worst medical condition that I have had. Well, that is not the way I see it. When I had the heart attack, I found that there was some pain but nothing that I could not handle. There was a way of curing it, and I was also gaining the position to a journey of a much more normal and healthier life as time progressed. If you die, then you die; but I was doing all I could to prevent that from happening. The best thing I could do in order to recover was avoid stress, and that was something that I did have control of. My cardiologist was surprised at the way I reacted to this situation, because of the lack of stress and concern that I was showing. He thought that I was in denial of what was happening and that I was far too happy for someone who had just had a severe heart attack. In reality, I was fully aware of my condition and felt that everything that needed to be done was being done, and if I started stressing myself out, then I was only going to make the matter worse. Let's simplify what stress is: Stress is when someone spends a lot of time concentrating on something that makes them feel miserable about themselves or on a bad experience that affects their life. The antidote to stress requires abandoning the concentration one has on misery and replacing it with dedication to the happy things that are happening in one's life. There are two sides to every coin: the head and the tail, the good and the bad. The most dominating story is the one which is considered to be the head. In my case, the possibility of dying from a heart attack is the head of the coin. If I die and have done everything that I could possibly do, then it is out of my control, and if I stress myself out, then it is only going to accelerate the journey to dying. The tail of the coin: I am alive, I am not in much pain, I have suffered much worse conditions when I had other medical problems. I have people who care about me and who are doing all they can to get me back to being healthy and well.

Getting back to the reason I consider hepatitis A to be the worst experience that I have gone through. The thing that bothered me most was the helplessness of having almost no control of it; apart from staying clear of alcohol, the only other thing I was able to do about it was have a very small amount of exercise, and the rest required having to succumb to the disease by lying helplessly in bed. As if that was not bad enough, I also needed to isolate myself from my friends because of my fear of them coming close to me and contracting this horrible disease. I didn't even ring them on the phone to let them know of the misery I was going through, and that was in case one of them decided to be the hero by deciding that it was a good idea to come over and see me, and encase they ended up by contracting the disease. All of my life I have had to fight battles and win battles in order to reach my next level of achievement, and this was the first battle where I had to succumb to it in order to win. When the spirit of battle is taken away from you, especially when you do not have the support of your friends, then the quest for the will to live also fades, although providing there is a light of hope by it gradually improving, then so is the hope to be able to return to some sort of a normal life.

Many years later; the allergy I had of taking alcohol, presented a fun side to it. What triggered the fun, is whenever the police pull me over for a random breathalyser test, and because of the fact that I have gone more than twenty years without any alcohol at all. So, when they pull me over, I take the liberty of informing them, that if the breathalyser shows even a trace of alcohol in it, then it is wrong. I believe that this is my time to relax and enjoy myself since they had the advantage of using my time.

Spurs in both heels. The symptom of spurs is a sharp pain in one or both of the heels in your feet. The pain you feel is caused by a small hook of bone that grows inside the base of the bone in the heel.

As usual, I found the library a resourceful place to do my research and found that the problem starts with the diet and believed that it was unlike gout, where there are several facts involved. I formed the opinion that only one food source was causing my problem, but in order for me to be sure that the food I was taking out of my diet was no longer affecting my body, I still needed to be wary of the possibility that another type of food could also be adding to the problem. This required my being prepared to spend maybe up to 3 weeks making certain that all traces had been cleared out of my system and clarifying whether it was the one causing the problem or not. As good fortune would have it, the first one I picked was potatoes, and I didn't need to wait 3 weeks. After 4 days of taking potatoes out of my diet, I found that most of the pain was gone, and after 6 days, all the pain was gone. It was a big relief from having that constant pain which I got in my heels every time they touched the ground. This seemed to be too simple. So, after a couple of more days, I tried one small potato, and within a few hours, I felt some of the pain coming back into my heels.

It wasn't until I was 55 years old that my body started showing the adverse effects of eating potatoes. I don't know why my body had changed to have that adverse effect, and I suspected that the problem may have been an extension of hepatitis A, a problem which causes the liver not to work as well as it used to. I also accept the fact that it is no longer smart for me to continue eating potatoes, because of the adverse effect of it activating spurs, which were in both my heels. So now I am left with two choices: to keep on eating potatoes and suffer a lot of pain in my heels, or to sacrifice the enjoyment of eating potatoes and have my heels free of pain. I chose the latter.

In regard to my history of eating potatoes, potatoes used to be the main source of my diet and were introduced into my diet when I was a child. I continued to enjoy eating them throughout most of my life. My thought on potatoes is that I used to love the idea of eating them, especially when they were roasted, and a big part of the excitement of eating potatoes came from the versatility of how they can be cooked. They can be boiled, roasted, fried (as in fried chips), served as hash browns, or presented as mashed potatoes, for which there are several good recipes.

In a relatively short period, I got past the want to enjoy eating my potatoes, and let's face it, there are other vegetables that can give me the same nutritional values; life still goes on in its own normal, healthy way (minus the potatoes). I am happy with the results and with being free of the spurs and the misery of pain, which the spurs used to give me.

Heart attack. On Saturday, 5/10/1996, at age 49, I had a heart attack and ended up in hospital for a few weeks.

A heart attack is when the wall of the arteries around the heart hardens, and the hardened area cracks and bleeds. The natural response of the body is to form a clot in order to stop the bleeding, thus creating a blockage of the artery and causing a heart attack. The hardening of the artery—or it can be the arteries—is a process that takes place over a long period. The long period is not referred to in hours or days or months; instead it takes about two years for it to form, or maybe longer, depending on the severity of the hardening of the artery or arteries.

I believe that the reason that I had the heart attack was that I was drinking 1–2 litres of full cream milk every day for 2 years. This lines up with both the time span and the damage which was done by the full cream milk. The sad part about it when it happened was that there was a lot of information which clearly showed me the dangers of taking full cream milk. This is one time I paid a very big price for *not* doing a fair and proper research on what I was being told when it came to the dangers of full cream milk. My distorted belief about the milk at the time, was when I placed far too much importance on the effect that the acid would have on me while I was working in the acid plant. I was overly concerned about how quickly the acid fumes damaged the weather balloon, which was in the factory. Unfortunately, I was also fully aware of how effective milk was in neutralising acid. One of the great things that I have learnt from my father is to learn from my mistakes. After having that heart attack, I got a wake-up call by letting me know that now was a good time to pay attention to that good advice my father gave me about learning from my mistakes.

In the introduction of this chapter, paragraphs 5–11, where I spent 7 paragraphs talking about a right-fighter, which is the very thing that I had become in regard to milk. There is also another story before a right-fighter that needs to be resolved, and that is the art of depersonalising the personal emotion that leads one to always want to be right. This requires viewing yourself as an object. So, the next time someone views themselves with an emotional problem that they find to be very close to them, try and see yourself as an object on the wall, where you can be everything, nothing, or something in between, although in fact, you are what the facts and the evidence align you to be.

So far, I have talked about what I believe caused the heart attack (by the way, my cardiologist also agreed that the excessive amount of full cream milk that I was taking at the time was the most likely cause of my heart attack). Now I wish to discuss what I believe triggered it. However, one needs to bear in mind that if I had continued down that path of drinking so much full cream milk, then as time progressed, so would the intensity of the damage which I was doing to the arteries, along with it resulting in being easier to trigger a heart attack. Doing the tough exercise that I was doing at the time accelerated the event, but it also prevented further damage from being done to my arteries by earlier waking me up to the damage which was being done at that point of time.

The work that I was doing at the time, just before I had my heart attack, was digging a trench at home for an electrical cable that needed to go into the ground. The trench started from the electrical meter box near the front of the house and went to the shed, which was situated at the back of the property. The electrical line that was being put into the trench was required for the electric light in my shed and the power points for the electrical appliances. The trench was 25 meters long, with a depth of 0.9 of a metre, which I dug with a mattock and a shovel (and sometimes there was need for a pick). At the time, I was working full-time with Ajax Chemicals, and the only time I had for digging the ditch which was on the weekends. I am not sure when I started it, although I believe that it would have been either the 14th or the 21st of September 1996. I remember that late in the afternoon, at the end of each day on the weekend, I would usually get a bit of soreness in my chest. Which I would put down to being sore muscles, because after I finished my evening meal, I would lie down and rest, and my chest would return to being free of pain.

On Saturday, 5/10/1996, when I had finished my work and had my meal, which was about 6 p.m., I lay down on the couch, and this time, the pain did not go away. Instead it continued to get worse. So, I said to my wife that something was not right, and I got her to drive me to Bankstown Hospital. My wife dropped me off before she parked the car, and I ventured into the emergency room while she found a place to park. The place was crowded, and the reason there were so many people was that on Saturday, many sportsmen have a tendency to get injured while playing their sport. I slowly walked to the front desk. The nurse said to me, 'Do you have chest pains?' and I nodded my head and said yes. I was then taken to the treatment room, where they did some testing on me by asking a lot of questions and putting anginine under my tongue. After doing a bit more testing, they rang up a cardiologist, who prescribed an injection that made the blood dangerously thin. I was instructed to lie still in bed, and a nurse had to keep watch over me at all times. At a much later time, the nurse who I first met in the emergency room explained that I looked grey and that it was her cue for understanding that I was in a lot of trouble. A couple of days later, I was transferred from Bankstown Hospital over to Royal Prince Alfred Hospital, and while I was undergoing angioplasty, it was revealed that I had a 90 per cent blockage in the right coronary artery. The angioplasty successfully repaired the damage done by the heart attack, and I was sent back to Bankstown Hospital until I was well enough to return home (I believe that the time I spent in the hospital was 4–6 weeks).

The loss of my physical abilities gave me a wake-up call. Because of the way my life may have been heading, there was a very real possibility that a lot of the physical activities I was previously able to do were going to be taken away from me. At the time, just after I got out of hospital when I had the heart attack, I was reduced to roughly 10 per cent of the physical capacity that I had before the heart attack. At first, I was only capable of walking about 20 steps before I needed to rest for a while in order to recover the energy that I had used. As time progressed, so did the distances that I could walk, and the time I needed for recovery ended up becoming much further apart. One of the most useful things that I found when I got home and when I went for walks were the small brick fences next to the footpath which I would walk on. I made a point of not being too proud to sit on them when I needed to rest. The most concerning thing at the time was how much of my physical capacity I would be able to regain safely. I was also aware of the fact that it was important not to overdo exercising, which could be adding to the damage by not letting one get enough rest when required.

The cardiologist arranged for me to have a few months of rehabilitation, which required me to be supervised on a programme with an exercise bicycle. This was very helpful because it gave me more confidence to safely push myself to exercise a bit harder than I would have (having the right procedure for doing the exercises is important,) and I worked harder than I normally would have, had the help from the rehabilitation not been available to me. The rehabilitation also included lectures from several specialists who dealt with the recovery of heart problems; they encouraged us to ask about any concerning questions that we may have had about our recovery.

Getting back to not knowing how much of my physical ability I would be losing, I knew that, at best, some loss of my physical ability was going to occur, even if you only take into account that some of the muscles around my heart had died when I had my heart attack and would never return. So, the trick here now was to work out ways to minimise the physical loss. With that in mind, I urgently needed to get a complete understanding of what my options were and to address the worst possible circumstance which could transpire. The first thing that came to mind was my losing a big chunk of my physical abilities. I did not appreciate the fact that 10 per cent was my starting point.

There was also another point that needed to be taken into consideration, and that was the fact that when you reach my age, you will age naturally and gradually lose some of that physical ability that you once had. As a result of that, it now became very important for me to be able to read and write with a good understanding of grammar, because I believe that there is a possibility of it being the only option left available to me. With that in mind and within a short period, I went back to learning grammar and writing at a vigorous pace, similar to the one I had at school. As time progressed, so did the pace that I was working at to improve my grammar. However, not all parts of the enthusiasm to my journey ran smoothly. I had dyslexia, which meant that I needed to be the teacher and the pupil at the same time, and I also had to deal with the common mistakes that dyslexics make. After about 9 months, the physical side of me settled down to where I remained to losing only about 10–15 per cent of my physical ability. However, I ended up losing about 40 per cent of my arm movement when it came to making big movements around the arm, but I was almost back to normal with small arm movements.

Arrhythmia. Not everything went smoothly after I had my heart attack. I returned to hospital five times with an irregular heartbeat (arrhythmia, or to be more precise, in my case, atrial fibrillations).

I got arrhythmia at the same time that I had my heart attack. Unfortunately, it came as a package deal in 1996. The technical name for my arrhythmia is atrial fibrillations. *Arrhythmia* refers to all the different parts of the heart that have irregular heartbeats, and it is the term that most people are more familiar with. *Atria* refers to the top part of the heart, and *fibrillations* refer to irregular heartbeats. No matter what part of the heart creates an irregular beat, it is always going to stand a good chance of creating blood clots in the bloodstream, which can cause serious problems with your health. I ended up returning to hospital 5 times for the treatment

181

of arrhythmia problems. I made quite a few visits to my cardiologist after being discharged from hospital and remember him telling me that when someone has had a severe heart attack like the one that I just had (90 per cent blockage to the right coronary artery), then they only last about 1 year. After I got past that year, I gloated to him that I got past that 1st year. He then said, 'Do you know what? Most people who survive that first year, nearly all of them die within the second year.' Well, I guess that the cardiologist was about 30 years older than me, and I have now gone 22 years past his last deadline. If he were alive today, he would be about 100 years old, and I truly believe that I have outlived him.

There was a time when I asked my cardiologist what causes my arrhythmia, and he said they do not rightly know. I underwent several tests that they gave me in order to see what they could do about it. Unfortunately, there was nothing that they came up with that gave me any satisfactory results, and I felt that one of the tablets they were giving me was making the situation worse. The cardiologist suggested that they put a pacemaker in me and a defibrillator. I declined both of them. The reason I declined them was that they required taking a lot more tablets, and they often had a lot of problems that one needed to deal with after having the operation and that don't always have satisfactory results.

One thing I put down to my dyslexia is that, people who have dyslexia work a lot more in the creative side of the brain than people without dyslexia, which sometimes proves to be a blessing and at other times proves to be a curse. Another way to put it is that it sometimes has big advantages to it, and there are times when you are confronted with some big disadvantages while writing. The one thing I constantly work on is when I am not able to find an answer to a problem that I am trying to solve and knowing that I am always going to need to have some sort of an answer to work with. This means that it is also important for me to bear in mind that the knowledge I am working with may need to be modified at any time, should the facts and evidence require adjustment. One thing I do know for sure is that nothing comes from nothing, and nothing ever can. So, I now need to do some serious investigative work in order to deal with the evidence and the facts of the problem at hand.

After going through the thoughts in my head about everything that had happened with the arrhythmia, I came up with the idea that the problem was in the breathing. This was because, in the past, when I had other medical problems that I couldn't work out, it quite often had a strong chance of being connected to the bad breathing problems that I have had throughout my life, and the more I studied this case, the more the evidence indicated it to be related to a breathing problem. I knew when I rejected the pacemaker and the defibrillator that what I was doing was not without risk, but it was a risk that I was prepared to take. I felt that the balance lay in the importance of the *quality of life* that I was able to have, which is very important to me, *not the quantity*. The risk of not taking what was being offered to me could have led to the possibility of serious health problems; the worst case that could transpire was that I would end up dead.

The next thing I did was to work on increasing the amount of oxygen that I needed to be putting into my lungs, as well as slowing down the breathing pattern at the same time; the short, fast breathing pattern was a big part of the problem that triggered the arrhythmia attacks. Unfortunately, slowing down the breathing pattern sometimes triggered panic attacks in the early stages of the exercise. In order to stop the reoccurring of the panic attacks, I had to temporary reduce the amount of slowing down that I did with the exercise; otherwise, the panic attacks would continue to occur. The key to this problem relied on being persistent with the number of times I did the exercise of breathing slower and deeper at the same time; it was important to be wary should any more of the early symptoms of panicking start to reoccur. I have now got to the stage where I do not have any more trouble with panic attacks.

After getting the panic attacks under control, I found that the arrhythmia problem had improved, but still, with the long term in mind, a lot more work needed to be done in order to get my heartbeat to be more constant so that I could sustain a regular pattern. The job of getting a good, steady beat was still a long way from being over, and all I had achieved so far was getting past the first stage. I continued dealing with the need for increasing the amount of oxygen I was putting into my lungs, in order to retain a steady rhythmic beat for my heart, by using two methods at the same time.

The first thing I needed to do was clear my bronchial tubes of any unnecessary mucus that was causing partial blockage. It is difficult to get air into the lungs when it is partially blocked, and it was a difficulty that needed to be removed. This required blowing my nose and clearing my throat, and sometimes this would require using a Vicks Inhaler. The inhaler would break up the mucus, so a clearer passage of air would go through the bronchial tubes. While on the subject of clearing mucus from the bronchial tubes, I feel that it is important to point out that while clearing out what is causing any partial blockage with the Vicks Inhaler, which is good for getting rid of excessive blockage when the mucus is sometimes hard to remove, I also believe that using it should be done sparingly and that blowing your nose with a tissue should be your first option. After all, there is an important reason for having a *thin* coating of mucus on the bronchial tubes at all times; otherwise, you will run into a host of other medical problems.

The second solution to this problem was to work out a way of improving the amount of oxygen I needed to get into my lungs. On this second leg of the journey, I thought that I had done a good job in figuring out how I was going to do that exercise—by going to one of the variety stores at the shopping mall and buying 25 party balloons for $2. The way I used the balloons was by blowing a balloon up as much as I could with one single breath, blocking the air from coming out of the balloon, and holding it in front of me to see how big I was able to make it. Then I would take all the air out of the balloon and blow it up again, trying to make it bigger than I had made it the time before. I would repeat this up to about ten times. This resulted in three things happening: it forced me to use the whole of my lungs and not only the top part of my lungs like most people have a tendency to do; it helped create a better breathing pattern, which also required me to use the whole of my lungs; and at the same time, it strengthened my lungs. In order for this method to be successful, I needed to do it often so that I could improve the new breathing pattern.

There were symptoms of warning, which I needed to pay attention too, that would let me know that I needed to get more oxygen into my lungs. The first warning was numbness in the fingers. A much more severe warning came when I would perspire and when the environment that I was in, was not one of feeling hot, along with having no good reason for me to be perspiring. This would usually take place when I woke up from my nightly sleep, and it was an urgent warning sign that I urgently needed to get more oxygen into my body. Fortunately, it was one of the things that I seldom had to deal with and is no longer occurring. Controlling my breathing pattern when I was asleep proved to be a hard task to deal with, but the way that I overcame it was, whenever I woke up, I would check and see if I was having any trouble with numbness in my fingers. Also, I would allow myself to wake up easily by trying not to sleep too soundly. This required getting up in the early hours of the morning; it could be 1 o'clock or 2 o'clock in the morning—it did not matter what the time was. It only meant that it was time to do something about my breathing. This required me to get out of bed, and go into the living room, and to sit down on a chair. Then I needed to go through the procedure of clearing my bronchial tubes and doing my breathing exercises of blowing up a balloon. A little warning regarding the balloons: After about the 40th or 50th times that you blow up the balloon, it will end up exploding, but this does not cause any harm, apart from making a loud noise and causing ripped pieces of the balloon to scatter. I am now roughly 17 years further down the track since I first started that procedure, and I have very little trouble with my arrhythmia and no more trouble with numbness in my fingers.

The only time I have trouble with the arrhythmia now is when I need to do a strenuous exercise. My definition of a strenuous exercise, since I have had my heart attack, mainly relates to big movements around the chest area, and the further the exercise is from the heart, the greater the reduction of stress is. I am now very wary of stress to the heart, which I take a lot of care to avoid, and consider myself to be doing very well with the care I take while looking after my heart. I am 66 years of age, and I am still working as a professional handyman, doing gardening, mowing lawns, doing carpentry work, doing small plumbing jobs, and sometimes chopping down small trees to below ground level, as well as slowing down to be semi-retired.

The only tablets I take now are one tablet for thinning my blood and half of one tablet to slow my heart down each night. Thinning the blood prevents blood from easily clotting, and the half tablet slows the heartbeat down and prevents the heart from beating irregularly. These are also safeguards that I have against another stroke. There is also another important reason I take this half tablet, and that is so I do not have to deal with the battle for the need to wake up in the early hours of the morning to maintain a slower and deeper breathing pattern that prevents arrhythmia attacks from starting up at a time when I need to be sleeping.

Stroke. In 2006, sometime in September, I had a stroke. There are two ways that you can have a stroke. The majority of strokes are caused by a blood clot in a blood vessel which is in the brain or lungs, and the other way that happens less frequently is through a blood vessel rupturing in the brain (haemorrhaging).

My stroke was caused by a blood clot in the brain. A stroke can affect you in many ways, depending on where it takes place—in the brain or in the lungs. The way mine affected me was that I lost half of my vision on the right temple side and half of my vision on the left nasal side. I worked out a way to get all my eyesight back after the doctor that I had, gave up on me.

The work I was doing at the time was as an acid plant operator, which required me too often use the forklift for the jobs I needed to do. The site was big, half a kilometre long and a little bit less than a quarter of its length wide. One day, when I was driving the forklift, I found myself having trouble focusing my vision; everything seemed to get a bit out of focus from time to time. When I came back from picking up a load, due to my bad focusing, I accidentally ran into the centre of the back of a big semi-trailer truck with the fork lift; I simply did not see it. I know that it is hard to believe that I could run into the back of a truck when I had a clear path between us, but nevertheless, that is how the accident occurred. I was only going slowly at the time due to my inability to clearly focus. The damage was minimal, so I apologised to the truck driver and headed to the office to explain the accident to the manager.

When I got inside the office, I found the manager and told him about the accident. I also included the fact that something was wrong and that I did not know what it was. The manager said to me that he would provide me with a taxi so that I could go home and see my local doctor, so that the doctor could work out what was wrong. Unfortunately for the company, it required travelling a 30-kilometre journey, for which the company paid the taxi fare. When I got to the doctor, I told him what had happened. He then did a hand test by running his hand across my face to see what vision I had, and it was clear to him that I had a blind spot. So, he sent me to see an optician for a *half-field test*.

A field test involves a piece of equipment that has a big dish that you look into. While you are looking inside the dish using one eye at a time, a laser puts a small lighted dot on the dish and repeatedly places it on different places on the dish. Each time you recognise where the lighted dot is, you push a button which lets the computer know that you have seen the lighted dot, and it repeats the process until it has covered the whole surface of the dish. Then it analyses how much of the eyesight may be missing, should that be the case. Fortunately for me, the optician would only follow the correct procedure, which required testing both eyes, and would not only test one eye like the doctor had requested in his written instructions, so, I agreed to the full field test. When I returned to the doctor, I gave him the results of the field test, and after reading the results, he became very angry with me, stating that I had gone against his instructions. He had only ordered a half-field test, and I had gone ahead and had a full-field test done. I found this response disrespectful and extremely excessive in the situation we were dealing with. First of all, it was not up to me to sort out the type of field test that was to be given. This was a decision for the optician, and with the benefit of hindsight, it turned out to be the correct one, because I had equal damage done by being half blind in both eyes, not just in one eye like the doctor thought. At that point of time, I was not concerned with whether he had or hadn't made a mistake; the only things that I was concerned with, was what permanent damage that may have accrued and what damage was still being done, as well as what could be done in order to repair the current problem.

He then took out my medical records and ran me down through everything he could find in it and also invented a few more of his own. He then told me that I had *permanently* lost half of my eyesight and that the only difference was that I would recognise where the blind spot was. I was astonished by the fact that the doctor refused to learn from his mistake and was going around trying to save a face that clearly was not worth saving. His stating that I had permanently lost half of my eyesight in both eyes meant that he had given up on me and left with having no way of being cured. Fortunately for me, he was wrong, and I did not believe him.

I was very vulnerable at this stage; this had me referring to a valuable lesson that I learnt in the past, and that was to spend as little time as possible being a victim. That came along with the fact that there was no time left for being angry and that I had a much bigger job that needed to be done urgently. My best possible outcome depended on taking back control of what was going on. Even though I did not tell my doctor, in my mind I did not accept that my damage was permanent, because I had watched a programme on television called *Catalyst*, which spoke about the brain being able to remap itself. This seemed a lot more palatable than sitting around and being a victim who was going to remain half blind for the rest of my life. So, I urgently concentrated on thinking of ways to make this remapping of the brain, in accordance with what I had seen on the *Catalyst* programme. The *Catalyst* programme gave a good demonstration on remapping the brain, and as good fortune would have it (let's face it, I already had enough of the bad fortune), I found a good exercise which happened to be a workable thing that I could do.

When I got home after having that rough ordeal and while I was

---

waiting for my evening meal, I turned the TV on with the remote control, and within a short period, I sat down and decided that I needed to use it again. When I looked back at the table in order to pick it up again from where I had just put it, I found myself astonished by the fact that I could not see the remote control anywhere on the table, and being fully aware that I had just put it there and that there was no obstruction that could prevent my seeing it from where I was sitting. It should have been easy to see, and I knew for certain that it had not fallen off the table. This gave me the inspiration to use this situation as an exercise for the remapping of my brain. I worked out that it was imperative that I find the remote control, regardless of how long it would take me to find it. So, the first time that I started looking for it took **10–15** minutes. I don't really know how long it took, but it was a long time before I found it. I also talked to my brain like it was a second person and kept on saying that it was imperative to find the remote control and that we must find a way to find it. I played this little game **10–15** times a day, every day, for the next three weeks, until I could find the remote control straight away. I did not need to go and have a second field test to know that I had won the battle with the stroke, although I did go back to prove that I had got my eyesight back. I had another full-field test done, and it showed that I had got *all my eyesight* back again.

The event of actually having the stroke and regaining all my eyesight was also confirmed by my neurologist, who I had a consultation with. This consultation took place three weeks after I had the stroke. His assessment was mainly reviewed by the evidence of the MRI scan and the two field tests that were done on me at the time I had the stroke. He also informed me that I had an **80** per cent chance of having another stroke if I did not use a blood thinner such as warfarin or Coumadin and that it would be reduced to about a **2** per cent chance of another stroke if I did take a blood thinner. Coumadin or warfarin are renowned blood thinners that have certain side effects that need to be managed on a regular basis. In my case, I am satisfied that the Coumadin I am taking is worth putting up with, because it most certainly outweighs the risk of not taking it.

In regard to the stroke, the reason I have my blood kept thinner is that I had a stroke and lost half of my eyesight in both eyes; this is what I am using for protection against another stroke. It also deals with other potential clots that may form, which, in my case, is triggered by arrhythmia. An arrhythmia attack can occur at any time, and it can even occur without my knowing that the arrythmia is occurring. The danger I have to watch out for is when an arrhythmia attack starts, which is unfortunately an event that sets the heart beating at a *fast and irregular pace*, which can cause clotting, therefore causing another stroke.

Having a stroke was something that I was able to reverse the first time, and I have no intention of running on the theory that I can keep on doing that forever and a day. The reason I am not prepared to take the risk of having another stroke is that the stakes are too high which are at the cost of being able to sustain a good, healthy life. Another thing that I am still very wary of is that I was able to remap the brain for the first time by repeatedly executing a simple exercise 10–15 times a day, every day, for three weeks. This also means that I am at the extreme edge, to the point of being a pioneer in regard to the remapping of the brain, and there are too many things that I do not know, such as: How many times can the brain be remapped? How many routes may already be blocked? How many routes are still left available to use that will do the same job? Does it keep dropping in efficiency each time a new route is used? And if the stroke attacks a different part of the brain, will I still be able to find another suitable exercise to remap the brain? I think it is always important to weigh the benefits versus the risk, and in this case, the benefits of having my blood kept in a thinner state certainly outweighed the risk of not having it thinned. In my studies, I have found in a lot of cases that after the brain has been remapped, it is usually slightly less efficient than it was before it was remapped, and there are often small differences in the results.

Something that I have noticed after recovering from my stroke is that I did lose a small part of my peripheral vision. I noticed that when I drive my car in reverse, that I don't do it as well as I used too, due to the partially diminished ability of my peripheral vision; however, I have recently noticed that my peripheral vision is slowly improving over time.

Gout. For those who are not aware of what gout is, well, here is a brief description of it: Gout is a condition which is caused by an excessive amount of uric acid in the blood, which creates crystals that form in the joints of your body. The crystals are sharp and pointed, and they dig into the flesh and cause severe pain. These crystals normally form in the lower joints, very often in the first joint of the big toe or in the ankle, although there is a small chance that they can form in any of the joints in our anatomy.

I have suffered from gout and have now gone many years free of it, and I firmly believe that I now have it under control, although going through many more years of staying free of it is the only way to completely confirm it.

There was one time when I had gout so severe that the pain caused by the crystals forced me into using crutches for three weeks. Even though I got some relief by using the crutches, the pain still remained severe, mainly when I moved the infected joint, and I was not capable of moving around without the crutches. It may not seem to be desirable to move the infected joint when you are feeling so much pain, but the sad part is that the crystals cause the pain to become more severe if you don't move the infected area enough. While I am venturing on the line of sadness, another problem that arises, which is more often than not, is that when gout attacks the first joint of your big toe, your foot ends up becoming so sensitive that even the sheet touching your foot while you are lying in bed adds to the pain; this is a common symptom for someone who is suffering from gout.

There is a tablet that you can take for gout that gives you some relief, although it comes at a price, with a side effect that takes place within a day or two. The factor of when it happens is directly related to how many tablets you take per day. You will end up having a continuous case of severe diarrhoea, and the number of tablets you take each day also determines the severity of the diarrhoea.

The symptoms that announce that you have gout include the continuous pricking you get from the sharp crystals each time there is any movement in the infected area. They have a habit of creating their own bit of fun by creating an inflammation that causes the lower part of your leg to swell, and in order to get the swelling to go down, you have to keep the leg elevated for a few hours at a time. It is important to get the swelling down; otherwise, if you leave it swollen for too long, it can end up causing some permanent damage in the swollen area. The reduction of the swelling will also give you some relief from the pain once the swelling goes down, "with *some*", being the operative word in regard to the relief of pain. The severity, as well as how long you have gout, varies each time you get it, but the one thing that stays constant is that you get a considerable amount of pain. Gout usually lasts up to about three weeks, although I do know someone who had it for six weeks. I guess she didn't make the right adjustment to her diet in order to make it go away.

I started my research on gout sometime after 2006, when I first started getting problems with gout. Not being keen on being someone who had to take medicine of any kind unless I find it absolutely necessary to do so, led me to wanting to apply the only other solution I had available to me in order to beat this gout, which was to see *what I could do about it* and to avoid relying on tablets. To achieve that goal also meant doing a lot of research on gout so that I could find some answers.

The library is a resourceful place for information, so I went there to see what I could find about gout. Fortunately for me, all the evidence relating to the problem kept leading back to diet. This strongly proved to be in my favour; I couldn't have asked for a better platform to be working from, because it put the solution in the very area that I had full control of, which was the diet. However, this was by no means a simple thing to fix. The most disappointing thing I had to deal with was the fact that in order for me to do any experiments, I needed to be suffering from gout. Otherwise, I had no way of knowing how the things I was changing in my diet was responding to the gout. Since this was an experiment that required travelling through a big field of pain, I decided that the quickest way to do it was by taking the personal element out of it. In other words, I did not see myself through the eyes of a victim, and instead I chose to look at myself as if understanding from the position of a second person; it eliminates the emotions that have a tendency of getting in the way of my being able to sort what I can establish from the experiment, in regard to whether the pain has increased or the intensity of the pain has been reduced due to the food I add or take out of my diet.

I was not happy with the doctor's solution for treating gout and was trapped into having to follow his plan because I didn't have a better plan to work with. Well, to be quite honest about it, I had no second plan at that point, but felt that I badly needed one. My alternative plan was to work on the problem of the excessive amount of uric acid that was going into my bloodstream instead of working on dealing with the symptom; I needed to find out why this monster was giving me so much grief and, even more importantly, find out what I could do about it.

One thing that concerned me about what the doctors were telling me was that they considered uric acid to be the bad guy. If we do not have uric acid in our body, we will die.

Let's have a look at the doctor's version of uric acid being the bad guy. If we eliminate all the things that can make uric acid, we will end up dying due to a lack of important ingredients needed for the body. What is required is to weaken the structure of the ingredients needed to make those unnatural crystals that are forming in the body. My thought was that there are certain types of foods which are needed to create the crystals, and my mission was to reduce the foods that are essential for the crystals to form, which I believed was a combination of several things.

I have also changed my version, from saying that the only bad guy that needs to be worked on is uric acid, to saying that the crystals are the bad guy and that uric acid is an important part of the catalyst for the crystals, along with it being what causes the anatomy—or to be more precise, the liver or the kidneys (or more than likely, both of them)—to distribute excessive amounts of uric acid to the bloodstream. The uric acid is administered by the liver and the kidneys, and then it is divided into three different parts of the body: the bloodstream, the bowel motion, and the urine tract.

The problem with solely dealing with reducing the amount of uric acid in the body is that it is loosely represented and does not make allowances for the other two areas that the uric acid is required to be in. It also does not prevent the fact that should you be successful in doing so, that it is only going to reduce it from the bloodstream; you would have no way of knowing how the reduction of uric acid would be redistributed.

Now it becomes more important to concentrate on looking for what is causing the problem and only pay minor attention to the symptoms; the symptoms may give the appearance that you are sorting the problem out, or it may very well be the case that all you need to do is work out a way to reduce the amount of uric acid that the body can make. Personally, I doubt it, because if it were as simple as that, a medical cure would be clearly understood and easily available.

While reading the books, I found out that the body does not necessarily need to have acid in order to make uric acid, although I believe that it is its first choice when doing so. The way I attacked the problem was by trying certain foods and waiting about 24 hours to see how they affected me. Obviously, I did not only eat one type of food—for example, only eating bananas. I still needed to have variety in the food I was eating, because imbalance of the diet appeared to be the leading cause of gout; and a balanced diet must remain a high priority. The problem I needed to deal with in regard to the dietary problem was the imbalance of the uric acid that is distributed from the liver and the kidneys, and the three ways by which it is distributed. One thing I know for sure is that I had too much uric acid flowing in the bloodstream, and I was not prepared to go along with the theory that all I needed to do was reduce the uric acid in my body.

I believe sorting the balance of the diet was more than likely where the bigger part of the answer lay, along with finding out why the body felt it necessary to put an excessive amount of uric acid in the bloodstream and why it was not directing it more to the other two places that it could be directing it to. However, those other two places were only a subsidiary concern.

I have done a lot of personal experiments with my diet while looking for the answer. The answer, I believe, lies in the liver not being able to cope with the workload that it has to deal with and is requiring assistance. Making the dietary balance better will contribute to lowering the workload. Experimenting with gout is not an easy task to perform, because it requires having to spend a lot of time working through a field of pain and having to wait about 24 hours—or sometimes longer—to get some sort of result from each experiment.

However, after saying that, and after a few times of having gout, I have noticed that *before you get gout,* there is usually a warning sign, which is a bit of stiffness in the lower part of the leg. That is providing that there is no other good reason for it to be stiff, as well as having established that you already have a history of gout; otherwise, the stiffness may have been caused by some other problem. Should you choose to ignore the warning signs by not making the necessary adjustments to your diet, then you stand a very good chance of having to take on the gout again, usually by the next day or the day after. The first thing I looked at as the culprit of the symptom was a slight discomfort and, on this occasion, was stiffness in one of my ankles' and the only fruit that I had eaten in the last 8 hours was a pear, which made it easy to identify the culprit. Should I have eaten more than 1 type of fruit in the last 8 hours. Then it would require me to stop eating all those fruits and testing them one by one. So far only the pears are the one to be causing aggravating stiffness around the lower leg. Unfortunately, pears are a fruit that I like a lot, so, from now on I will need to eat them very sparingly or end up having to avoid them altogether.

While I have been studying gout, I have found it important to pay attention to making my best effort into making sure that I do not end up creating other problems as a result of solving the first one. I have found that the best way to avoid that situation is by looking at the worst possible risk that could transpire from the action I was taking and then comparing it with the best possible benefits that could be gained and sorting out where the balance lay.

The dietary things I have worked on while trying to maintain a good healthy balanced diet, that will make the workload of the liver and kidneys easier, came from one of the books I have read which claimed to be helpful in curing gout, and they are red or purple varieties of fruit, which I am very keen on. These are blackberries, cherries, blueberries, and strawberries, and the good part is that they can be eaten as canned or fresh fruit, although the canned fruit has a drawback of having added sugar. So far, while experimenting on these red and purple fruits, I have found that there is no further increase in pain after eating them, and I believe that the information is correct. However, I also believe that a balance still needs to be maintained, and should you go on eating them in excess, then it is going to leave you with a strong possibility of having some side effect or even a possibility of having the reverse effect of what it first had on your gout. The one type of food that I have found that quickly adds to the pain is citrus fruit. So far, the changes to my diet involve accepting that red fruits are good for me, providing I don't eat them in excess. Citrus fruits have quickly proven to increase the pain after I eat them, and I have excluded them from my diet, along with pears.

While doing my experiments on gout, I ventured into the concerns about the acid which forms in the mouth. I am still not sure as to what type of acid it is that forms in the mouth, and I have no intention of doing a lot of research to find the different names of the acid or acids that accumulate along the journey of the bronchial tubes while entering and being discharged from the mouth. The thing that concerns me is that the acid in the mouth has a strong possibility of going back into the bloodstream, and I also believe that it has a very good chance of turning into uric acid, which ends up in the bloodstream. The acid in the mouth is something I have a way of controlling and it is also the body's way of cleaning the mouth and teeth, and it is important to be sure not to cause the neutralising of the acid in your mouth to reach the point where it is stopping the acid for long periods at a time. Instead-try and get the balance of acid to a satisfactory level. After all, it does have a good purpose for being there in the first place.

The method I use for neutralising the acid requires putting half a mouthful of milk in my mouth and swirling it around for a minute or two. If it is low-fat milk, then just drink it when you are finished. If it is full cream milk, then it may pay to spit it out when you are finished; otherwise, you may end up with a cholesterol problem further down the track. My belief is that when some of the acid forms in your mouth, it may end up being a contributing factor to gout when it becomes excessive, and it needs to be controlled. I identify the strength of the acid by the taste in my mouth.

The next thing I need to deal with are the things that are harmful to the liver or that give the liver an excessive amount of work to do. Most people who have gout are overweight, which extends the problem of making the liver have an urgent need to work overtime due to the burden of the excessive weight. The excess weight also creates another problem, which is that the uric acid stores itself in the fat cells. This is one of the ways that it ends up returning to the dreaded excessive amount of uric acid in the bloodstream. So now keeping your weight at a healthy level is a lot more important. There is another thing that ends up being harmful to the liver, and for some people, they may find it not so easy to deal with. That is alcohol, which is addictive. Let's face it, even small doses of alcohol can add strain to the liver, and the bigger the level of alcohol that is consumed, the bigger the strain will be on your liver. You also need to stay clear of any other substance that can give your liver a hard time.

Dental plaque. This is an unwanted hard coating that builds up on your teeth. It was an odd way how I came about fixing this problem of plaque on my teeth. As a matter of fact, it came from the study I was doing on gout. While I was working on trying to slow down the amount of acid that was forming in my mouth, I noticed that one of the side-effects was that it fixed the problem that I was having with the plaque on my teeth.

Getting the dentist to clean the plaque off my teeth had turned into an annual event over the course of many years, and each time the dentist needed to clean the plaque off my teeth, they would always find a lot of plaque that needed to be taken off and always made a point of telling me so. I thought that since I had that great side effect from dealing with gout, I would take this study a bit further. That was because not only did the plaque stop building up on my teeth, but it also slowly came off. The only thing that I did differently, between when I had trouble with the excessive amount of plaque on my teeth and now being almost free of plaque, was neutralising the acid in my mouth.

I already had a head start in dealing with some of the dental problems, because I knew, from when I was a child at school, that milk is always good for your teeth. I say that because I was told by one of the football coaches that if you ever get a tooth knocked out, you shouldn't throw it away; it can be saved if you wrap it in a clean piece of gauze and leave it soaking in cool milk and place it inside a clean container. This also requires getting it to a dentist within a few hours from when it gets knocked out. They can usually save the tooth by putting it back in your mouth. I am now almost free of plaque on my teeth.

I haven't done a lot of research while dealing with the plaque that I used to get on my teeth, apart from the research I did while working on solving the gout problem, and the neutralising of the acid in the mouth is the only clear evidence I have that shows the result of getting rid of the plaque on my teeth. I have now gone 8 years without plaque build-up, as well as having stopped my gum line from receding. I have also had two teeth that were starting to come a bit loose that have gone back to being firm again. All those good results gave me the satisfaction that I had done enough in researching on plaque.

This is my self-analysis of what happened when I stopped the plaque. The acid around your teeth is most harmful to the teeth, when the moisture has dried up around them, and this is obvious when you find you have a dry mouth. It also could be that the mouth is producing too much acid even though the teeth are being properly cleaned. Cleaning the teeth properly is very important, but if your body is producing too much acid in your mouth, despite your best effort to keep them clean. I believe that you need to find a way of neutralising some of the acid. Remember that it is important to make sure that you don't try to eliminate all the acid in your mouth, because your teeth are always going to need a small amount of acid in order to stay healthy. I believe the key to stopping the plaque is to deal with acid when you first feel the taste of excessive acid in your mouth and not just because there may happen to be a more convenient time to neutralise it. The times I have noticed that I do have a lot of acid in my mouth which needs to be neutralised or that my mouth is drying up is often in the early hours of the morning, when I need to go to the toilet. My attitude when getting up at 2 or 3 o'clock in the morning and neutralising my mouth with milk is that I am going to be a lot healthier for doing it and that I now have a good reason for going back to sleep with the contentment of sleeping better than I did before.

Another important thing that needs to be taken care of is to make sure that the teeth always have a protective coating of saliva on them, because when the teeth dry out, the acid starts attacking the enamel on them, along with the other impurities that dry out on your teeth. There is also a possibility that you may have a solution of sugar left in your mouth that could be causing problems. This is the theory I have on it. It does not necessarily make my theory right; neither does it necessarily make it wrong. However, all the facts and evidence point in that direction, along with the fact that I no longer have any more trouble with plaque. It has proven to be the case for the last 8 years.

Painkillers. I thought that while I am on the subject of medical problems, I will talk a bit about painkillers. Painkillers can sometimes be a very necessary thing to take.

When I was 18 years of age, I had a motorbike accident wherein I sustained two broken legs. On the right leg, I had a broken shin bone (tibia), and on the left leg, I had broken off the bone around the ankle (fibula), which needed to be screwed back together. The pain I suffered from the two broken legs was very severe, and the hospital relieved my pain by giving me morphine. The morphine was great; within the first hour, it relieved my pain by 100 per cent. But that was as good as it got, because after 1 hour the pain quickly returned to how it first was. The story only gets worse, because I then needed to wait a total of 4 hours before I could get another shot of morphine (the reason for the delay was so that I did not become addicted to the morphine). After about a week, they gave me a different drug for the pain. I am not sure what it was called, because that would mean being able to recall its name when it happened in 1965, some 48 years ago. If my memory serves me correctly, it was called hydrocodone. Even though I am uncertain about the name of the painkilling drug, one thing I remember very clearly is that this new painkiller only gave me about 80 per cent relief from the pain and lasted about 3 hours. This meant that I only had to wait 1 hour before I was eligible to have my next shot after the 4-hour waiting time. I found this to be much better, than when one compares it to the morphine, which would only last an hour. Getting that 80 per cent relief for an extra two hours was heaven compared to getting the morphine's relief for a much shorter time.

When I look back on the research that I have done on painkillers and when I refer back to the time when I had two broken legs, I find myself feeling very grateful to the nurses and doctors who kept me honest by making sure that I waited 4 hours before the next injection. When one does not wait for 4 hours and takes them sooner or continues to take them over a long period, especially when they are taken sooner than 4 hours which will almost certainly make that person who is taking the drug into becoming a drug addict from the painkillers, and left with the misery of having to get themselves off the addiction from the painkillers, which are setting you for a very unpleasant time. It is many times easier not to get addicted to them in the first place. Personally, I have not gone through the experience of being addicted to them but have seen the misery of many people who have.

The results from studies of doctors who have done research on painkillers clearly show that it is best to avoid painkillers when you can, which means that it is best if one works hard to try to avoid them as much as possible. The side effects are that they are addictive and that they can end up reversing the job they first started doing for you (*recreating the pain you had in the first place*). Over a short period, if they are correctly managed, the user is usually successful in avoiding becoming addicted to them. The danger of the addiction is, when someone does become addicted, they are not aware of the addiction which is happening to them and, worse still, will argue with someone who knows the signs of addiction and who is not able to break through the reality of them being addicted.

One thing people using painkillers need to be wary of is that painkillers *mask the pain* and do not cure the existing problem. As a matter of fact, it can eventually be a reason for making the problem worse. When someone has pain without painkillers, they would naturally nurse the infected area so that they do not suffer more pain from it. When someone takes a painkiller, they are only masking the pain. Once the painkiller has masked the pain of the infected area, one no longer has a reason to protect it, and that could end up doing more damage because of the lack of protection it is receiving. After all, pain is a warning that something is wrong and that something needs protecting, and you cannot protect that which you are not aware of. Using a painkiller is a bit like turning off the smoke alarm in the belief that it will put out the fire which is causing it to go off in the first place.

INR test. There are a lot of people who spend many years taking Coumadin or warfarin in order to ensure that their blood is kept thinner than normal; this is done to prevent stroke, heart attack, and other thrombotic diseases that block the arteries. This tablet is taken daily. Even though it has gone through many tests to find the right dosage required, the blood can still quickly venture into a dangerous level of thickness or a lack of thickness, and someone could end up dying. If it is too thick, you can end up dying from the disease that the thinner blood was trying to protect you from. If the blood is too thin, you can end up dying from haemorrhaging. INR (the international normalised ratio) testing is required to be done under the supervision of a doctor because of the dangerous risks that are involved, especially when it comes to how quickly it can get out of control.

To the many people who have been having INR tests and who may need to have a test once a fortnight—or sometimes more often—over a period of many years and who still do not understand what the INR acronym for testing means, well, you are not alone. I remember travelling the same journey and have had to undergo many years of being subjected to INR tests. I remember asking most of the girls who took the blood what it meant, and the bulk of the replies were that it was too difficult to explain. Even when they did explain the words of the acronym, it did not make a lot of sense in describing the procedure which was taking place. Here is a simple explanation of the procedure of the INR test, when you leave out the words of the acronym.

The INR test is done by taking a sample of blood and having it tested at a laboratory. The people who use this service are people who have had severe problems with clotting; they can be people with heart problems, people who have had a stroke, and people who have had some problems with thrombosis.

When someone's blood is tested *without* the use of blood thinners, such as Coumadin or warfarin, then the normal range is 1. The number 1 represents one minute for the blood to clot when done under laboratory conditions. When someone has an INR test, a new standard for normal is set up to be 2–3. This will mean that the new normal range for the blood clot is now two or three minutes, depending on the number from the INR test.

Let's get back to the abbreviation and the major reason I believe people are having so much trouble medically understanding the acronym of INR testing. An acronym is also referred to as an abbreviation. In this case, the abbreviation *INR* has been abbreviated by leaving out 3 characters from the front of *INR*. The full abbreviation is *PT/INR*, and the meaning is *prothrombin time and international normalised ratio*. So, what I am seeing at this time is that the two words that were left out, *prothrombin time*, are a lot more important than the other three words. I also run with the feeling that it is no wonder that the acronym is confusing; this is due to the fact that it sadly lacks information needed to understand the procedure of PT/INR (prothrombin time and international normalised ratio) testing.

I thought it would be appropriate for me to give you a direct quotation of the definition of the first two words from the *Medical Oxford Dictionary*. I did not bother with the last three words because they are self-explanatory.

According to the *Medical Oxford Dictionary*, *prothrombin time (PT)* is 'the time for blood clotting to occur in a sample of blood to which calcium and thromboplastin [blood thinner] have been added'.

There is more to the definition that I have just given from the *Medical Oxford Dictionary*. However, it is clear from the information which I have just given that calcium and thromboplastin are chemicals that will make your blood thinner, along with giving a new standard for how long it takes your blood to clot; that new standard comes from PT/INR testing. The rest of the information only relates to what I have already told you. This untold information relates back to a different standard for the amount of time it takes for someone's blood to clot. Both standards are internationally accepted, and it is important to separately recognise the two standards. If someone is having trouble with haemorrhaging, they need to use the original standard of time that it takes for the blood to clot (1 minute) and most certainly do not want to work from the PT/INR standard of time for clotting. Alternatively, it is important to use the PT/INR standard method when it is necessary for you to safely keep your blood much thinner than normal, with the new normal being the standard from the PT/INR testing (2–3 minutes).

My Philosophical Way of Solving Problems

The way I sort out my medical problems is by working out what I believe I need to do. If it is something, I can do for myself, I carry out the required experiments on myself and work on analysing the worst thing that could happen with the changes I make versus the best outcome of the problem I am dealing with. My theory is also to accept mistakes as a good thing, providing something is learnt from them. I was taught by a wise person, "that a person who never made a mistake never made a goddam thing," and that making a mistake the first time is not necessarily a bad thing, although repeating the same mistake definitely is.

One thing that I would like to point out is that all the successful medical results that I have managed are contained. The same thing often happens when you see a medical doctor; the problem is contained, and should you continue doing the thing that made it occur in the first place, then that same problem will recur. I am not a doctor, and the only medical studies I have done have been through books, along with numerous other ways that I have been able to find in order to gain further medical knowledge.

I can't even guarantee, if you have a similar problem, that you will get the same result, because the studies of the experiments I have done were on myself, apart from the outside help that I have received from books, doctors, etc. A good example of what I am referring to is that I am highly allergic to alcohol taken internally, and even very small amounts can give me the symptoms of one who has severe liver problems. Some people can be allergic to peanuts or strawberries, and there are also many other things people can be allergic to. Personally, for me, I can eat as many peanuts or strawberries as I like, and I do not get any adverse effects from them.

CHAPTER 16

My Reasons for Wanting to Be an Author

People want to be an author for many reasons. Some may think it is an easy way to make money, and some may think that it will make them famous—or both. My reasons have very little to do with fame or money or how many book sales I can make; instead it has a lot more to do with me having a heart attack and battling through the stigma of being haunted by dyslexia.

In regard to my attitude of wanting to be an author, first of all, I would like to clarify a question that many people may be asking: why in the world would someone with dyslexia even think of wanting to write a book when they are encumbered with such a heavy burden of getting their grammar to the standard of where an author needs to be and then still be left with the task of writing the book?

My story of wanting to be an author has a very bad beginning to it. It would have been very doubtful, prior to the heart attack, whether I would have done anything in the field of writing if it were not for the life-changing circumstances of a heart attack, because nearly all my skills, required doing jobs that involved some sort of physical activity. However, it still would have been smarter of me to have devised some sort of a plan to have in the later stage of my life even if I did not have a heart attack. Because as you get older, your body will no longer be able to do the physical work that it did before, and you always need to have something to work on in order to have a way to maintaining a healthy life. (I am a firm believer in the idea that, when it comes to understanding the human anatomy, if you do not use it, then you will lose it, regardless of what part of the anatomy one refers to.)

At the age of 49, in 1996, I had a heart attack. The heart attack was severe, and it created a 90 per cent blockage to the right coronary artery at the back of the heart. Even though they cleared the blockage through angioplasty, this still left me very weak in the first few weeks, and I was only able to walk about 20 steps before I needed to stop and have a rest so that I could recuperate the energy that I had just used. My physical ability was reduced to about 10 per cent of the original amount of physical energy that I had before the heart attack, and to compound the problem even further, I needed to be hospitalised 5 times because of arrhythmia (irregular heartbeat).

In regard to the permanent amount of physical energy that I was going to lose and how much energy I was going to recuperate, it was not an easy answer to get. I did not consider 10 per cent to be a good starting point, and the answer from my cardiologist as to how much physical energy I was about to lose turned out to be a dismal story. He said to me that at the minimal, when someone has had a heart attack, they lose some of the muscles around the heart, which die and never grow back again, and that only time and what I do with that time will establish how much physical energy I will get back. He also informed me, in one of his consultations, that when someone has a heart attack as severe as the one, I had (90 per cent blockage to the right coronary), it usually results in them being dead after one year of having the heart attack. When that one year was up, I gloated to him that I had got past that year. His story still did not have a happy ending, because he then told me, 'Guess what? Most people who get past that first year, nearly all of them die in the second year.' If he is still alive, well, I hate to break the bad news to him, but I have now lived 21 years past that deadline, and I am still in line for many years to come. I would also like to wish him all the best, should he still be alive.

Losing a substantial amount of my physical abilities was a very concerning thing to deal with, especially since I relied so heavily on it for my way of life. Thinking about the things that I might no longer be able to do converted me into accepting the options I had left available to me. I considered that the best option was to work from the worst possible situation and work my way up so that I did not set myself up for disappointment. The only option I could think of was to be a writer, although that was stacked with a heap of problems.

All those problems can be explained in one word: *dyslexia*. The symptom that identifies my having dyslexia comes out in the grammatical material that I write. A friend of mine who is a professional editor once recently said to me that when it comes to grammar, I am very good at it when I present it verbally, but it is laced with a lot of minor errors when it comes to writing. Since dyslexia presents a lot of confusion to many people regarding what it really is, along with it being a dominant feature of my character and a big influence on the way I write, I consider it important to try and explain the reason for my dyslexia and why it is taking so much time to write one book.

The first notable signs of stigma from my dyslexia started when I was as young as 5, at the time when I first started school. Dyslexia was something which was completely unknown at that time, and even I was unaware as to why I was struggling with my reading and writing. This meant that I was not able to always keep up with the lessons that my peers were doing at school. Reading out loud was a scary thing to do, and when it came to writing, I constantly found myself making a lot of simple errors that I shouldn't have been making. Yet there were times when we were having a lesson at school were I would come up with answers that my fellow peers found too difficult. Dyslexia simply means that you are over creative, to the point where it ends up creating more problems than it solves, or to put it another way, you create so much information that you are no longer able to effectively process all the information that you have and are left to unravel a lot of fragmented information.

Another thing that added to my difficulty was the method teachers would often use when teaching; and that was by teaching a small bit of information, skipping a bit, presenting you with another piece of information, and then go back to the beginning, and piece it all together. Due to my dyslexia, and the problem that I had with this method, was that when they skipped past the first bit of information, I was no longer able to proceed with the lesson. That was because my brain was locked into trying to find out what I did not understand, and I was no longer able to progress past that point. This was not a conscious decision that I was making; instead it was an involuntary decision that I was left with. When I was presented with all the information, then I was left with a surge of new information that continued while the rest of the lesson proceeded, which presented a huge job of being able to quickly understand all of what I was given but not having enough time to process what I missed out on. The problem would continue to worsen; the teacher would continue with the rest of the lesson, and I was left trying to work out what I had missed out on in the earlier segment while at the same time trying to process the new segment of the lesson which was being presented. The problem had yet to reach rock bottom. If I asked too many questions, I was considered to be deliberately disrupting the class. This left me as a young child who was left with the only option of having to be the teacher and the pupil at the same time, which is always a major struggle when it comes to getting good results at that young age. The repeated minor mistakes that I made created a chain reaction that led to the stigma of me not appearing to be too bright, and since it was very difficult to understand, it became a lot more comfortable for people to downgrade me to the *lowest common denominator* with my reading and writing. In regard to my higher achievements, it was much easier to pass them off as, just *me being lucky*. So I was left to be perceived as someone who was not too bright when it came to the department of intelligence. The areas where I struggled most was in my writing and when I read out loud. Reading out loud was something that I found very scary, and I have given a good explanation of it in the dyslexic article.

Like any stigma, it has a flow on effect, and the closer someone is to you, the more it hurts to hear degrading remarks, such as 'You will never amount to anything good' or 'You will always remain a hopeless case'. This happened at an early stage in my life, when I was learning and trying to get ahead; it was mostly done by the people who were trying to teach me and who were frustrated because they believed that they were not getting their message through to me while trying to teach me. The driving force that got me through this difficult period kept looping back to the state of wanting to be normal and was what I would seek in order to have some peace of mind. I know that I was better than the stigma that was constantly thrown my way, because in most cases, I would understand or know the answer to the mistakes I was making. Wanting to be perceived to be at the standard of normal has turned into a battlefield that has continued for more than fifty years. It doesn't matter whether I do some difficult things that others struggle with or are not able to work out, such as having a good, structured plan of what I have written. The focus on how well I write something is always going to revert back to the many minor errors that I have made, such as being bad at spelling, missing a word, or adding an unnecessary word, along with other minor errors that certainly compound the problem.

There is an intelligent person buried in that writing, and it is tough to work hard on trying to eliminate all the minor errors I have spent many hours working hard on correcting over many years. It is seldom that I do not know the answers to the errors I have made. More often than not, I do have the answer in my head; it's just that I am not picking up on the errors. Even when I revisit what I have read, I can still end up making the same mistake in the same place as before. It is not until I let it go for a few hours and come back and have another go at it that I may find a few more of the mistakes.

It hurts when you are being constantly downgraded, and the closer someone is to you, the greater the intensity of hurt you are going to feel from suppressing who you really are. However, I do not believe that wanting to be a victim is the answer either. I believe that the answer to it is working out a way to qualify for the status of who you can and need to be. When someone wants to stay a victim, the problem is that they are not prepared to do anything for themselves, and if someone else will not do something for them, neither will they do anything for themselves. However, as we progress through life, we are all going to find ourselves subjected to being a victim from time to time. One needs to be wary of the consequences of wanting to stay a victim, which is not being prepared to do anything to get out of that predicament, which leaves one in a bad situation with no way out until they get out of the predicament of being a victim.

Let's talk about the hurdles I am faced with and the things that people who have dyslexia have to contend with. First of all, I need to clarify that dyslexia is not a black-and-white thing we are dealing with. As I said earlier, it is about over creating, and there are many ways that one can create. So, when one evaluates dyslexia based on the symptoms, as opposed to the root of where the problem lies, they are going to end up with many different answers. It also comes back to the point of the degree that you have dyslexia, as well as the method that you use to over create as opposed to someone who does not have dyslexia and who uses a lot more direct information when it is more appropriate to do so. Another important aspect that needs to be taken into consideration is how far you are prepared to take on the role of a victim or how far you are prepared to battle through your problems. The different types of attitudes have an equally big range to the many different outcomes that can develop.

The quality of my grammar when I first started improving it after having my heart attack was equivalent to the standard of a seven-year-old. This was mainly due to the fact that although I had lots of useful words that I needed to use, not only could I not spell them, but I was also very often at a loss in finding a way to spell them. I know that the most obvious choice is to go to the dictionary. However, the dictionary is very savage to anyone who does not know the spelling of the first 3 or 4 letters. A good example of this is the word *especially*. If you want to put it to the test, try and find the word *especially* in the dictionary when you only have the belief that *especially* begins with the letter "*a*". The thing that was getting in the way of my doing better with my grammar was the mountain of minor errors that I was not picking up on. With most of those errors, I would have known how and why they were made, but I could not recognise the errors until somebody pointed them out to me. Another problem that compounded the situation was that I badly pronounced my words, even though I had a lot of great words that I knew and should have been using.

When I reviewed the journey of my dyslexia many decades later, I found that the hardest thing to deal with was that nobody knew that I had dyslexia at the time, including myself. I never understood what dyslexia was, until the age of about 60. A big part of the stigma I am referring to is that dyslexic people very often come up with answers that most people who first meet us would not give us credit for being able to achieve, due to the fact that we make a lot of simple mistakes that we shouldn't be making. This very often leaves the people who do not understand us thinking that we are just lucky with the answers that were more difficult to create, and once again, we get downgraded to not being all that bright. Not knowing that I had dyslexia until I was about sixty years of age certainly made it a lot harder to unravel the problems that it created, because you can't change what you do not acknowledge.

The truth of the matter is that the majority of people with dyslexia are bright and intelligent people, although some do quit because they are unable to handle the constant juggling from the excessive information that they have in their head. We have to be able to work out whether the extra information in our head is needed or if some of it needs to be rejected. Maybe something needs to be added, or more than likely, the information needs to be rearranged while we are exercising our reading or writing. So now we have two choices: to quit with a lack of spirit and end up filling in the requirements of what we have been accused of, or to keep battling on and fight for the right to present the intelligence that we have buried in our heads. However, people with dyslexia need to know, before taking on that big hurdle, that they need to establish that it is doable. If they do not come up with that answer, it would be a very good idea to re-evaluate it, because it will have a major effect on the outcome of how the rest of their life is going to be determined when it comes to who they are really going to be. Dyslexia; is never going to let us off the hook, for the need to do a mountain of work in order to get through it.

Having normal intelligence may seem trivial to most people without dyslexia, but one thing you can be sure of when you have dyslexia is that when you are told consistently over a long period that you are lacking in intelligence and that you always will be, this leaves you battling with a feeling of hurt and embarrassment that you desperately want to climb out of, providing you do not quit.

Before setting up my goals for being an author, I would like to tell you briefly how I got on with the physical side of my life from the age of **49**, when I had the heart attack. After about a month or so of having the heart attack, I returned to having about **90** per cent of my physical energy again and went back to my previous employment at the chemical factory, working as a labourer. I was later transferred to being an acid plant operator, which lasted for a total of **11** years. Then the factory was closed down, and I was made redundant. I then spent a period being unemployed for the first time in my life and later found my way back into the workforce by being self-employed and working as a professional handyman.

In regard to my credentials for being a handyman, well, I started off working on the family farm as a young boy. One of the requirements for working on the farm was having to sort out our own maintenance problems as they occurred; very often, if the family did not find a way to fix their own maintenance problems, there was a good chance that work would not get done. When I left home and went out to work, I also continued doing handyman's work for myself and my friends. Maintenance was a big part of the many jobs that I did throughout my life, which continued to enhance my handyman skills.

When I started my business, I worked out a good strategy for working as a handyman. I told all the customers that I wear many hats (*do many different types of jobs*), but I concern myself with two things only: *to do a good job and to make the customer happy*. I have taken these two things very seriously, which has supplied me with a lot of job satisfaction and a great work environment for everyone involved in the jobs that I do for them. Since the age of 65, I have been semi-retired and no longer put out flyers, which I used to rely on to increase business. I now solely rely on the ongoing customers that I previously had to supply me with work, and I spend the majority of my time working on improving my grammar and writing up articles for my book.

Another concern that has plagued me throughout most of my life was that I felt I was in a mental prison that stemmed from my childhood, which was the negative labels that were continually thrown at me, such as 'He is not very bright' or 'It would be good if only he tried a bit harder' or 'He is never going to be too smart at anything'. The thing that made it even harder was having all the people I knew locking me into that situation, throwing away the key with the conclusion that I would never be able to do any better. Something that ventured closer to home was that even my mother threw away that key. I suppose that I should explain it a bit better. The key and what it locked—well, these were the downgraded thoughts and beliefs that everybody had me locked into.

In regard to my Mum, well, there was nothing mean that she did to me. I believe that my mother thought while she was working hard at trying to help me through my schooling that she had done everything that could be done. Unfortunately for me, the longer that thought stayed with her, the stronger the lock became, because I further believed that she did not want to have that belief of me in the first place. This was a place she found hurtful to her, and she thought that nothing more could ever make it any better. I didn't say she was right, only why she had locked herself into that position. Over the last five or six years, I sent her numerous copies of things I have done which showed the improvement in my grammar. I also spent quite a few hours with the two or three times, when I returned home to New Zealand and did a lot of hard work on the computer, or in the early stages, on the word processor, which was one of the major tools I used to improve my grammar.

This did not change the fact that Mum still kept me locked into that same box of not being too bright. I had the feeling I was never going to be able to get out of that depressing situation. Just recently, I sent her seven articles from the book that I am writing. My Mum is now 93 years old, and she said to me for the first time *that she could see a huge improvement in my grammar.* Prior to that announcement, she did tell me a few years before that she had noticed that I had made a big improvement in other areas of my life. I am sure that she has no idea how great it was for me to be able *to earn* my way over that mammoth hurdle; had she said something like that to me without authentically believing it, it would have meant nothing. There was only ever going to be one way out of that box, and the key was to earn my way out.

When I reviewed the breakdown of my goals in writing my book, which I still have not yet written, and when I placed a percentage value on the progress made in each step, I found that the first step was being able to find the words I was unable to find in the dictionary, which amounts to **20** per cent. Being able to construct written text with the words of the message I intended to use while writing is **20** per cent (this is referring to wrongly used homophones and words that were left out or put in unintentionally). Having Mum upgrade, me from not being too bright to doing well with my grammar is **40** per cent. The other **20** per cent is to continue working and to make sure that my writing is correctly done and, last of all, to do a good job of writing the book, with the intention of selling enough copies to pay the expenses and to make a little extra pocket money, which will always come in handy.

One might say that it is a poor attitude for an author to have, but my main goal has always been to shed the idea of me not being too bright; that has been a big Part of my motivation for all this work in writing my book and other articles that I might write. I also believe that I have valuable information to pass on to others through the experiences that I have had in my life. However, since I have already got results from the many goals that I have achieved, this also means that I do not need to go around proving the authenticity of my successful goals. For example, I have the written results of my field test, but if someone asked me to produce them so that they could have proof of what I said, I would decline. I believe that I have already put in all the facts and evidence needed to determine whether the reader wants to see it as useful information or dismiss it as just a story.

If this book is going to have any success, it is going to need a good marketing plan to make it work, and that is something that I do not have at the moment. Besides, I believe that I have already achieved the most important part of my goal and that I have now reached the standard of being perceived as normal or better by the people who are close to me. I have always believed that I have good material to work with for writing a book. My biggest problem was in trying to be understood and sorting out the fragmented mess I had in my head. Worse than that, before the age of 60, I didn't even know that I had dyslexia and believed that I was gathering my information the same way that everybody else received their information. All I knew was, despite my best efforts, and with my writing, I kept on coming out with a mountain of mistakes; it would take ages to work out the mistakes, and even then, I would still be left with a few mistakes after doing all that checking. The last thing that I would like to say about the book is why I have such a low value on the sales of copies, which would establish how successful my book is. This all comes back to my attitude and my view on that, is that there are many great books that have been published that have turned out to be considered flops due to the lack of sales, and there are also a great many books that have been published that have very little value of contents in them and were not even well presented and yet have been considered successful and have sold a lot of copies. As far as I understand it, it all comes down to a thing called *marketing*. So, should I be able to sell a lot of copies of my book, the only real success I believe I can claim is that I did a good job of *marketing* it and *possibly* a good job of writing it.

An advantage that I feel I have going for me in my life is that I almost always question everything that I am told in my head in depth if I feel that it is important. It also means that I have very little interest in the shallow version, regardless of who it may come from or whether that person's source of information is considered right or wrong. That information can come from a professor, a doctor, or anyone certified with high credentials; throughout my life, I have known them to be wrong from time to time. Let's be realistic, regardless of who anybody is, they are always going to be a human being first and their profession second. Human beings are always very prone to making mistakes, myself included, and the one who by far receives the heaviest criticism, whether it is right or wrong, is myself, which I judged based on the evidence of workable results. So, getting past the hurdle of not being afraid to ask questions of someone with higher authority gives me an edge to sorting out problems, because there is always a chance that they might be wrong or that they are mentally going down the wrong track in regard to solving the problem. The trick here is not to verbally consult them but to run it through your head and show respect at all times, because it will give you a lot more mileage than someone who thinks they know it all. After all, if they can be wrong, so can you, and allowing them a lot of latitude is normally the safest way to go. It beats the hell out of trying to unring a bell.

I would like to exhibit three examples to explain why I am not afraid of higher authority and why I have no concern about challenging them in my mind when I believe that they are wrong. I usually find that there is nothing to be gained by confronting them. The results, coupled with evidence and logical facts, are the things that allow me to make the decision of whether they are right or wrong. Another thing that needs to be carefully considered is that I find that keeping the answer to myself is the best way to proceed, unless I think that they may want to hear the other answer.

One of the first times that I recall someone of high authority being wrong was with an orthopaedic surgeon. I was at the age of 18. This took place when I had two broken legs from a motorbike accident. On the left leg, I broke the bone that goes around the ankle (the bottom of the fibula), which was screwed back together. It was correctly done. With the right leg, I broke the main shin bone (the tibia). The normal procedure was to put the leg in traction in order to keep the muscles stretched so the bone grows straight. Failing to do so would cause the leg muscles to pull together too tightly, and the bone would end up healing in a crooked position and would more than likely require rebreaking in order to get it straightened again.

The orthopaedic surgeon failed to follow normal procedure and came up with his own idea of how he was going to repair the broken shin bone (tibia). The new procedure required putting me under anaesthesia (putting me to sleep). He put a pin through the bone in my heel and wrapped my foot and my whole leg in cotton wool. Then he stretched my leg by pulling it from the pin that went through the bone in my heel and wrapped it with plaster while maintaining the pressure and allowing it to dry. I do not believe that one needs to have a lot of intelligence to know that cotton wool is going to absorb most—if not all—of the pressure needed to stretch the leg so that it does not have the bone healing in a crooked position. The result from that procedure is that my leg healed 1 inch or 25 millimetres short. If the normal treatment had been exercised, when it comes to how much my leg would have shortened, other people I have talked to explained that it would have been a lot less. This also caused a lot more pain. I remember asking the orthopaedic surgeon about the procedure, and he said to me, 'The less you know, the better off you are.' How very convenient it was for him to make that comment.

The second example is when I had an accident at work while driving a forklift. I had ended up driving it straight into the back of a large truck which was parked in clear view and which was easy for a normal person to see. The fact that I did not see it there and yet still ran into the back of it was not normal in anybody's books. So, after it happened, I looked around, and after noticing that there was only minor damage done to the truck, I then apologised to the driver and continued on to do the next most important thing that I felt needed to be done, which was to see the manager and report the accident. After telling the manager what had happened, I said to him that there was definitely something wrong and that I didn't know what it was. So, he arranged for a taxi to take me from my place of employment at Seven Hills to see my local doctor in Riverwood, where I resided. The company was kind to me and paid the taxi for the 30-kilometre trip to Riverwood. When I got inside the doctor's surgery, he tested me by running his hand across my face and found that I had a blind spot. So, he instructed me to go to the optician with a letter of reference for me to have a half-field test, which happens to be the testing of only one eye. When I went to the optician, she said that they do not do half-field tests and that they only do full-field testing. So, I agreed to accept the full-field test, and it was fortunate for me that they did a full-field test, because it concluded that I had lost half my eyesight not just in one eye like the doctor thought was the case, but in both eyes.

When I went back to give the doctor the results, he was very upset that his instructions were disobeyed, with me having a full-field test done instead of having the half-field one that he ordered. At the time, I wasn't concerned as to whether I had a full- or a half-field test done on me, because I was too busy trying to figure out what was wrong with me and what could be done in order to fix the problem. This was until he started presenting me with his angry feelings about me having the full-field test done. He then took out my medical records and ran me down for everything he could find and, in his mind, what he considered I had done wrong. I was astounded that he was so interested in saving a face that wasn't worth saving. Instead of accepting the mistake that he made so he could avoid making the same mistake in the future, he chose to focus on bullying me when I was at my weakest moment by taking out my medical records and rubbishing me for all he could. He also told me that I had a stroke which would give me the permit disability of losing half of my eyesight and that the only thing that would change was that I would recognise where the blind spot was, and that there was nothing I could do about it. First of all, he had no right to close the door on my condition, because he was only a GP and not a neurologist, who is better qualified to make that decision.

Even though I kept the opinion to myself, I did not accept that there was nothing that could be done about my stroke, because I had already learnt that the brain can be remapped, from a television station on channel 2 with a programme called *Catalyst*. I did not have any previous knowledge about how to remap the brain, only the good description that I received from the *Catalyst* programme. So, I said to myself that there was no point in worrying about what I haven't got at this point, because remapping the brain was the only chance I had of getting all my eyesight back. After the visit when I had the stroke, and when I got back home from seeing the doctor, I picked up the remote control and then sat down at the table. Within a few short moments, I decided to pick up the remote control of the television again so that I could change the channel, but when I looked back to pick up the remote control, I was unable to see it on the table even though I knew for certain that it was there. This gave me a great exercise which I believed was my best chance to reprogram the mapping of my brain. So, the first time that I looked for the remote control, it may have taken me about 10 to 15 minutes to find it, when it should have only taken one or two seconds. I am really not aware of the time span, only that it took a long time and that it was imperative to get all my eyesight back again. Another thing I did at the time while I was looking for the remote control was that I talked to my brain like it was a second person, telling it that losing half my eyesight was unacceptable and that it was imperative to find a way to get it back. I played this little game about 10–15 times each day for about 3 weeks until I could find the remote right away. That was when I knew that I had won the battle against the stroke and the need to have another full-field test, which was now only a formality and which would confirm what I already knew.

The two things the doctor did do right was that he ordered an MRI scan and made an appointment for me to see a neurologist; he got it half right when it came to having a field test. It took three weeks before I saw the neurologist, who confirmed that I had now got my eyesight back to normal. This was confirmed by the two field tests and the MRI scan, and this also contributed to letting the neurologist know the extent of my stroke. After the neurologist had confirmed that I had lost half my eyesight in both eyes and that I had got it all back again, he then said that if I did not have my blood kept thinner than normal, I had an 80 per cent chance of having another stroke, but if I did keep it thinner than normal, I only had about a 2 per cent chance of having another stroke. So now I am on warfarin for the rest of my life, and I am not prepared to take on round two of remapping the brain. Let's face it, I am on the extreme side of being a pioneer in the knowledge of remapping the brain. The thing I now concern myself with is that there are too many things that can go badly wrong to which I may or may not find an answer. The important thing to take on board is that if I had accepted my doctor's version that there was nothing that could be done and then had sat around, being the victim and feeling sorry for myself, then I firmly believe that I would have been left with only half of my eyesight in both eyes for the rest of my life.

Now for the last example. This one annoys me every time I hear it. 'You are what you eat.' Unfortunately, a lot of the people who say it are supposed to have high intelligence and experience in the nutritional value of food when they make that statement. So, let's analyse this phrase: You are what you eat. Let's take an apple for example, which is supposedly very good for you. If I only eat apples for a very long period, there is no way in the world that I can ever become an apple. What is more likely to happen is that you will end up with an excess of acid in the body, which will largely contribute to getting into bad health problems and dying a lot sooner than one needs to due to the lopsided choice of my diet. To correct that statement, what one needs to say is that you are a by-product of what you eat, which is controlled by your DNA. So 'you are what you eat' is not even close to being right, and I fail to understand how a phrase so far off-track could ever be helpful. At best, it is a bad way to start someone off who wants and needs to improve their eating habits. They are more than likely to end up having—for want of better wording—an extremely lopsided diet. There is not a food on the planet for human beings that you can keep eating in excess and disregard the balance of where it is good for your health. Because once you continue past that healthy point of balance, it will turn around and become bad for your health. The more you continue past that point, the more your health is going to decline in the value to being healthy, and the most important part, to the balance of your diet, will be thrown right out the window.

The thing which needs to be taken into consideration and which is not being addressed is that people who are living with bad eating disorders are very likely to drift from one bad habit to another by thinking that if a certain food is very good for you, then the more you have, the better it will be for you, and by failing to understand the importance of balance. Since they already have a history of making bad decisions when it comes to food, this leaves them badly prone (exposed) to developing another bad food habit. Any food or drink taken in extremes is no good for you. For example, having 10 litres of water a day, if you were capable or close to being capable of drinking that much, over a period would cause you to have swelling in the ankles, and if you continue doing so, you will end up with further complications. Let's take another thing that is very good for you: oxygen. If you started taking oxygen in excessive amounts, you would eventually end up fainting, and if you were still able to continue taking further excessive amounts of oxygen, you would end up dying. I believe the trick is to eat the foods that most benefit you and to get the balance of what you are eating right for you.

Summary

So wanting to be an author has taken me from being very embarrassed and feeling very degraded because I was only able to write up to the standard of a 7-year-old and the time span that I am referring to with the low quality of work that I had when I left school at the age of 16, up to when I was about the age of 49, which was when I started making big improvements in the quality of my grammar. I still need to make some big steps forward in order to reach the standard of grammar that an author should be able to produce. As the years progressed, so did the hard work I put into improving my grammar, which has been rewarded by the good progress that I have been making. I believe that I have now advanced to the point of someone who has just completed college, and if you are capable of accepting the overall standard of the work and ignoring some of the minor errors that may occur, then you might say I am doing well with my writing.

CHAPTER 17

The Advantage of Being Nice

There are two stories about being nice that I would like to present. The first one is about a car accident that happened to me in 2012, when I was 64 years of age.

The second story took place when I was roughly 38 years of age, while I was working in the maintenance crew as a rigger/trades assistant in the acid plant in ICI. This was a place where the crew often had a lot of spare time. One of the fitters got a bit bored and decided to use me as entertainment by calling my mother a whore, and I clearly won the battle of that verbal confrontation by being nice. But I will discuss more about that story later.

My Car Accident and What Being Nice Got Me

This is another one of those 'being nice' stories that I have written within some of my articles and where I have demonstrated after having a car accident and some of the great advantages, I have gained by taking the high road and being nice. On this occasion, it involved being in a car accident, which was not my fault. There was nothing I could have done to prevent it. There were a lot of things that went wrong due to the poor attitude of the young girl that hit me with her car. I believe that for most people, when they have so many bad things happen to them that they don't deserve, then they want to lash out at that person and make them pay in any way that they possibly can, for all the hurt that they have been receiving. Yet I chose the option of being nice. By doing so and looking back at the event with all the business of the accident completed, I find that financially, I got the best possible result, as well as emotionally getting the best possible result by being happy with how I conducted myself in difficult circumstances and being able to look back at the incident with a good and happy feeling of achievement with everything that could have gone in my favour.

This accident occurred when I was at the age of **64**. One day, I was driving in Sydney, in a suburb called Revesby, where I went to pick up a couple of bags of topsoil. I have this habit of being sociable with most people I meet, and this time, it happened to be a truck driver I got to chatting with, who was waiting at the same office as me to organise his paperwork for the load he was carrying. I left just before him and proceeded to go back home along the River Road (it is a six-lane road). While I was travelling along the road and getting near the crossroad at Milperra Road, a female driver came out of a small side road on my left-hand side, crossing my path. She proceeded to do a right-hand turn across the road that I was driving on. At first, I thought she was one of those drivers that charged the intersection then stopped suddenly, but unfortunately for me, she didn't hit the brake at all. She just kept coming at quite a high speed and drove into me, hitting me on the passenger's side between the front door and the rear door but closer to the rear door. The impact caused my car to spin a **180°**, leaving me facing the traffic in the opposite direction of the lane I was travelling in. Fortunately for me, while doing so, I managed to keep my car from drifting across to the wrong side of the six lanes to that road, where the other three lanes where traveling the opposite direction. This could have very easily have ended up very badly for me, where I could have been hit by a truck who might have been traveling in one of those lanes that I should not have been in, and been badly hurt or even killed. She didn't stop or even hit the break at all. She just kept on driving and then turned off the road and proceeded down the freeway towards the city. I later found out that she didn't even live on any of the roads connected to the freeway. As soon as I was able to get out of the car, I ran down the road, unsuccessfully trying to get her licence number. Fortunately for me, the truck driver I was talking to before I left the place that sold the soil, stopped me and gave me the registration number of the number plate from the lady who had hit me with her car. I wasn't hurt, but I was still facing the wrong way in my traffic lane and needed a decent gap in the traffic in order to turn around, providing the car could still be driven. While I was waiting, an attractive young girl in her mid-twenties opened my car door and asked me if I was all right. I was pleasantly surprised that someone of that young generation had taken the time to show that she cared. I told her that I was all right and thanked her for her generosity of care and commented that she was a very nice person and that I very much appreciated the help she offered.

While I was thinking and waiting for a break in the traffic so I could turn the car around the right way, I remembered a scam that happened to me a few years ago, wherein a driver set me up so that I would crash into the back of his car. But that's another story for another time. It did remind me of a good smash repairer who was not all that far from where I had just had my accident. I also remembered that they did it for a very good price, as well as doing a good job.

My car was just driveable, and when I arrived at the smash repair yard, I found that the tyres had gradually deflated because of the damage to the two rims, but were not deflated badly enough, so that I was not able to drive on them. Further damage to the car included a big dent on the passenger's side between the two doors, a small crimp in the chassis, scratches on the front bumper bar, and also a damaged back wheel bearing on the passenger's side. The repair people were nice and helpful. They allowed me to use their phone so I could ring the police and report the accident. After that, the smash repairs gave me a quote of $4,660 for the damage on my car, which is a 1996 Subaru Impreza hatchback. One thing that was in my favour was that this happened on Thursday, 19/1/12. It was easier for me to get a hired car because it was during a weekday and not the weekend when there was more likely no cars available.

The accident was classed as a third-party accident claim, with me being the third party. The police said that the other party had been in touch with them but would not say whether they had been summoned or if they had gone there of their own accord. The driver's name was Ashley Kozarovski, and her date of birth was 19/11/93 (she was 20 years old). She had accepted responsibility, and they were insured with AAMI. The police said that I had to negotiate with the insurance company for the right to hire a courtesy car while mine was out of action. Because I am a professional handyman and cannot work without a vehicle, given my circumstances, I went and hired one anyway. The way I figured it was that I had a very good case for meeting the requirement of getting a courtesy car, and after renting the car, the remaining question was whether the insurance company would do the right thing or whether they would not do the right thing. However, I thought it smarter to do a little bit of homework before I got the rental car. If I had got it, say, from Avis rentals, it would have cost $84 per day, and even if I had got it from Budget, they also would have charged $84 per day. I believe that a lot of people at this stage would be looking at how much they could make someone pay for all the bad things that had happened to them and the hardship that was thrust upon them while they were doing nothing wrong. Now here was where being nice came into play. Not only did I not go for the most expensive car I could get, but I also looked for the cheapest one. Fortunately for me, the smash repairer told me about a cheap car I could rent from a rental called Rent A Bomb, which could be found on the Internet. I decided to ring them up and found that Rent A Bomb only cost $22 a day. When I got there, I found that it was not a bad sort of a car at all. Even though it had no air conditioner and no radio and was a 1991 Holden hatchback, it was a neat, reliable, and tidy car with plenty of power. I did it for two reasons. Even though I was fairly confident they would pay for the rental, I still could not be certain. The other reason was that it gave me a lot of extra bargaining power that I would not have had, if I had hired a more expensive car. This proved to be very helpful further down the track.

I managed to drive around to the place of the girl that I had the accident with, and she told me that she still hadn't got all the details yet and that it was her father's car. *When we had the accident, she didn't even touch the brake.* So, I explained to her that whenever there is an emergency or when something is wrong, you hit the brake, not the accelerator. I don't think she appreciated me telling her that. I figured that I had the right to tell her, because if I had not been able to control my car by keeping it on the correct side of the road which I was driving on and had I allowed it to travel across to the other side, then I could have been hit by a passing truck and could have ended up in the Promised Land. The next day, her father rang me up, yelling at me in a hostile manner and saying that I was rude to his daughter, and he accused me of yelling at him. I calmly replied that all I did was tell her that she needed to use the brake in an emergency, not the accelerator, because she did not touch the brake throughout the period of the accident. I told him that considering she could have had me killed, it left me with the feeling that I had the right to tell her, and by the way, you are the only one who is yelling. I tried to exchange further details of the accident, but he went on to tell me that he was doing me a favour. That was a bit too much to hear, so I explained that having that accident certainly did me no favour; as a matter of fact, it was nothing but a headache. He ended up hanging up on me. About two hours later, he rang up and apologised. He then gave me the claim number, the most important thing I needed to have. I thanked him for ringing back and said that in future, we need to talk to each other in a calm and respectful manner. We finished our business, and thank goodness I didn't need to deal with him anymore.

The assessor took 13 days before he looked at the car, which was not a comfortable feeling when you don't know for sure whether you are going to get paid for the rental car. I thought the quote that I got from the smash repairer was low, and I was surprised when AAMI wanted to tow the car away and get a second quote. The next day, the assessor told me that the car was a write-off (one of the things AAMI does when repairing a car is to guarantee all their parts that they use for 3 years). I guess the write-off was largely influenced by the extra money of the guarantee for 3 years that they may or may not have to pay for further down the track. He said that they would pay me the market value of the car, $5,000 minus $110, should I need them to get rid of my car and that I could do what I liked with the car. I then needed to talk to the head office, who misread the report and gave the wrong information when they said to me that the car could no longer be registered in NSW. This put me in a really bad situation, because trying to get another car in a similar condition to mine would have cost about $10,000, and that was not a financial journey that I could really afford to go on, especially since I had not done anything wrong in the first place. So, I spent the rest of the day fighting to get out of that mess. The one thing that I thought I had going for me was that the bloke from the smash repair yard said that the damage to the chassis was minor and was not a reason to write off my car. So late in the afternoon, I eventually managed to get hold of the assessor again on the phone to tell him that he had not told me the truth when he said, that I could do what I wanted with my car, because I did not consider that after I had repaired my car, that the only thing it was good for was sitting in the garage and that I couldn't afford to replace it. Then he enlightened me as to where the problem lay. He said that he had filled out a standard form, and there was one part where he filled in a box on right of registration. If he ticked the box 'nonapplicable', that meant that the registration was the same as before the accident, but if he ticked the box 'applicable', that meant that the registration was cancelled and could not be renewed in the state of NSW. In my case, I did live in New South Wales. He had ticked the box 'nonapplicable', which meant I was dancing through hoops that I didn't need to be dancing through (getting stressed out). However, it did have one upside to the smash in having a second quote, and that was that they had reduced the bill from $4,660 to $4,100. The next problem was sorting out the courtesy car. I rang the head office again and told them of the undue stress they put me through, and I proceeded to discuss who was going to be paying for the financing of the courtesy car, and if they were paying for it, and if so, for how long would they be prepared to pay for it. They said that they would pay for it up to the time I received the cheque from the writing off on my car, which was usually within two days. I explained to them that they were not being fair, because I had done nothing wrong and had even gone out of my way to keeping the cost for them as low as possible. I explained that I had already done my homework on the figures and had worked out that I had already saved them $300 by getting Rent A Bomb, so they said that they would pay for a further week. Then I said, 'Oh no, that's not fair at all, because you know that it takes two weeks for the smash repair to get all the parts, and also, they need to send it to the mechanic.' He said, 'OK, we will do it for two weeks.' I said, 'No, that is still not right. It needs to be until I get my car back.' He eventually agreed. So, I believe that not trying to slog the insurance company with all the money you can get out of them leaves you in a much better bargaining position, and when things don't go nicely for you, you still need to be the bigger person and stay nice.

The smash repairer did a marvellous job with the car. It looked better than it did before the smash, and also, they took another $100 off, making it $4,000. They even repainted the back-bumper bar, which they didn't have to do. When I took the car for a drive after the repairs had been done, I managed to pick up a noise from the other rear wheel bearing, which had to be replaced. Since the car was written off, there was no way the smash repairer or I could get any more from the payment of the insurance company. I looked at all the charges and took into consideration that I had got a very good deal, with quite a bit of change to play with, so I thanked the smash repairers for the great job and happily paid the $300 for the repair of the other rear wheel bearing. With hindsight, I feel that by being nice, despite all the inconvenience and the fact that it was completely not my fault, I ended up being paid the best deal I could get.

When I take into consideration the money that I had saved by being nice, it worked out to be $700 from the repairs and $308 from the rental car—in all, $1,008. So, if you just look at two currencies, (being nice socially) and (gaining monetary value), you will see how valuable being nice got me and how costly it would have been to be sour by trying to make them pay for the misery I was put through.

The Second Story

The fitter who tried to get his entertainment by talking badly about my mother

This story is about a fitter who I worked with, who got bored and tried to use me as entertainment. The story took place around 1980, at ICI, in the acid plant where I was working as a rigger/trades assistant with the maintenance crew. In regard to the maintenance cost of running the acid plant when it was shut down, well, it cost about $200,000 an hour. The company was not too concerned if the crew had very little to do each day, providing that everything was ready to go when it was required.

Consequently, this sometimes created a situation wherein some of the crew would get bored because of a lack of something to do. One day, one of the fitters decided to use me as entertainment by calling my mother a whore. For him to achieve his goal of entertainment, it meant getting me angry and getting me to defend my mother from being called a whore, though neither he nor I believed that story to be true.

After he called my mother a whore, I very politely asked him where he had met my mother. He replied, 'I haven't.' So I said to him, 'That shows you how dopey you are.' Then he said, 'But,' I quickly interrupted and said, 'Don't *but* me. Grow a brain, then come back and talk to me.'

He lost in every way possible. He did not achieve his goal of making me angry, instead I stayed polite. He also never got me to defend against the accusation of my mother being a whore; instead I made him do it for me. Another way that he could have got a victory would have been if I would have tried to defend my mother from being a whore, because had I done so then he would have said that there must be some truth to her being a whore otherwise I would not be defending her. The mere fact that both of us know that it was not the reason for me defending my mother, would have made no difference to him because his victory in this case, was that it was able to create some doubt, A few weeks later, I got another victory, which I consider a bonus, when I heard him discussing with his friends, saying 'Don't mess with him, he is mad'. This meant he still had no idea how I verbally defeated him.

Most people, upon hearing such a nasty false accusation, would verbally or physically strike back with an instant emotional response. This was what he relied on to happen so he would win both victories like he had done in the past.

I took away his victory by exposing the lack of credibility of his false accusation and, more importantly, responding with politeness and kindness, which left him confused and out of his comfort zone.

CHAPTER 18

The Philosophical Balance of My Life

Even though this book is my autobiography, this does not mean that an autobiography is going to automatically guarantee that you are going to have interesting material to read. The thing that I believe makes my book interesting for the reader is the strategy that I have developed over time to deal with the many challenges that I considered to be essential to battle with in order to have success in the journey of my life.

The life strategy that I developed started with a golden rule of not accepting any worthwhile goal as an option to quit. I was fortunate as a young child to have the weakness of quitting pointed out to me, and I guess perceiving myself as already being in a weak mental state which had the potential to control the rest of my life was also a big contributing factor to my not wanting to see quitting as an option.

I had dyslexia and was not aware of it until the age of sixty. I am now writing this story between the ages of **60-69**, and the parts of the story that I have presented before the age of sixty come from the luxury of having hindsight, along with the ability to resolve and understand most of the problems that were laid before me over a large span of time.

The biggest problem dyslexia gave me, besides having to constantly work with mixed results while writing and not knowing that I had it, was that it inhibited my ability to correctly pass on the written knowledge that I had available to me. Instead I had to battle with messages that were usually well constructed but entwined with a lot of minor grammatical errors, which I believe was the reason I did not feel as mentally strong as I believed I should have been.

There was also another big contributing factor which was created by the schoolchildren in the two schools that I attended, who relentlessly teased me about having a long nose and red hair. It made me take on the assumption that I was perceived as being abnormal. Now for me to proceed to having a normal life also meant getting past the perception of being mentally weak.

Let's face it, the mental stress that I was dealing with was only a paper tiger (something which appears to be powerful but in reality, is weak). The paper tiger in this case was designed to make me feel powerless and bad about something which was normal, and they felt if they repeated the phrase often enough, then I would sabotage my perception of about being normal. Mental stress only becomes real when you are prepared to accept it as real. Take away the things that you believe are making you emotionally stressed, and you also take away the perception which you could have created. In my case, I allowed the constant harassment of being told that I had a long nose and red hair to affect my judgement; I was made to believe that it was shameful and that I was some kind of freak because of my nose being slightly longer than most people's and because of my having red hair. (Some stresses are harder to deal with than others, such as when you lose a loved one who has passed away.)

However, in reality, there was nothing abnormal about me having red hair and a long nose, and neither one of my body parts were even close to being in the category of being abnormal. Even if one does have some form of abnormities, it is something you need to come to terms with and not an issue you should be spending a lot of time focusing on, because it slowly, and persistently works on altering the great qualities of who you really are. The people who are *trying* to take away your fundamental emotional beliefs, such as the way they tried to categorise my hair and nose as abnormal, can only do so when you alone, give them permission.

The person tormenting you is trying to control you by trying to control the emotional beliefs that you have about yourself. Most often, their mentality is directed at wanting to emotionally put you down; in their twisted way of thinking, they are trying to equalise themselves, thinking that the more they pull you down, the smarter they believe they become. However, they can only be successful in that dim-witted belief if you are prepared to accept that provocation (the act of being tormented). Once that provocation has been rejected, you have the ability to remain in control of the situation. If they have already beaten you to some degree at this point, you need to take back the authentic emotional beliefs that you used to have of yourself and regain the control you so rightly deserve to have in your journey of life and accept that the only thing you have done wrong is allow that harassment and misguided information to be *temporarily attached* to part of your emotional beliefs. The only one who has control of your emotional beliefs is you. Other people only have the chance to influence it, should you give them permission to do so.

There is a sad part to when someone perceives that they have been emotionally hurt by someone and when that hurt is allowed to continue for many years after the event. The perpetrator who started the hurtful event will more than likely have it so far in the back of their memory that they will, at best, only have a faint memory of it. You, being the victim, will take on the role of doing the bully's job for them, and as time progresses, you end up doing a better job of bullying yourself than the original bully did.

I know that I have the antidote to emotional stress, because it has already worked with me. I have also studied it by studying psychology and neurology, which deal with a type of emotional stress similar to what I have been talking about and which also have the same way of dealing with it.

The simple version is to go back to what was wrong (what was tormenting you) and to replace it with what is right. There was nothing wrong with my nose or hair, and there was no evidence to support the fact that there was. My nose being slightly bigger has some advantages: it is easy to breathe air into my lungs, it does a better job of filtering the air I breathe, and it also does a good job of conveying the different scents that register in my brain. As to the colour of my hair and the way I perceive it, I can listen to some misguided person who is prepared to tell me that it is weird in some way, or I can see it as a nice colour and remember that some people go and get their hair dyed red and are happy with the extra attention that it sometimes creates. I did not ask for the colour of my hair or any other parts of the anatomy that I was given. We have two choices to make with the body that we have. We can embrace it, or we can try and find a way of seeing some kind of fault with it. The first choice has happiness attached to it, and the second choice has a lot of misery attached to it.

There is another point of view to be wary of while sorting out about debating, which is not only applicable to my case but also applies to any debate on any given topic. This is a mistake which is often made by many

227

people who do not first qualify their statement to being correct, when there is a good chance that it may be incorrect. Even if only part of the statement is incorrect, the incorrect part of the statement is going to make it a lot more confusing and harder to sort out. Gaining a successful result also means working with what is correct. When you continue a debate with wrong information, it will compound the results and make it go wrong, until you acknowledge the things that have been wrongly stated and replace it with ones that are correct (you cannot change what you do not acknowledge), which will then avail you to the chance of having a successful result.

Even though I did not consciously know it at the time, dyslexia proved to be a very big influence in my life, which was a bit like a two-sided sword. On one side of the equation, while writing, I would create a lot of fragmented information which would constantly float around in my head and which would lead the way to the many minor errors in my grammar which would frequently occur. The upside was that it would create a much deeper level of thought to work from.

Starting my life off by having dyslexia where neither the schoolteachers, my parents, nor I, or as a matter of fact, did anyone else who was associated with the events in my life—had any knowledge about dyslexia, This was due to the fact that for at least the first couple of decades in my life, the dyslexia problem was not recognised. However, it does not pay to travel too far down the field of feeling sorry for myself, because it also definitely had some big advantages that went with it.

Being unaware that I was so over creative to the point where it ended up becoming disruptive to what I was writing and not knowing why, especially when I was at a young age, when I first started going to school and beyond. This turned out to be a very hard problem that needed sorting out, and I had nobody to help me sort out my problem; as a matter of fact, they did quite the opposite. The people who were available (mainly the adults in my life) and who were supposed to be supporting me ended up spending a great deal of time ridiculing me about my problem and left me with no answers for solving it or any way of being able to improve the situation. The response was caused by the use of ridicule as a diversion, because those people did not have an answer when they believed that they should have an answer. It is a very common occurrence that I still see happening in our everyday life.

The teachers were the ones that everybody appeared to be looking to for answers to this unknown problem, and it was assumed that they were the most knowledgeable when it came to dealing with the problem that I was having in school. Writing was my number one problem that needed solving, and the thing that was causing the problem was given very little to no thought by anybody who was involved in my life. Unfortunately for me, the teachers also led the campaign of ridiculing me, and the other people of authority who were supposed to be helping me through these troubled times went with the assumption that the teachers had the best way of solving my learning problems. In reality, the teachers were a long way from having the answers to dyslexia and inadvertently added to the dyslexia problem by forcing me to be even more creative in creating a way of dealing with the ridicule.

The other part of this loop was that the teachers were also trapped by the need to constantly produce positive results. Unfortunately, the only way you can identify dyslexia is through the problems it creates, which most likely discouraged them from wanting to spend a lot of time going down that negative path to understanding the problem of the few people who were having that problem. I guess that it was more convenient to not believe that a genuine problem even needed to be addressed and their best way of trying to get pass the problem was by trying to find a way of trivialising it.

There was also another problem which involved my not knowing that I had dyslexia, which stretched over a large span of time. It more than likely started at the age of about four or five and continued till the age of sixty. Even though I still have dyslexia, I have also gained a lot more control of its advantages, along with having resolved a large amount of the disadvantages at a rapid pace. This excessive habit that I have of being over creative, which constitutes having dyslexia, also happens to be the very same thing which gives me the ability to solve some difficult problems and come up with some workable solutions that are accompanied by a lot of fragmented information that constantly needs to be sorted out. Having a very creative brain also requires thinking at a deeper level than most people who do not have dyslexia and who have a strong tendency to think at a shallower level. While analysing what I have just said, bear in mind that the short definition of someone who has dyslexia is someone who overuses the creative side of the brain.

Let's face it, the results that we create in our life are derived from the established knowledge of information that we have accumulated, along with new information we have to add in, which is referred to as creative information. The problem that a person with dyslexia has is that they have exceeded the balance of creative information to the point where the brain can no longer process the information efficiently. Unfortunately, it also means that if a dyslexic is pressured into doing more creative activity, it is going to increase the degree of how dyslexic they are. A good example of that is when I was relentlessly teased and was pressured into finding a way to sustain a realistic emotional belief of myself, which comes with the chain reaction of the need to be more creative. On the other side of the coin, if you reduce the amount of creativity that you have to work with enough, you will end up not having dyslexia at all. I think this analogy will give you a better understanding of what I have just discussed: Water is a very important component for our ability to live, and without it, we die. Yet it is the amount of water that determines whether it is going to contribute to giving us a healthy life or whether it is going to damage our anatomy in some way. It also has the ability when we have too much of it, to kill us through the method of drowning.

When someone who does not have dyslexia sets out to solve the problem of having dyslexia, they will more than likely view it by the short version and say that all a dyslexic needs to do is cut back on the creative activity that they do. However, when you venture through the deeper version, it takes into account all the valuable hard work that a dyslexic has accomplished over a long span of time. They would be exposing themselves to the possibility of, at best, losing some of that valuable information that they had taken so long to gather or, at worst, losing all of it and left with the need to try and start all-over again.

Since this is going to have a very big effect on the way that I am going to understand the strategies in my life, I believe that there are three things I need to consider, not just one. I also believe that it would be wise to fully evaluate the choices before making that important decision.

1. There is a danger when you choose the option of getting rid of a lot of creative thoughts without knowing the point where that theory starts becoming more destructive than useful to you.
2. There is also another danger when you run with the theory that you have the right balance while you are eliminating your creative thoughts; you stand a big chance of not being able to decide how much creativity

you need to retain for future use. The problem with that theory is, if you are wrong, there is a very big price to pay for it.

3. The most favourable option in my opinion, is the third choice, which is to battle through the problem by unravelling the defects and turning those defects around so that they become advantages. I know that the theory is easier said than done, and that is the same reason it is referred to as a battle which is worth pursuing.

When it comes to using the computer and spell check properly, the trick is to learn why you have made a spelling error, how you can correct it, and what you can do to prevent it from happening again. There is little to no advantage in getting the message correctly presented if you do not understand how to do it without the use of the spell check on the computer. The spell check is there to help you and is not designed to be an extension of your brain. Your wisdom only extends to what you can work out for yourself.

Finding out about dyslexia much later in life, at the age of sixty, was far from helpful when it came to managing it (because you cannot change a problem which you do not acknowledge). There is also another reason one is not able to solve this dyslexia problem which is causing them to be so excessively creative.

Unfortunately, when one consults the majority of the medical profession about the understanding of dyslexia, usually it is most likely that the doctor will be describing the symptoms of the dyslexia and not the problem which is causing it. So, when someone is working on the problem of dyslexia from the symptomatic side, they are working with one creation at a time. This means that there will be many creative answers that will line up with someone being correct, because there are many ways of being creative; each individual is going to have their own way in which they choose to be creative. The problem with working from only understanding of the symptoms is that you only understand part of what you need to know in order to resolve a complex problem which is hard to resolve even if you had all the relative information that you needed for solving it.

I have listened to what a lot of professional people have had to say while passing on their explanation of what dyslexia is, as well as a lot of non-professional people. Overwhelmingly, they inevitably explained the symptoms instead of what causes the problem. For example, it is possible that when you ask about what dyslexia is from 12 different doctors who can be supplying you with **12** different answers, wherein each answer is correct because each one is an answer created by an individual dyslexic person. I also believe it to be the reason so many dyslexic people have trouble coming up with a satisfactory answer which is going to give them the most profound way to work with their dyslexia.

There are two directions in which we proceed through life. From the time we are born, our aim in life is to live by learning mental and physical skills and by understanding the thoughts and events which will give meaningful purpose to our lives. On the other side of the coin is to stop learning and to stop being active, which will accelerate our journey to death. Personally, I am in no hurry to go there, and besides, that is a pretty permanent choice to make. (There is a basic theory which I firmly believe in regarding the anatomy, which says, 'If you don't use it, you lose it.' So if one continues losing different functions of the anatomy, which most definitely includes the functions of the brain, then the only thing left to do is to head down the path to dying.)

For a dyslexic, to enjoy that quest of living involves having to continue battling through the many fields of fragmented information that one has constantly floating in their head, along with being able to unravel it for the purpose of making sense of English grammar—for themselves and for the need to do a much better job of unravelling it for anyone else they wish to communicate with.

This fragmented information magnifies itself when it is transformed into written form, for several good reasons. First of all, when you transform it into written form, it is going to require additional information, such as the way the word needs to be spelt. There are homophones, homographs, prefixes, suffixes, punctuation, and the correct way to construct a sentence—all these need to be correctly used. My problems do not end there, because after rechecking my writing many times and going with the belief that I have transformed it into a defragmented state which has been written in a grammatically correct way—well, unfortunately for me, that seldom happens. Even though I put my best effort into correcting the mistakes, I very often find myself knowing the corrections to the mistakes that I make, but my brain, at that point, is not capable of acknowledging the obvious mistakes which are clearly visible to most people. The upside to it is the progress that I have made in improving my grammar through the hundreds of hours that I have spent studying my grammar.

One thing I have always strived to achieve in my life are the goals which I believe are going to gain the achievements to my life's fullest potential. This means that I need to embrace the constant battles so that I can gain the success to the wisdom of goals that are worth pursuing. The battle also includes the importance of being able to align with a scale of measurement which shows where you are coming from and the success of achieving your goals, which will enable you to gain momentum so that you can continue battling on to your next victory.

On the other side of the battle, one needs to accept that results are not going to be success only, and like everyone on the planet, it comes down to how well you are able to deal with the failures that come your way, which are reference points that let you know how successful you are becoming. For example, when a one-year-old baby first learns to walk, the baby repeatedly falls over in its journey to being successful while learning the art of walking. That does not mean that you give up on the baby and say 'You are too stupid' and 'You are never going to learn'. Instead you continue to encourage the baby until it eventually masters the skill of walking. The easiest thing to do is quit, which is usually accompanied by a lot of inaccurate statements that try to justify the quitter's reason for quitting. However, the problem with the quitter's theory of taking that so-called easy option is, if you go too far into the business of successfully quitting your goals, you will end up with the ultimate goal, which is to die. I believe that it would be wise if you take the time to step back from that trend of goal making and reconsider before you go down that path, because it is eventually going to be a one-way journey and you are going to end up being there for a very long time (try the thought of being there permanently).

Another aspect that needs to be addressed while taking on the challenge of making goals is the decisions you need to make, such as: Is this what I want to do with my life? Is it worth the time that I am spending on it? How do I get past a certain hurdle? How do I gain more knowledge on the subject? There are a host of other questions that probably need to be answered. However, the most important part is to see it in your mind as being doable, with a realistic time span attached to it which allows you enough time to evaluate your goal. It is also important to be aware that when you repeatedly get into a state of procrastination (being unable to decide, which also creates a loss of time), you will inevitably prevent yourself from reaching that goal. When you are young, you usually have enough time in your life to sort it out. But as you get older, depending on the time span of the goal you are working on, where you are more often than not able to achieve some of the goals. This will now come with a price tag that includes not being able to do all the things you could do when you were younger, both mentally and physically, along with the amount of time you lose in your life by not living with the success of achievement that you deserve to have from that goal. There are big variations in the time spans of each goal, and the largest contribution to the time span is the position of where you consider it completed enough for your satisfaction in the completion of the goal you wish to set for yourself.

I have a basic rule in my life which I call my ABC. It is a theory which I have adopted over the last few years. I am not saying that it is not possible that it has been said or written in some other book before me, although I don't recall hearing about it or reading about it anywhere else. But also, given the fact that I spend a lot of time watching the Dr Phil show, it's plausible that it was the place where I first heard of it.

The ABC that I am referring to are the ones that I talked about in the dyslexia article: *attitude, balance,* and *choices.* For example, let's take the case of someone who wanted to learn how to use the computer. This person happened to be very good at playing the piano and can also play some tunes which were are played at a very fast pace. Yet after I had shown her in detail how to double-click with the mouse, and when she was still struggling with it the next day, she told me that she can't do it. This was something well within her range of ability, and her attitude was the only thing that was letting her down.

Let's analyse what had happened. Her attitude was wrong, because she took the quitter's attitude, saying that she can't do it. To achieve nothing is a very easy goal to accomplish, and this also applies when only doing part of a requirement that needs to be accomplished. *Can't means that you do not want to do it* and that you are no longer prepared to meet the requirements needed to be done; it very often has little to do with what you are capable of doing, and there is a far greater likelihood of you looking for the easy option which will present you with an excuse for your lack of achievement. Had she said, that she did not remember or asked what she was doing wrong or what else she needed to do in order to be successful, then she would be working with a different attitude, wherein her attitude would present her with a very good chance of succeeding. In this case, the balance came into play when she failed to stabilise the mouse enough so that it did not move while she was double clicking. Had she stabilised the mouse as instructed by putting her thumb and finger on either side of the mouse and pushing them down on the desk so that she can stop the mouse from moving while she was double clicking, then she would have been successful. The balance lay between holding the mouse stable enough or not holding it stable enough while double clicking. The choices are what you make from your attitude and the balance in which you work.

Throughout this book, the main theme has been based on philosophical problems in my life and that of other people who have been involved in my life. My philosophical beliefs are designed to encourage the individual person to work a lot more on what they can do for themselves and rely a lot less on what someone or something else can do for them.

Remember when I talked about the word *balance*? Well, this is a good time to remember it, because so far, the bulk of my discussions have been about creativity. The balance of the other side of it is, while we are researching something, we will also need to rely on some information which has already been established. This new piece of established information will need to be validated through logical reasoning that aligns with facts and evidence which you have gathered. *If* it is going to make a big change in your life, then it needs to be validated through a pros and cons list, which can give you the best path in which to proceed. The success of these many events rely on what you control, and *the only thing you control is yourself.* The things you say and do, can, and usually do make an impact on the way someone will respond to you and other people who are associated with you.

While you are researching the new information, it becomes important to validate the information you are working with to the best of your ability, which one usually deems to be correct. However, because we are human, it means that human beings are prone to making mistakes. Furthermore, it means that you need to leave yourself open to the possibility that some of the information that you have deemed correct may still be wrong and will need modifying, or that it may even be completely wrong and that you may need to restart from another position, as opposed to automatically believing that your first line of reasoning is still correct in your mind. A very common practice that often occurs is when one lies behind a fear of being wrong and then tries to avoid that fear by trying to turn wrong into right.

This often happens when someone is debating the research with someone else. They will often resort to filling it in, with some meaningless answer such as 'It is just how it happened' where important parts of the information are left out, leaving the answers to being only partially correct.

When someone is in denial of something which they know is true, they are also destroying the most important tool of communication required for resolving a debate. One of the toughest parts to correct is when you believe that you have established your original thought as correct and now find out that your new evidence is going to require some modification—or worse still, it may need to be completely changed. Human beings have a habit of perceiving that they are always right and will very often go to great lengths to maintain what they first thought to be right and disregard the new facts of evidence which may prove them wrong. But it is necessary to establish when one is wrong so that they can change it to the correct result which one is seeking. Then it becomes equally important to reunite one's energy of concerns to the replacement of the correction and the things that can sustain that correction for the future.

Most people, during their journey of life, pass on good personal advice to other people that they care about, yet when it comes to following that same good advice for themselves, they quite often fail to do so. When one asks why that is so, they are only left with a few answers. That they did not understand what they were talking about could be their plausible answer, and this will depend on who you are talking to. The more likely option is that they are making the same mistake or that someone close to them in their life is making that same mistake, and while working with a shallow thought of it in their mind, they are still not prepared to accept the reality of that mistake which is still occurring. However, should they choose to work with a deeper thought, they would be able to attach reality to the embarrassing situation which they are not able to cope with.

I have found that the best way to get past that hurdle of not being able to follow your own good advice is by depersonalising it, which requires being able to see yourself as a second person. The details of how you view that second person are not important, although viewing the image of that second person in your mind is. Usually, in my case, especially when it is very personal, I mirror an imaginary image of a person on a structural object, which usually appears as a shadow or it could be simply just a dot on the wall. Disassociating from your own personality and working through the personality of a second person will now allow you to see things which your own personality was preventing you from seeing. The thing which was blocking you was your inability to get past being personally wrong, and this has now opened the door to viewing your problem in a more objective way. The things which are important are the facts and the evidence, not the things which you may have personally got wrong. By the way, while doing this exercise, it is a good idea to do it silently; otherwise, when you express your personal thoughts out loud and when someone else hears you, they may end up gaining the wrong impression of your mental health.

I am now sixty-nine years of age and have achieved a lot of valuable and successful goals in my life. No man is an island unto himself, wherein he can completely rely on being able to achieve everything he has accomplished with his own creation. Every new creation is going to need, at the very minimum, to be filtered through some established information that you have gained access to. The resource could come from a family member or a friend or maybe from a book or something that you may have viewed on the television or some professional person you have met along the way. In order to create this new invention, one needs to steer clear of understanding the information in parrot-like fashion (to gather information by automatically processing it without thinking or by thinking it through mechanically or through the mentality of mindless thought). This means that a person who understands what they are doing in parrot-like fashion lacks the important ability to understand the basic requirements of reasoning and therefore is unable to make any amendments, should there be any reason to change the original message. Bear in mind that parrots are not very smart.

My father had a bad start in life; his mother died when he was three, and his father died when he was eight. He was brought up by his grandparents for a couple of years in a place that mainly lacked in getting love, which is very much needed when you are a young boy. The grandfather kept a whip at the dining room table and maintained heavy discipline, and if one of the boys said something that the grandfather did not like, they would get a flick from the whip. After two years the grandparents found the boys to be too much to handle and turned him and his two brothers over to be wards of the state (orphans). Most of the time, he was mainly adopted into families who owned farms. In the period of 1916 to about 1923 (and more likely well beyond that period), the main requirement of the many orphanage homes and farms they were sent to—and to some degree, this type of parenting also applied to the grandparents—was how much work they could get out of them. Homework and their schooling took a very distant second place in their lives. As bad as that situation appears. Being able to survive was nowhere as easy as it is today and that extra help from the boys was badly needed.

When it came to the order of age in the family, my father was the middle one. He was also the leader, and he did a good job of helping his two brothers and himself through a difficult period in their lives. Another thing that was important to the boys was for the three of them to avoid being split up; they believed that by consolidating their family unity, which would give them the best chance of having a successful life, and they placed a lot of importance on what was left of the family bond. So even though my father had a poor education, which was no fault of his own, he was still able to substitute that loss with the ability of being very streetwise. Well, it actually went beyond just being streetwise; he also had a great capability of deeply understanding how and why, about most of the things that happened in his life. A good example of that would be when I was between the ages of about eight and twelve.

My Dad taught me many great lessons that proved to be valuable throughout my journey of life. Knowing about the stupidity of taking illegal drugs was and is important, which I will talk about a little bit later. Another valuable lesson he gave me is an area I still find astounding to understand, by the way in which so many people who should know better still get caught in this trap, and the trap I am referring to is the one of being conned (*con* is an abbreviation for *confidence trick*).

The advice my father gave me was that there is nothing in this world that is "free". When he told me that, I laughed and said, 'What about the free cup of tea that I had at Mrs Russo's place?' His answer came as a surprise. He said to me, 'No son, *that cup of tea was not free*, because if you have any decency in you—and I believe you have—then not only will you pay that cup of tea back again, but you will give her another one as well when you can.' Even though I did not understand the real meaning of *free* before he made that statement, it only took a short period for me to wake up to the fact that his statement was true and accurate. So, continuing what my father was saying to me, once you wake up to the fact that nothing is free in this world, means that you can no longer be conned. The thing you always need to do is look back down the trail to where this so-called free thing is coming from, and you need to ask yourself the moral question: Are you still happy receiving it when you know that there is no free money or that there is no free gift? Someone had to pay for it somewhere down the track and does it come from honesty? Another important fact to consider: Is it right and fair that you should receive it?

In order to be conned, one needs to attempt to take advantage of something they are not entitled to. This is usually by falsely believing that they have the right to gain a sum of money. Once again falsely believing that they have found a shortcut to making a big gain by leaving out the propriety of the things that are not convenient for one to know about. As well as the things that are a disadvantage to hear about, which will be the very thing that causes one to be conned. Both parties work with false expectations.

The person conning you has probably picked you because they see a flaw in your code of ethics, and this flaw that you have in your code of ethics is more than likely something you do not recognise or admit to. If the person conning you is right about their assessment of you, then they win and you lose. When you closely look at the situation, you will see that the person attempting to con you has little to lose, and that you have a lot to lose; which is the reason they are trying to con you in the first place.

Another thing I learnt and accepted as a child is that your Mum and Dad are always right, unless proven wrong, and a parent's brain is fully developed or more developed than a child's brain, which becomes fully developed at the age of 25. Unfortunately, with the modern child of today, that trend is often reversed, wherein the parent is wrong until proven right. *A good metaphorical example* of what I am talking about is a situation wherein a child happens to be standing close to a cliff edge and the parent says to the child that it is dangerous and that they need to get away from the edge of the cliff.

This is just one metaphor that I have chosen to use; there are many more that can show the reason it is important for the parent to start off by being right, which is going to allow the child to have their best chance in life.

Does that child really need to retain their position of always being right? Or does the parent, who has developed insight from a more mature brain, and who has a better chance of predicting a bad outcome which is likely to occur? A good thing to remember is that if your evaluation has gone with the point of view that the child needs to perceive themselves as right, and should your assessment end up being wrong, that child may very well end up dead or having something bad happen to them, with you no longer having the option to re-evaluate your original answer.

In regard to taking illegal drugs, all my father said to me about it when I was about eight years old was 'Don't touch them son, because you don't need them to live on, and they will wreck your brain'. So, wrecking my brain by trying or experimenting with something that I neither needed nor required to live on meant that there was no way that I was going to try them. Dad was also good at being able to intensify the strength of his message with the humour that he had, and his humorous comment was 'You only have one brain, and even that one is in doubt'. After hearing that humorous warning about the destruction of the only brain that I have, coupled with a lot of the dyslexic problems which I was struggling to understand and wishing that I had a better ability for sorting these problems in my mind, then it became very clear to me. It most certainly left me with no doubt that I had no intention of wrecking the only brain I have with some silly drug that I neither needed nor required to live on. It does not matter even if you do not have dyslexia; there is a lot of evidence that shows it is a dumb idea to take this unwanted and destructive substance into your body.

Years later, and after reviewing his witty comment that he made and seen the dangers that happen to the people taking illegal drugs. Let's not leave out the destruction that it causes to the loved ones around them and the loss of happy times with the family, which are replaced with having to deal with a drug addict who tears the family apart with family problems that did not exist in the past, such as being lied to, having that person steal from them, and no longer being able to trust what they say. Their values in life have now been transferred into stealing money or anything of value in order to get the next fix for their drug habit. Every good moral value that you once shared with that drug addict will eventually be taken away from you, and the only loyalty they have left is their loyalty to the drug habit. To make matters even worse, when you try to help them get over their problem, they will lie to you and find ways to make you feel guilty about yourself, which will weaken your confidence in your ability to help them. They will be left with the sole interest of being able to get another fix from the drug.

Even though my Dad died in 1970, I will always remember the lessons he taught me and will always be very grateful to him for providing me with the most powerful way that he could have helped me fully understand that important message. It was only a short message, but that is quite often all it takes to get a powerful message across. I guess having dyslexia and struggling badly with my grammar constantly reminded me about the tendency I had, which pulled my intelligence level in a strong downward direction with the minor mistakes I was making, which also strengthen his message. This is one way to get the children to understand the unnecessary need for taking illegal drugs

Dad also had another powerful weapon at his disposal and that was when Dad asked me to do something, I would do it first and ask questions later. He could have very simply said 'Don't touch the drugs son, because they are no good for you, and I forbid you from taking them'. Fortunately for me, he was very wise when it came to fully understanding the message he was passing on and knew that the way he presented it would be the most effective way for me to understand the dangers of drugs.

In regard to the warning my father gave me when I was growing up—about the drugs, as well as the many other traps where curiosity played a big part in my life—as I write this story, I find it stressful to think how bad my life could have turned out to be, had I not received all that good advice from my father, who was able to steer my choices of curiosity in the right direction when I was a child who was growing up in the real world.

The modern problem I see with drugs is that most people do not start at the beginning of the problem of taking drugs. Too often, the problem is addressed when someone is addicted to drugs, or they concentrate on putting the drug dealers in jail. While still going with the theory that these problems need to be constantly addressed, one still cannot get past the fact that the drug problem is many times easier to fix when you start at the beginning—by simply not taking the drug in the first place. If the potential drug user is taught before taking the drug that it is a nasty drug that causes damage to your brain and that it quickly becomes very addictive and that, by far, the majority of the time that you are taking the drug, you are not aware that you are caught up in the strength of its addictive power and very often will be in denial of the addiction to the drug, and they will follow up by saying that they have it under control and will quite often say that they can stop it any time that they want too, along with adding that they just do not want to stop taking it and are not aligned to the lack of understanding about addiction to that drug at the time of making that statement and lack of awareness of the amount of damage that is happening to *their brain*.

When someone first starts taking the drug and makes the statement that they can stop at any time, well, it could very well be true in the *very early stages* of taking the drug. However, when someone has already been taking the drug for a long time and is saying that they can stop at any time, addiction is more than likely to have taken place. When they still say that they can stop at any time, unless they actually put their theory to the test by staying off it for at least two months and that does not mean taking the odd one in between that period. Because, then their statement becomes invalid, and are in denial of the addiction which is taking place. To proceed along the line of thinking that it is all right to take it sometimes is also very dangerous. The danger occurs for two reasons. If they continue taking it, they definitely will get addicted and will take a long time before they are prepared to admit or believe that addiction is even taking place. The second reason is, if you are the one trying to prevent them from being a drug addict, you are more than likely also be unaware of how addictive it has become, and to make matters worse, there is a big variation in each case of how quickly that drug is becoming addictive to that person. However, the one thing you know for sure is that in the early stages, it's easier to break the habit. As they continue taking the drug, the more addictive it will become, along with it being harder to get off it. The endgame is that they will have an early death.

Each time they first take the drug, it will give them a short boost of pleasure. As they continue along the journey of taking the drug, when the brain's normal function is disrupted then they are left with the difficulty of finding it harder to create new creative thoughts, or their new thoughts will have a tendency to be irrational. They end up paying a very heavy price that they are not aware of. Their lies will continue so that they can protect their continuous supply of drugs, and they will want to stay in their safe haven of being in denial that they are addicted while the drug continues to destroy them.

My mother taught me very early in life that an ounce of prevention is better than a pound of cure. Going on that theory, *if* there is no market for the drug, then the drug addicts and the drug dealers are left with no business. One cannot sell something when there is no need for that product.

Another illustration which relates to the illegal drug business is when a teenager gets into a car and does a burnout and ends up killing himself, as well as his three mates. He also stood a chance of killing other innocent people. When it comes to the funeral, his parents talk about what a good guy he was, which is a very natural response to make. However, the only thing which is going to prevent a similar drug problem from occurring is pointing out *that "if he had not taken the drugs in the first place, they would all still be alive."* Since only the message of him being a good person has been announced, there is a strong chance that with the modern mentality of the young people of today, they are very likely to say to each other, 'We are going to also take some drugs in honour of his memory.' The cycle of the drug problem ends up becoming worse, not better, and the only message which could have prevented the same thing from happening again has been lost.

I am aware that some of my views in life may not be popular, and I understand that I have gained a lot of successful results in my life, especially in the medical field. The most successful goal I believe that I have achieved is curing the problem of a stroke, wherein I lost half of my eyesight in both eyes, when the doctor gave up on me, and I was left to find my own answer and regained all my eyesight again. I have also sorted out the problem that I had with spurs in both of my heels, as well as with gout. When asked the question of if I have ever indulged in taking illegal drugs or abused the taking of prescription drugs, *the answer is no*. This does not mean that I personally need to take the drugs in order to have knowledge about them.

I am quite happy—especially knowing the damage the drugs can do—to rely on the successful research of others. Most of the research from which I have knowledge of drugs come from the Dr Phil show. He has a highly qualified team of experts who have done an intensive study on the brain and have compared the normal brain (free of illegal drugs) and a brain which being supplied with drugs. This test clearly shows the damage which is being done with the drugs, along with knowing the history of how the drugs are being used at the time of being tested. Dr Phil fully understands the requirements of getting a drug addict off that addictive drug and has provided some drug addicts the chance of going to a rehabilitation centre that frees someone from that addictive habit. Another reason why it is senseless to take drugs to start with, is because even should you be successful in the rehabilitation centre and when you get back to normal life. There are triggers that are still out there which can cause you to relapse, which will require going back and getting further treatment.

Dr Phil is the presenter of the show and is also very qualified in clinical psychology and forensic psychology.

Index

CPSIA information can be obtained
at www.ICGtesting.com
Printed in the USA
BVHW030954250419
546530BV00005B/12/P